PRAISE FOR
ANATOMY OF A BREAKTHROUGH

"Those feeling stuck in their circumstances will find several paths forward."

—*The Wall Street Journal*

"Rooted in science and enlivened by stories, *Anatomy of a Breakthrough* offers insight after insight and the rallying cry of 'action above all' as an antidote to enemy #1: inertia."

—Angela Duckworth, PhD, #1 *New York Times* bestselling author of *Grit: The Power of Passion and Perseverance*

"This book is something special: it's as captivating as it is constructive. Adam Alter demystifies the science and practice of uncovering motivation, unlocking creativity, and unleashing change. If you've ever felt like you're languishing, these pages hold the keys to regaining momentum."

—Adam Grant, #1 *New York Times* bestselling author of *Think Again* and host of the podcast *ReThinking*

"Adam Alter marries research-based solutions with genuine insight. This book is an invaluable guide to turning hurdles into breakthroughs."

—Scott Galloway, professor of marketing, NYU Stern School of Business, and *New York Times* bestselling author of *Adrift*

"A deeply researched and compelling guide to breaking through the inevitable obstacles on the path to meaningful accomplishment."

—Cal Newport, *New York Times* bestselling author of *Digital Minimalism* and *Deep Work*

"*Anatomy of a Breakthrough* is important, entertaining, practical, and timely. Alter reveals how to turn sticking points into breakthroughs in pursuits as diverse as entrepreneurship, art, music, writing, athletics, friendship, and personal relationships."

—Arianna Huffington, founder & CEO, Thrive Global

"A brilliant detective story about the sources of human creativity. I loved it."

—Malcolm Gladwell, #1 *New York Times* bestselling author

"Whether in a career, a creative project, or a relationship, everyone will get mired in a rut at one point or another. *Anatomy of a Breakthrough* brings the often-private struggle to get 'unstuck' into the light, and provides a handbook for moving on from your personal plateau. Adam Alter is simply one of the best science communicators at work."

—David Epstein, #1 *New York Times* bestselling author of *Range*

"A useful guide to getting past barriers to progress . . . Alter's advice is solid and confidence boosting, with a heartening message that's grounded in clear scientific research. This is persuasive and practical."

—*Publishers Weekly*

"A useful look at how to get 'unstuck' . . . In a wide-ranging package, Alter offers practical advice on how to break free of inertia and blaze a new path."

—*Kirkus Reviews*

"[*Anatomy of a Breakthrough*] tackles the internal factors that keep you mired in the mud . . . [Alter] demystifies the experience of being stuck [and] provides a primer on changing ingrained habits."

—*The New York Times*

ALSO BY ADAM ALTER

Irresistible

Drunk Tank Pink

ANATOMY OF A BREAKTHROUGH

How to Get Unstuck
When It Matters Most

ADAM ALTER

SIMON & SCHUSTER PAPERBACKS

New York   London   Toronto   Sydney   New Delhi

An Imprint of Simon & Schuster, LLC
1230 Avenue of the Americas
New York, NY 10020

First Simon & Schuster trade paperback edition May 2024

SIMON & SCHUSTER PAPERBACKS and colophon are registered trademarks of Simon & Schuster, LLC

Simon & Schuster: Celebrating 100 Years of Publishing in 2024

For information about special discounts for bulk purchases, please contact Simon & Schuster Special Sales at 1-866-506-1949 or business@simonandschuster.com.

The Simon & Schuster Speakers Bureau can bring authors to your live event. For more information or to book an event, contact the Simon & Schuster Speakers Bureau at 1-866-248-3049 or visit our website at www.simonspeakers.com.

Interior design by Carly Loman

Manufactured in the United States of America

10 9 8 7 6 5 4 3 2 1

Library of Congress Cataloging-in-Publication Data has been applied for.

ISBN 978-1-9821-8296-0
ISBN 978-1-9821-8297-7 (pbk)
ISBN 978-1-9821-8298-4 (ebook)

For Sar, Sam, and Is, who inspire my greatest breakthroughs

CONTENTS

THE FIRST RULE IS THAT YOU WILL GET STUCK

Brianne Desaulniers was born in Sacramento, California, in 1989. She was homeschooled by her French-Canadian father and American mother and was drawn to Egyptology and magic—but most of all to acting. At age six, she enrolled as the youngest student at San Francisco's American Conservatory Theater, and three years later appeared in a skit on *The Tonight Show with Jay Leno*. That brief appearance inspired other TV roles, beginning with guest appearances, then minor recurring roles, and eventually starring roles on popular TV shows. Reviewers praised her TV acting, which paved the way for film acting, directing, and writing.

A couple of years later, Desaulniers—now known as Brie Larson—became the seventy-fourth woman to win the Academy Award for Best Actress, the highest award in acting, for her role in *Room*. In addition to her Oscar, Larson has won more than seventy other acting awards, and the blockbuster title role in Marvel's *Captain Marvel*. Larson's trajectory is the stuff of fairy tales: a precocious start followed by dozens of small steps that culminated in towering success.

The problem with this account of Larson's career path is that it ignores decades of frustration. Like many actors, Larson was stuck for years before she broke through. She struggled with rejection and body-image concerns and admitted to "feeling ugly" for most of her life. On the home front, her parents divorced, and her mother moved with Larson and her sister, Milaine, to Los Angeles, to be closer to Hollywood. "We had a crappy one-room apartment," Larson recalled. "The bed came out of the wall and we each had three articles of clothing." She auditioned hundreds of times for dozens of roles that eluded her, from commercial work to TV gigs.

What makes Larson different from most A-list actors is that she's transparent about her struggles. On August 13, 2020, she uploaded a fourteen-minute YouTube video titled "Audition Storytime! (pt. 1)." "I thought I'd talk a little bit about my process," Larson says to the camera, "because I think a lot of the time there's been a lot of focus on my successes, and not on how hard it was, how much I was rejected; and you never know all of the jobs I didn't get. So I thought it might be interesting to talk about that."

The video and its sequel cataloged twenty years of disappointment, beginning with Larson's first audition for a commercial role at age seven. Jammed into a room with other young hopefuls, Larson was dismissed after spending just a few seconds with the casting director. She sobbed because he didn't ask her to perform her rehearsed mono- logue. "Later," Larson said, "one casting director told my agent I was so bad she'd never bring me in for anything ever again. And she didn't." From there, Larson lists the roles she didn't get: *Gossip Girl*, *The Hun- ger Games*, *Tomorrowland*, the *Star Wars* movies, *Smart House*, *Spy Kids*, and *The Big Bang Theory*. Larson punctuates each title with a laugh, but if you pause at the right moments, you see micro-expressions of pain. These aren't happy memories, and they remain despite her subsequent success.

In the second part of "Audition Storytime," Larson hits her stride, rattling off dozens of failed auditions. "I got down to the final round," she says, "on *Juno*, *13*, *Brink*, *Smart House*, *Tomorrowland*, *Pitch Perfect*, *Into the Woods*, *Youth in Revolt*, *Peter Pan*, *Halt and Catch Fire*, *The Big Bang Theory*. Oh my gosh. That's a lot of heartbreak, folks. Here I am still standing." The numbers aren't pretty, Larson admits, but she ends with a note of hope: "I got told no ninety-eight to ninety-nine percent of the time. I know that's hard to fully wrap your brain around—to think I've been on thousands and thousands and thousands of auditions."

Larson is the embodiment of acting success. She has the awards, the fame, the money, the critical acclaim, and the list of credits. But even she hit walls, by her account, 99 percent of the time. Larson's YouTube videos attracted hundreds of thousands of views and inspired dozens of media pieces. It was notable because it was so unusual in revealing the wrinkles beneath a journey that from afar appeared unbroken. Getting stuck isn't a topic that celebrated actors and successes in other fields routinely discuss in such agonizing detail, so we're often left feeling lonely and isolated when our own paths seem so much bumpier.

———

People get stuck in every imaginable area of life. They get stuck in jobs they'd prefer to leave, and in relationships that leave them unfulfilled. They get stuck as writers, artists, composers, athletes, scientists, and entrepreneurs. Sometimes they're stuck for days, and other times for decades. Sometimes they stumble on breakthroughs, and other times they remain mired for life. We hear relatively little about these stubborn cases of stuckness because we're bombarded by popular success stories. These successes lead us to believe that other people face fewer barriers than we do. Every now and then a star like Brie Larson will dispel that myth, but most of the time the experience of being stuck seems like a glitch that plagues us more than it does other people. In truth, we all face roadblocks—and being stuck is a feature rather than a bug on the path to success. So why is it so much easier to recognize our own barriers than those that face other people?

There are at least two reasons. The first lies in the headwinds/ tailwinds asymmetry, a psychological phenomenon named by researchers Shai Davidai and Tom Gilovich. The asymmetry suggests that we pay far more attention to our barriers (or headwinds) than our blessings (or tailwinds), which leads us to believe that we face more opposition than we actually do. Davidai and Gilovich illustrate the idea with the case of a Scrabble player who draws unfavorable letters. Imagine getting the tiles U, U, I, I, I, Q, and W. Unless you sacrifice a turn to draw fresh letters, you'll be stuck with those tiles for many rounds. Each time you try to make a word, you'll ruminate on your bad luck. In contrast, a good draw doesn't last long. You play the tiles as soon as they hit your rack. The same is true in other contexts. If you're driving in heavy traffic and pick the slower of two lanes, you'll watch with frustration as dozens of cars zip by in the other lane, whereas if you were in one of the cars zipping by, you'd be focusing on the road. We also devote more time and energy to barriers because that's the only way to overcome them. You can't improve your Scrabble performance or make up for lost time in heavy traffic unless you consider and act on your options.

Davidai and Gilovich also found that while we're focusing on our own barriers, we tend to overlook the hardships that plague other people. In one experiment, the researchers asked pairs of Cornell University students to play a trivia game. Some of the questions for each contestant were drawn from easy categories—like TV sitcoms and famous cartoons—whereas others were drawn from difficult categories, like Baroque music and Russian literature. After the game, the contestants did a much better job of remembering their opponents' easy categories than they did their opponents' difficult categories—a bias they tended not to show when recalling their own questions. This pattern holds in other domains, too. For example, in another study Gilovich showed that people tend to believe taxes and regulations hurt them more than they do other people—even when that isn't objectively true.

The second reason we believe our barriers are unusual is that it's difficult to see others' struggles. People tend to wrestle their demons privately, either behind closed doors or within their own heads, and what we ultimately see is the polished outcome of that process. We see Brie Larson's Oscar, but not the decades of struggle that preceded the award. Meanwhile, the media devotes far more time to titanic success stories—Roger Federer and Serena Williams; Jeff Bezos and Mark Zuckerberg; Meryl Streep and Daniel Day-Lewis—than to the billions of strugglers who are more typical and therefore less interesting. Our social media accounts are similarly cluttered with the most glossy and popular accounts, and even the micro-influencers we follow share refined versions of their lives that skim the best moments and leave the wrinkles behind. Struggle is harder to see in other people's lives, so we mistakenly believe it troubles us more than it does them.

———

In early 2021, Airbnb's market capitalization topped $100 billion, making it one of the hundred largest publicly traded companies in the world. Its three cofounders, Brian Chesky, Joe Gebbia, and Nathan Blecharczyk, were worth more than $13 billion each. Of those three, Chesky is the face of the company, and its CEO. Like Brie Larson, Chesky has been transparent about Airbnb's challenges, and his own sticking points as the company grew.

Airbnb was born of necessity. Chesky and Gebbia met in college, and after graduation Chesky moved to Los Angeles, and Gebbia moved to San Francisco. Their postcollege jobs were uninspiring, so Chesky moved into Gebbia's apartment in San Francisco so they could try their luck as tech entrepreneurs. "At the time, I had one thousand dollars in my bank account and I drove to SF," Chesky recalled during an interview at Stanford University in 2015.

This was in 2007. Upon arriving in San Francisco I had learned my portion of rent for the place we had was twelve hundred dollars, so I literally didn't have enough to pay rent. At the same time, there was this international design conference coming to SF, and on the event page it showed all of the nearby hotels were completely sold-out.

We had this idea that the designers coming to attend the conference needed a place to stay. We had no money, so what if we created a bed-and-breakfast for the design conference? The problem with this idea was we didn't have any beds—however, we did have three inflatable air beds. This is where we came up with the name Air Bed and Breakfast, and our first site was airbedandbreakfast.com. We ended up hosting three people in our home during the conference, and at the time we thought this was a cool and funny way to make some money.

After this experience, Joe brought in Nathan Blecharczyk—one of his old roommates—and we decided to do this as a company. The core idea was, What if you could book someone's home just like you could book a hotel room, anywhere in the world?

Put this way, the idea seems like the sort of dinky "business" a few postcollege guys might throw together on a whim. Even Chesky laughed when he began the interview by admitting that a number of people had told him, "Airbnb is the worst idea that has ever worked."

At first, the company faltered. "We launched three separate times in 2008," Chesky remembered. After the third launch, the team was introduced to fifteen angel investors. "Seven didn't respond, four said it 'didn't fit with their thesis,' one said they didn't like the market, and three just passed." Chesky and Gebbia funded the company with a string of credit cards that they stored in a baseball-card sleeve and were soon bogged down with more than $30,000 in debt.

Like Brie Larson, Chesky was open about his barriers. In the summer of 2015 he shared screenshots of those original rejection emails in a Medium blog post. They're peppered with such phrases as "not something we would do here," "not our area of focus," "the potential market opportunity did not seem large enough," and "we've always struggled with travel as a category." Obviously Airbnb weathered these early storms and emerged intact. The team met with dozens of its early hosts to learn what did and didn't work about the product. That year, the founders lived in Airbnb-hosted apartments to experience the service firsthand. What made the difference between a three-star experience, a five-star experience, and—as Chesky likes to call a sublime review—"a seven-star experience"? Airbnb eventually grew, first in

New York, and then in other US cities, and investors began to take the company seriously. The company raised $620,000 in 2009, $7 million in 2010, and $112 million in 2011. Despite its many hiccups, most people most of the time focus on the company's successful destination rather than the barriers that hampered its journey.

Airbnb isn't unusual in its bumpy path to prosperity. Take another behemoth, Amazon, and you'll find the same hurdles. Dan Rose managed retail divisions at Amazon from 1999 to 2006 and helped launch the Kindle. In September 2020, Rose posted a thread of tweets recalling how the company teetered shortly after he joined, in November 1999:

> Amazon launched in July 1995, and every Xmas was a near death experience for the first 7 years. I joined in '99 and got to experience this first hand. Starting in late Nov, all corporate employees were shipped to fulfillment centers to pack boxes for 6 weeks. Here's what I saw:
>
> Despite efforts to plan ahead, the company literally couldn't keep up with holiday demand. 40% of all annual orders would come through in 6 weeks from Thanksgiving through New Year's. . . . Xmas '95, every employee including [CEO Jeff] Bezos packs boxes for 6 straight weeks, then vows to never let that happen again. . . . By the time I joined in '99 it was an annual tradition. . . .
>
> Picking items, packing boxes, wrapping gifts for 10 hours/day x 6 days/week is fucking hard work. I have immense appreciation for the people who do these jobs. Your legs ache, your eyes go blurry. . . . [It's] exhausting.

Jeff Bezos ultimately brought in Jeff Wilke, who saved the growing company from itself. Wilke's background in manufacturing gave him the tools to turn Amazon's warehouses into finely tuned machines, ultimately allowing the company to promise the same-day and next-day delivery options that fueled its Prime membership service. Wilke's role was so instrumental in Amazon's success that he ultimately became the company's CEO of worldwide consumer business—a position that placed him second in charge behind only Bezos himself. In an interview Wilke gave shortly before he retired in January 2021, he remembered those early days when Amazon's fulfillment process was stuck:

> So I took the playbook that I had, which came from manufacturing, and implemented it in retail. It was really the first time that some of these techniques had been applied in a retail environment. And fortunately, they worked, [producing] very short cycle times, lower waste, lower defects. And that's what enabled us to launch Prime. Prime is basically a subscription to this.

What we focus on is Amazon's immense success, rather than its struggles. But what might have happened in an alternate reality where the company failed to overcome these early hurdles? In this universe, like so many other fledgling companies, Amazon might have collapsed beneath the weight of its own success. By its third or fourth holiday period, in the late 1990s, this alt-Amazon was receiving hundreds of thousands of online book orders. Its ersatz fulfillment team was forced to work twenty-plus hours a day to keep up with demand. Many orders arrived late, and customers were furious. Kids were denied the latest Harry Potter book on Christmas morning, and their parents were left without Stephen King's holiday bestseller. The company had gone public in May 1997, but by 1998 or 1999 its stock price tanked in the wake of terrible reviews. (Even in reality, many early reviews of the company were quite negative. *Slate* called the company "Amazon.con," and the *Wall Street Journal* called it "Amazon.bomb.") By the early 2000s, alt-Amazon imploded. And since it no longer captured the attention of major newspapers, websites, and reviewers, its struggles faded from view. The company was stuck, but, as with the thousands of other companies that close every day, nobody was there to document its decline.

The bottom line is that entrepreneurial struggles are hard to see regardless of whether a business succeeds or fails. Success eclipses the struggles that preceded it, while failure is so commonplace that it tends to escape our attention. Instead, we're exposed to story after story about Apple, Google, Facebook, Netflix, and an elite group of similarly exceptional successes.

———

Brie Larson, Airbnb, and Amazon are just three examples, but you don't need to cherry-pick. Just dig one or two layers deep into our culture's most prominent success stories and you'll find frustrated protagonists. A young Fred Astaire complained of being stuck after a Hollywood producer rejected him with the statement "Can't act. Slightly bald. Dances a little." When Walt Disney's first studio, Laugh-O-Gram, went into bankruptcy, he endured five years of inertia before designing a cartoon mouse who would go on to become his new studio's mascot. Photorealist painter Chuck Close suffered what he called "the event" in 1988—a seizure that partially paralyzed him from the waist down. For decades his hyperrealistic paintings had relied on fine motor movements that were now impossible. Close was initially despondent, but in time he learned to paint in a new, expressive style with a brush strapped to his wrist. As he emerged from the fog of grief, Close famously claimed, "Inspiration is for amateurs; the rest of us just show up and get to work. If you wait around for the clouds to part and a bolt of lightning to strike you in the brain, you are not going to make an awful lot of work."

Closer to home for me, stories of chronic writer's block are legion. Ralph Ellison wrote the classic bestseller *Invisible Man* in 1952 and failed to write a follow-up before his death in 1994, more than half a lifetime later. During those four decades, he amassed two thousand pages of notes for his planned second novel and complained to his friend and fellow writer Saul Bellow that he "had a writer's block as big as the Ritz." Harper Lee flirted with a similar fate. She published *To*

Kill a Mockingbird in 1960, at age thirty-four, and only published its sequel, *Go Set a Watchman*, in 2015, a year before her death at age eighty-nine. Though much of *Watchman* was written in the mid-1950s, before *Mockingbird* was published, Lee "polished" the manuscript for fifty-five years. "I've found I can't write," she told a friend. "I have about three hundred personal friends who keep dropping in for a cup of coffee. I've tried getting up at six, but then all the six o'clock risers congregate."

George R. R. Martin, the author of the A Song of Ice and Fire book series, which inspired the *Game of Thrones* TV show, released the series' first three books in 1996, 1999, and 2000. The fourth and fifth arrived in 2005 and 2011, and to date—more than a decade later—the sixth and seventh books are nowhere to be seen. Martin has been candid about his struggles. "I know there are a lot of people out there who are very angry with me that [the sixth book] isn't finished. And I'm mad about that myself. I wished I finished it four years ago. I wished it was finished now. But it's not. . . . What the hell is happening here? I've got to do this."

Martin isn't shy about his battle with writer's block, but even in a case as public as this one, success is brighter than struggle. At its peak, the average *Game of Thrones* episode attracted around 44 million viewers. To those fans, the richness of the world Martin created, and his skill as a fantasy writer, eclipse his writing demons. What they see primarily is a man whose writing inspired a $3 billion entertainment empire.

Writer's block has plagued humans for as long as they've been writing, but its formal origins lie with poet Samuel Taylor Coleridge. Coleridge commemorated his thirty-second birthday, in 1804, by complaining that writing inspired in him "an indefinite indescribable Terror." A year had passed "with scarcely the fruits of a month," and Coleridge had succumbed to an opium addiction. "O Sorrow and Shame," he wrote, "I have done nothing!" In 1949, an Austrian psychiatrist named Edmund Bergler coined the term *writer's block*, which he understood through a Freudian lens. Bergler believed writers who were denied milk by their mothers, or who were bottle-fed, would encounter blocks whenever stress forced them to divert valuable mental resources to cope with panic. Today some experts argue that writer's block isn't real—that it's the natural product of procrastination, poor planning or strategy, or the extended absence of good ideas. Whatever you call it, though, the sense of being stuck as you pursue creative output is familiar to almost every writer.

The same "block" affects other creatives, too. For most of his sixty-seven-year painting career, Claude Monet was a model of productive success. Between the 1860s and 1920s, Monet painted around twenty-five hundred works and inspired the term *Impressionism*, and hundreds of English art lovers voted his Water Lilies series Great Britain's favorite paintings. But even Monet suffered an extended bout of creative block. Late in the spring of 1911, his second wife, Alice Hoschedé, died, leaving Monet distraught. Following her death, Monet destroyed dozens or perhaps even hundreds of his canvases and was unable to paint for two years. Other artists, from Jackson Pollock to Pablo Picasso, described similar periods of creative frustration, struggling to produce a single work for months or even years. Still, we remember them, as we remember Coleridge and Monet, for their triumphs rather than their struggles.

What we see today in Brie Larson, Airbnb, Amazon, and famous but sometimes-frustrated writers, artists, and composers are the glossy "after" shots. The "before" shots, which are usually hidden, are rougher around the edges. They're laden with uncertainty and anxiety. Each of these colossal successes had an excellent chance of failing before ultimately getting unstuck. For every public success story there are hundreds or thousands of private stories of frustration.

———

In early 2020, just before the COVID pandemic descended, I distributed an online survey to hundreds of people. I'd read of the frustrations of prominent actors, writers, and entrepreneurs, but wanted to learn more about how the rest of us experience getting stuck. Some of the people who responded were living in poverty, but others were obscenely wealthy. Some were unemployed, but others were business titans. Some saw themselves as chronic underdogs, but others were Olympic champions. Some were trapped in bad relationships and mind-numbing careers, but others were happily married and prospering at work.

I learned at least three things from the people who were kind enough to respond to my survey.

First, I learned that being stuck is ubiquitous. Every one of the people I asked told me she was stuck in at least one respect at that moment. Some were stuck in bad relationships; some in stagnant careers; some were incapable of losing or gaining or maintaining weight; some were struggling to start a new business or to apply to school or to pay off loans or to save for their futures. Some sought creative solutions to enduring problems; others felt the solution was obvious but they were "frozen on the spot."

I measured how long people took to respond to each question in the survey and found that, on average, they needed less than ten seconds to identify a sticking point. Seventy percent of them said the sticking point came to mind "very easily" because it sucked up a big chunk of the mental energy they expended every day. Half had been stuck for years or decades, and 80 percent had been stuck for longer than a month. Seventy-nine percent felt "very or extremely negative emotions" when thinking about this situation, and—striking because most of them weren't wealthy—many were willing to pay thousands of dollars, and to sacrifice a large portion of their assets, to free themselves.

The second thing I learned is that people don't realize how common it is to be stuck. Many people said they felt lonely and isolated, imagining that the rest of the world was making progress while they were fixed in place. They described a mixture of anxiety, uncertainty, fear, anger, and numbness. Psychologists call this a classic case of pluralistic ignorance—the tendency to believe you see the world differently from other people when in fact you feel the same way. For example, if you ask college students how comfortable they are with the drinking norms on campus, most will tell you they privately believe that students drink too much, but that the average college student is quite comfortable with campus drinking norms. The problem arises because behavior is visible, but attitudes and beliefs are hidden from view. Most college students don't visibly protest campus drinking norms—and some visibly drink too much alcohol—so students are left believing their views are unusual. In the case of being stuck, I found the same pattern: people imagine others are gliding through life and only they and a minority of other people feel stuck.

The third thing I learned is that the diverse instances of "being stuck" my respondents described fall into two categories: those that are imposed from outside, and those that originate within the individual. Externally imposed constraints can be intractable. If you want to travel from New York to Paris during a pandemic and the borders are closed, you're physically stuck; if you want a Ferrari but can't afford a used Honda, you're financially stuck. These instances of inertia reflect constraints that aren't always surmountable, and they're largely beyond the scope of this book. They're also relatively uncommon—in the survey I learned that truly intractable inertia is surprisingly rare, accounting for around 10 percent of all cases of chronic immobility. People want plenty of things they can't have, but they're plagued by the things they feel they *should* or *could* have. I'm far more interested in these internal roadblocks—the 90-plus percent that are surmountable. They may be difficult to overcome, but they're ripe for intervention. To give you a sense of how they sound, here's a small sample from my survey:

Respondent 6: "I'm in my 30s. I can't seem to save up money. I always find ways to spend in the moment and can't get myself to stop. Saving is impossible for me. I'm anxious and fearful about how I'll afford to live in the future."

Respondent 107: "I've been trying to learn how to play the piano.

I was making steady progress, but in the last couple of years, I feel I haven't improved at all. I continue to practice the basics but I feel stuck, and it is making me worry that I'll never improve. It feels as if I'm wasting my time."

Respondent 384: "I'm stuck in a thankless job and want to be able to start my own business. I want to take the leap, but I'm worried about my finances and the uncertainty of going out on my own. Thinking about this leaves me numb and devoid of emotion."

Respondent 443: "I'm an artist. I've hit a plateau and can't seem to improve further. I need to practice—to put my nose to the grindstone—to improve my skill in drawing portraits and landscapes. I need to learn how to be more creative, and to find creative solutions to my problems."

You can hear the frustration as you read each account. Respondent 6 lacks the willpower to save money more responsibly. Respondent 107 has plateaued on the road to learning a new skill. Respondent 384 is scared to leap from a stable but uninspiring job to a risky business venture. And Respondent 443 is grinding through a period of creative block. Theirs are four brief stories among hundreds of responses, and surely among billions of humans across the globe. Each of these people was willing to pay hundreds or thousands of dollars to get unstuck— including, paradoxically, Respondent 6, who says both that he doesn't know how to save money and that he'd pay $500 to get unstuck.

—

As the respondents to my survey showed, to be alive is to battle stuckness. People get stuck at home and at work; financially and intellectually; individually and interpersonally. They get stuck as creatives and entrepreneurs; as athletes and thinkers; alone and in groups. The term *stuck* covers a broad range of contexts and experiences, but to be stuck, as I think of it, means three things: (1) that you're temporarily unable to make progress in a domain that matters to you; (2) that you've been fixed in place for long enough to feel psychological discomfort; and

(3) that your existing habits and strategies aren't solving the problem. Being stuck, then, is more than brief discomfort that can be remedied with the diligent application of old ideas. Getting unstuck requires the right blend of emotional, mental, and behavioral tools, and *Anatomy of a Breakthrough* is a strategic guide in the war against stuckness—a war with four distinct battles that make up the four sections of this book.

The first section, "Help," demystifies the experience of being stuck. Once you accept that being stuck is universal, you're primed to ask how it could be a feature of progress, rather than an uncommon glitch. Why is being stuck a natural default state, while consistent progress is vanishingly rare? Why do so many public success stories begin with extended, private bouts of hardship? Why do barriers block the paths of people across so many disciplines, from entrepreneurs and athletes to actors, artists, and writers?

The book's second section, "Heart," focuses on the emotional consequences of stuckness. It's painful, it's anxiety provoking, and it can be lonely. That's because friction is naturally isolating. It forces you to focus sharply on whatever's blocking your path, so it's easy to overlook the millions of other frustrated people and organizations stuck in their own separate bubbles. Mastering your emotional response to being stuck is a critical step in getting unstuck, and many of our intuitive responses entrench us further rather than propelling us forward. Sometimes slowing down, and questioning our intuitions, paves the best path forward.

The book's third section, "Head," moves from hot emotional states to calculated mental strategies. Getting unstuck is, to a large extent, a matter of following the right mental scripts. Being stuck complicates your life, and often the best way to move forward is to simplify the problem, to identify opportunities to deviate from an existing path, and to recognize that input from many brains is often—but not always—better than your own ideas alone.

The book's fourth and final section, "Habit," focuses on the actions that take you from sticking point to breakthrough. The most important principle is to take action even if you're moving sideways. Action is the great unsticker because it necessarily replaces inertia with movement. Some actions are more helpful than others, and this fourth section examines the most fruitful of those, and the best order in which to pursue them.

But before you can start working on your heart, head, and habits, you need to understand what it means to be stuck, why being stuck is so common, and when, during any extended experience, you're most likely to get stuck. Enter the work of an American psychologist named Clark Hull, who studied the mechanics of stuckness.

PART I

HELP

1

WHY GETTING STUCK IS INEVITABLE

Clark Hull spent his academic career studying rats in mazes, which was poetic because his youth was littered with dead ends. By the age of eighteen, Hull had been forced to join—and managed to escape—a religious sect. He battled typhoid and polio, one after the other, and almost lost the ability to walk and to see. "My eyes were so weak," he remembered, "that my mother began reading William James' *Principles of Psychology* to me." Hull dabbled in mathematics, physics, chemistry, and engineering, but nothing clicked until James' classic book launched Hull's stellar career as a research psychologist.

Hull spent three decades as a professor at Yale, where he studied maze running in rats. He and his colleagues would bet milkshakes on which rat would run each maze fastest. Hull was incredibly productive. According to his friend and colleague Carl Hovland, Hull was by far the most cited psychologist in the late 1940s and early 1950s. "Hull's scientific work comprised [several] phases," Hovland said, "each of which constituted what other men would be proud to consider the work of an entire lifetime."

Hull spent decades watching rats run mazes because, like many psychologists at the time, he was interested in learning and behavior. The mazes allowed him to measure how fast the animals were moving in a controlled environment. Over and over he saw the same pattern: the rats moved quickly when they neared the end of the maze, but moved slowly or stopped altogether at its beginning and middle. The end of the maze was like a magnet that pulled them more strongly as they got closer. This was true regardless of whether the mazes were long, straight tunnels or complex webs of trunks and branches. Hull called this pattern the *goal gradient effect*. Though the maze was completely flat, the rats seemed to experience it differently as they went along. They appeared to struggle as if running uphill during its early sections, but sprinted as if running downhill when the goal was in sight.

In the ninety years since Hull described the effect, psychologists have shown that it applies to people, too. In one experiment from a paper published in 2006, researchers tracked how quickly customers bought ten cups of coffee on the way to a free eleventh cup. The interval between the first and second cup was 20 percent longer than the interval between the ninth and tenth cups, suggesting that coffee drinkers were significantly more motivated as they approached that free eleventh cup. In another experiment, people who visited a music-rating website were offered a $25 Amazon voucher for rating fifty-one songs on fifty different scales—a total of 2,550 ratings. Raters were forty times more likely to quit early in the task than closer to the goal, and they rated more songs each time they visited the site. Those who required four visits to complete the task, for example, rated an average of six songs on their first visit, and an average of eighteen songs on the fourth and final visit. As with Hull's rats, they were slower and more likely to stop the farther they were from the goal.

I first learned about Hull's goal gradient effect as an undergrad, more than twenty years ago. The professor told us he'd seen evidence of the effect in his own lab rats, but that the effect was more complicated than Hull believed. Most rats move more quickly as they approach the end of the maze, but many also move quickly when they first begin running. Instead of just running faster and faster as the maze continues, they seem to follow a *quick-slow-quick* pattern. They buzz with excitement when they enter the maze, but soon seem to get stuck when the maze is more complicated or longer than they expect it to be.

This quick-slow-quick wrinkle in Hull's original effect applies to people, too. In one experiment designed by my NYU colleague Andrea

Bonezzi, students who proofread nine essays for typos were 20 percent slower to find typos in the fifth essay than in the second and eighth essays. In a second experiment, students tried to find as many shorter words as they could within nine longer words (for example, the word *manager* includes the words *man*, *game*, and *name*, among others). On average they found 19 percent fewer words on their fifth attempt than on their second or eighth attempts. As the researchers noted, people seem to get "stuck in the middle."

As researchers continued to monitor goal progress in other domains, the goal gradient effect kept appearing. No matter the domain, people seemed to slow down or stop midway through the task, and to speed up when they thought they were approaching the goal. That was true when people decided how much to give to charitable appeals, how many pieces of unappealing but healthy broccoli and cauliflower to eat, how much credit card debt to pay off, how loyal to remain to businesses as they approached reward milestones, and even how quickly to walk toward a product they had decided to buy. People are also more likely to behave unethically or to compromise their morals to make progress when they're stuck midway to a goal—at moments when they feel especially hopeless and therefore willing to sacrifice the high ground for a desperate step forward. Across almost every imaginable context, people advance slowly or stop altogether when goals feel far away, and they move more quickly when those goals appear to be within reach.

It's easy to understand why we get stuck in the middle if you imagine an ocean liner traveling between New York and Southampton. As the ship leaves New York, its captain looks back to see the Empire State Building recede farther with each mile of progress. The incremental value of each mile is clear because New York's landmarks look different all the time. Two weeks later, Britain's southwestern tip appears, and the captain watches as his ship enters the English Channel, steers between the coasts of northwestern France and southwestern Britain, then hooks a northerly left turn past the Isle of Wight on to Southampton. That final segment of the journey is dotted with landmarks that show the passage of each mile traveled. In contrast, New York and the British and French coasts are separated by thousands of miles of open water. The same miles that register at the beginning and the end of the journey barely register when the captain sees the same blue-gray panorama hour after hour, day after day. If New York is the goal's origin, and Southampton is the goal's end, it's easy to see why sailors might lose motivation as they traverse the oceanic expanse between them. If you're trying to lose 100 pounds or save $10,000, the 45th pound and 5,010th dollar barely register as meaningful progress.

One remedy for the midpoint lull is to shrink or eliminate the middle altogether. The easiest way to do that is to divide larger experiences into smaller subexperiences. This is known as narrow bracketing. You can bracket any experience broadly by thinking of it as a single, long event, or narrowly by thinking of it as many smaller subexperiences. Take the case of a marathon. At the broadest end of the bracketing spectrum, the marathon is a single stretch of 26.2 miles. At the narrowest end, the same marathon is a chain of thousands of individual steps—about sixty thousand for the average runner. Many runners play the "one step at a time" mantra on repeat during the darkest moments of marathons and ultramarathons in part because there's no room for a midpoint lull when you bracket the distance so narrowly.

You can apply the same logic to any extended goal using one of two approaches: either you can audit the goal by breaking it into small chunks that reflect real subdivisions of the goal, or, if the goal can't be broken down naturally, you can craft those subdivisions artificially. Say the goal is moving from a job you hate to a job you love—a sticking point for many people. You might break the process down into making a list of alternative jobs; writing a list of pros and cons for each of those jobs relative to your current job; creating an ordered wish list of those jobs from "most desirable" to "least desirable"; deciding which jobs in your list fall above a "threshold of desirability"—in other words, they're better than your current job to such an extent that it's worth applying for them; and, finally, applying for those jobs and keeping your fingers crossed. These are real, material chunks in the job-upgrading process, and you can mark the completion of each one with a cupcake or a glass of Scotch, or however else you like to celebrate small victories. Other goals aren't easy to break down naturally, so you need to create your own narrow brackets. If you're trying to save $3,000 for the first payment on a new car, you can create a chart that splits that sum into ten smaller chunks of $300—and, again, reward yourself with a cupcake or a glass of Scotch as you complete each subgoal. The rule here is that you can't get stuck in the middle if you eradicate the middle completely.

———

Middles are problematic in other contexts, too. One of Clark Hull's intellectual heroes was a Prussian psychologist named Hermann Ebbinghaus. Like Hull, Ebbinghaus believed you should investigate what makes animals tick by observing their behavior. Whereas Hull measured motivation through maze-running rats, Ebbinghaus studied learning and forgetfulness. "A poem is learned by heart and then not again repeated," wrote Ebbinghaus. "We will suppose that after a half year it has been forgotten: no effort of recollection is able to call it back again into consciousness." He was fascinated by the tendency for information to vanish forever, never to return, so decided to use himself as a test guinea pig. For days on end, Ebbinghaus forced himself to memorize and recall thousands of three-letter nonsense syllables, or trigrams. He'd sit and stare at small cards with trigrams like GOS, FID, and CUV for hours at a time, before trying to remember as many as he could the following day. Mirroring Hull's goal gradient effect, Ebbinghaus tended to remember the first and last words in his long lists more often than the words in the middle. Somehow, the words in the middle blurred together or escaped his memory completely. Like Hull, Ebbinghaus was stuck in the middle.

Ebbinghaus tried to improve his memory, particularly for words in the middle of the list, by studying them tens or even hundreds of times. The task was mind-numbingly boring and mentally taxing, but he persevered. He discovered that beyond a certain point there wasn't much value in learning the list one or two or even ten more times. His brute-force approach to learning had its limits, and so was born the plateau effect—the tendency for techniques that work well at first to lose their value over time. Ebbinghaus didn't spend much time considering why his ability to learn trigrams plateaued, but he was meticulous about showing that the same approach used over and over eventually stopped working. The same technique that drove you forward yesterday will leave you stuck in place today.

Plateau effects—like goal gradients—are everywhere. Ebbinghaus studied memorization, but his intellectual offspring have shown plateaus in hundreds of studies across dozens of mental and physical pursuits. If you're trying to understand why people get stuck, and how to unstick them, you have to understand that even the best strategies and approaches need to be revised from time to time. If you're trying to lose weight, build stronger muscles, or learn a new language, you can't keep eating the same foods, following the same exercise routine, or using the same techniques to memorize new words. That's a problem for our species because we're creatures of habit. Once a technique works, we tend to use it over and over rather than revising our approach. That makes sense—starting from scratch requires time and energy—but those same techniques eventually stop working. The same diet, exercise regime, or language-learning schedule that worked in the past will progressively lose its power over time.

The best recent evidence for the plateau effect comes from a study of fifteen thousand people who followed an "ultra-minimalist" training plan for up to seven years. Fit20, the Dutch company that devised the plan, described it as "personal health training in 20 minutes per week . . . no hassle with changing/showering." It involved a circuit of six simple exercises repeated once a week that initially seemed to be effective. Exercisers gained strength quickly for the first year or so, but then gains came much more slowly or stopped altogether. The same was true for men and women, older and younger participants. The researchers pointed out, too, that competitive powerlifters gain strength rapidly for about a year, before reaching a similar sticking point, so the plateau effect isn't just restricted to this one training program.

As the training program suggested, we hit plateaus for at least two reasons. The first is habituation: if you're, say, training certain muscles, your muscles adapt to the same exercises and stop developing unless you introduce a new approach. In the case of dieting, your body learns to cope with less food, so your metabolism slows and you stop burning calories as quickly. The smaller portions that pushed you to lose weight are now metabolized more slowly, so you stop losing weight and need to try a different diet. The same is true of any other process that teaches you to become more efficient. It's the struggle up front that drives you to lose weight, gain physical fitness, or engage deeply enough to learn new skills (or lists of trigrams). The best way to short-circuit habituation is to try new strategies.

A second cause of plateaus is that we're myopic, or shortsighted. We prefer an adequate solution now to a great solution in the long run. Bob Sullivan and Hugh Thompson—a writer and a mathematician who wrote the book *The Plateau Effect*—explain this with an example: Imagine you're rushing to a meeting twenty blocks north of your current location in Manhattan, money is no object, and you have two options. You can either jump in a cab right now, or you can walk south two blocks to a subway station, where you'll wait for a few minutes for the next train, which will then carry you uptown. Seasoned New Yorkers who are in a rush know the subway's far quicker than a taxi, so they're willing to walk backward because they'll travel more quickly in the long run. Tourists, on the other hand, will choose the option that allows them to make *immediate* progress, though they'll ultimately cover those twenty blocks much more slowly than the seasoned local. Tourists hit a plateau when their taxis are stuck in traffic, while veterans sacrifice brief, early progress for sustained, consistent progress later. In most domains, unfortunately, humans are more like tourists than veterans. We avoid going backward now even if that ultimately makes us quicker in the long run. The solution here has two parts: habitually question whether you're privileging short-term progress over long-term gains, and make a point of learning the difference between paths forward. Most tourists may opt for the taxi over the subway, but those who do their homework will know the subway's usually a better option.

When you add goal gradients to plateau effects, the sum isn't pretty. The goal gradient slows us down in the short and medium term, whereas the plateau effect slows us in the long term. The silver lining is that you can plan for both effects because they happen at predictable points during an extended process. If you know to expect them, they're less likely to stymie your progress. This same desire to weaken setbacks by predicting them before they arrive is at the root of many models of human progress. Fifteen years after Hull's death, a Canadian psychoanalyst named Elliott Jaques noticed a predictable dip in progress that mirrored Hull's midpoint lull in goal progress. The difference was that Jaques wasn't focused on a single maze or a single task; he was interested in progress and friction across the entire human life span.

———

In 1965, Jaques noticed that dozens of creative geniuses lost their mojo just before they turned forty. He pointed out that Bach's creativity ebbed after he turned thirty-eight; Goethe's genius abandoned him when he was thirty-nine; and Michelangelo produced little art beyond his late thirties. This, Jaques explained, was how some middle-aged adults responded to the specter of their own deaths: they experienced a "midlife crisis." Midlife crises express themselves in different ways for different people, but most commonly, Jaques argued, they lead people to question whether their lives are meaningful. For many people, approaching the age of forty is the first time they confront the idea that life won't last forever.

Though Jaques was broadly right to suggest we find the specter of death overwhelming, the midlife crisis concept was too narrow. We experience the same sort of crisis whenever time seems to run away from us. When I was twenty-nine years old—a decade before Jaques' definition of midlife—I had the same sense of being stuck. With almost three decades under my belt, I felt paralyzed by how quickly the rest of my life would streak by. The solution, as I saw it, was to inject my life with fresh meaning by adopting a long-term goal: training for and running my first marathon while raising money for a medical charity.

Several years later, my colleague Hal Hershfield and I discussed how my experience as a twenty-nine-year-old mapped onto the concept of the midlife crisis. It made us wonder whether approaching any major landmark in aging—not just midlife—might create existential friction. Because most of the world follows the base-ten number system, we wondered if each new decade of life starting with age thirty might inspire a fresh crisis of meaning. We decided to search for signs that people question the meaningfulness of their lives shortly before the arrival of a new decade, when their age ends in a nine—twenty-nine, thirty-nine, forty-nine, fifty-nine, and so on. (We called these nine-ending ages.)

The evidence mounted across a range of contexts and measures. When thousands of people around the world completed the World Values Survey, a global research project that studies people's values and beliefs, one of the questions asked the extent to which they wondered whether their lives were meaningful. As we expected, people who were nine-enders were more likely to report questioning the meaningfulness of their lives.

This life audit has different consequences for different people. Some feel pleased by how they've spent their time, and optimistic about the years that remain. Others are less pleased when they examine the past, but—as I did by running a marathon—find productive ways to unstick themselves. We found, for example, that people with nine-ending ages were overrepresented among first-time marathon runners, and people who ran multiple marathons ran faster at nine-ending ages than they ran a year or two earlier or later. A third group, though, found this audit intimidating. Among this group, we found evidence of destructive behavior: the suicide rate rises ever so slightly among nine-enders, and nine-ending men are disproportionately likely to use Ashley Madison, a dating website for people seeking extramarital affairs. (The same may be true of nine-ending women, but we only had reliable data on males.)

Some people experience this crisis a little earlier or later. Although these behaviors peak at nine-ending ages, the data pattern looks more like a wave: people's concerns about meaning start to rise at eight-ending ages, crest at nine-ending ages, and begin to fall at zero-ending ages. For many, these concerns inspire a crisis that fixes them in place. Instead of moving forward, or finding ways to get unstuck, they turn to nihilism and self-destruction.

Though the effect is subtle, other researchers have replicated and refined the basic pattern. In one study, people increasingly emphasized broad, long-term facets of health and well-being over momentary happiness as they approached the transition between two decades in age. In another, researchers noticed that, although people question the meaning in their lives more intently when they imagine the end of a decade, they don't necessarily perceive their lives to be more meaningful at those points in life. For many of them, this introspective experience was threatening and overwhelming.

These results are important because the behaviors we examined were highly consequential. If people are slightly more likely to seek extramarital affairs or even to end their lives as new decades approach, mental health practitioners and policy makers should be aware of this pattern. If we understand that many people struggle when evaluating their lives, we're better prepared to encourage them to deal with this struggle constructively rather than destructively—by, for example, taking up a new form of exercise, eating healthier foods, saving for retirement, or donating to charitable causes.

Though nine-ending crises are easy to anticipate, many other barriers are harder to foresee. These are the sticking points that often do the most damage because they arise without warning, often when we least expect them. These unexpected jolts are what Bruce Feiler has called lifequakes.

———

Bruce Feiler describes himself as a "lifestorian"—a collector of personal-life stories the way a historian collects historical artifacts. For decades Feiler's life was "ascending." He became an immensely successful writer and TV personality, he worked in a circus and traveled with Garth Brooks, and got married and fathered identical twin girls. Then he seemed to hit a string of roadblocks. He was diagnosed with a rare form of bone cancer that required sixteen rounds of chemo, invasive surgeries, and several years of recovery. Pummeled by the Great Recession, he almost went bankrupt, and his father attempted suicide several times. People seek comfort in different ways, but Feiler's comfort came from conversations with friends and strangers. His mantra became "When in turmoil, turn to narrative."

"I felt stuck, and so I went out looking for stories," Feiler told me. As soon as he was healthy enough to travel, he spent three years traipsing across all fifty states while collecting 225 life stories. These stories formed the basis for Feiler's bestselling book *Life Is in the Transitions*. Each life story was unique, but with a large enough sample Feiler began to see consistencies amid the noise. "Doing these conversations all day every day, it became clear that there was this pattern," he said.

Far from being unusual, Feiler's setbacks were mirrored in the stories he heard around the country. He discovered that every life story was dotted with small and large life disruptions. There were no exceptions. Young, old, rich, poor, professional, laborer, urban, rural—

disruptions were universal. Most of these setbacks were unchosen, like losing a job or battling an illness, and most were unwanted. Some were minor—these happened every twelve to eighteen months for most people—but roughly every tenth disruption was a major life event. He struggled to find a neutral term that captured these disruptions in all their diversity, but ultimately settled on the term *lifequakes*.

"These are the wolves that upend our fairy tales," Feiler wrote about lifequakes. Lifequakes are sticking points, Feiler noted, because they place roadblocks in whatever path we are following. They prevent us from pursuing the lives we previously imagined living and so leave us stuck as we attempt to construct revised lives in their wake. He combed through the stories he'd heard to organize the various lifequakes by type and frequency. In roughly descending order of regularity, people reported medical issues; deaths and personal losses; the end of relationships; financial setbacks; job losses or changes; natural disasters; and personal shifts in response to movements like Black Lives Matter or the Tea Party. Seven in eight lifequakes were personal events, but one in eight affected a group of people. Feiler finished writing his book shortly before the first cases of COVID-19 emerged, and he told me that the pandemic was the biggest collective lifequake "in a hundred years." As roadblocks go, he believed it affected more people across the planet more profoundly than any other event in living memory. He also discovered that six in ten lifequakes are involuntary events that arrive suddenly, and six in seven involve a shift from stability to volatility. This volatility shakes people and leaves many of them stuck. Lifequakes are so disruptive that they last for an average of five years. "We spend a huge percentage of our lives in transition," Feiler wrote. "If you consider that we go through three to five lifequakes in our adult lives, and each one lasts four, five, six years, or longer, that could be thirty-plus years we spend in a state of change. That's half a lifetime!"

The most important feature of lifequakes is that they're hard to predict. You don't plan for a lifequake the way you might anticipate an impending plateau, so instead you need to develop a general tool kit for managing unwanted change. "Life transitions are a skill," Feiler wrote. "They're a skill we can, and must, master." A particular lifequake may take you by surprise, but recognizing that lifequakes and other profound sticking points are inevitable puts you several steps ahead of the many people who respond first by asking, "Why me?!" Feiler told me that "Why me?!" exclamations are a modern, privileged response to sticking points. "The fact that we believe [being stuck] is noise rather than signal is a historical anomaly of the last one hundred and fifty years," he said. Much of this reflects "the myth of progress"— the largely Western idea that things improve over time. With the rise of science, modern medicine, and stock markets that grow an average of 7 percent yearly, we've come to believe that every problem can be solved, cured, or resolved. In Feiler's words, we're saddled by "the myth of human dominion over the natural world." When you look back in time or sideways to developing regions of the world, you'll see populations that expect disruption. When and where religion and philosophy dominate science, people are open to the idea that the world can be unpredictable and unkind. Where science and narratives of progress rule, societies are lulled into an illusion of invulnerability.

When Feiler released his book, he wasn't sure which aspects would resonate most with readers. Most of the emails, comments, and questions have focused on lifequakes. "I would say that the number one reaction I'm hearing from people is 'Whew!'" People felt liberated by the concept of the lifequake for two reasons. First, it gave a nonjudgmental label to a concept that affects all of us. Naming our experiences gives us a sense of control and makes us feel less lonely. Once a concept has a name, the logic goes, it can't be something that lives only in our heads. The second and I think more important reason is that the lifequakes concept recognizes that life is messy. Unlike with, say, the five-stage Kübler-Ross model of grief (denial, anger, bargaining, depression, acceptance), lifequakes can happen anytime with any order of emotions. Feiler was wise to recognize that there's no one-size-fits-all blueprint for disruption across the life span. Sometimes you'll avoid a lifequake for ten years, and then three or four will appear simultaneously. Feiler wrote about a young minister from Virginia named Erik Smith: "[Smith] preached at his mother's funeral, his father's funeral, left the church to become a special-needs teacher, had suicidal thoughts, got addicted to painkillers, and lost sixty pounds—all within two years." These are the stickiest of sticking points because they stretch your coping resources across not just one but many profound disruptions. The biggest challenge is knowing how much energy to devote to each one so you have enough left for the others. Meting out limited resources is a critical component to getting unstuck—and it's particularly important when you're most depleted, just before you reach the finish line. That's true metaphorically, as you cope with lifequakes; and it's also true when you're running on empty toward a literal finish line.

———

Chandler Self is a good marathon runner. She isn't an Olympian or a national champion, but she sometimes wins marathons and half-marathons, and she's considered "sub-elite." In 2017, she won the Dallas Marathon in a time of 2:53:57, though her victory came with an asterisk. Four miles from the end of the race Self passed her dad, who gestured to tell her she was in first place by a comfortable margin. Self was elated. "I was so excited!!" she wrote later. "Then I looked at my time, and thought, geez I might even get a [personal record]!! I declined fluid at the aid station. I was running so well, I didn't want to interrupt my pace with silly water! It wasn't hot outside and I didn't think I was sweating much. Then I was coming into the finish! I saw the finish line! And it was UPHILL. My legs gave out."

The footage of Self's legs "giving out" is hard to watch. "This is our winner, ladies and gentlemen," the race commentator says. "This is not normally what you expect to see at the finish of a marathon." Having completed 99.57 percent of the race, her body couldn't carry her another step. A seventeen-year-old high school student, who was running a relay race within the marathon, stopped running and generously helped Self to her feet. Self collapsed several more times, but, carried by the high schooler, ultimately crossed the finish line in first place. The race officials ruled that, since help had come from another competitor rather than a spectator or official, Self's victory was legal.

If you were grading Self's performance, you'd say she scored 99.57 percent. She was *so* close to apportioning her energy perfectly. Watch enough marathons and endurance races and you'll see dozens of athletes collapsing just as they reach the finish line. Some, like Self, collapse just before they arrive. It isn't a coincidence that they tend to fold within a few hundred yards of their goal. They're guided by teleoanticipation—literally, knowledge of an approaching end point (or telos). Teleoanticipation isn't an exact science, even when you know precisely how much ground you'll need to cover, so even seasoned athletes sometimes expend a few too many calories before they finish a race. Self's body, as it crumpled, was the perfect physical embodiment of stuckness.

Teleoanticipation was first described in 1996 by a German researcher named Hans-Volkhart Ulmer. "If the athlete runs too quickly," Ulmer wrote, "he will not be able to finish because of early fatigue, but if he runs too slowly, he will not reach his . . . optimal racing time. Therefore, the athlete has to arrange his energy consumption per unit time with respect to a finishing point." Ulmer described the behavior of athletes in his paper, but also wondered how migratory birds managed to fly for thousands of miles without landing. His paper is full of complex calculations and graphs because the problem of anticipating an ending is complicated. A migrating bird needs to pay attention to wind conditions, how much food it's consumed, when it's likely to eat again, the air temperature, and so on. Marathoners are saddled with a similar task. In addition to anticipating hills, wind conditions, and air temperature, you need to know whether you're feeling unusually strong or weak. If you're a runner, you'll know that on some days your legs feel like pogo sticks, and on others like concrete. Teleoanticipation isn't easy even when you have a precise finish line.

When athletes aren't aiming for a finish line, they move more slowly. If you don't know when an event ends, you can't expend your energy reserves. In one study, cyclists who completed two thirty-kilometer (eighteen-mile) time trials finished an average of almost two minutes, or 4 percent, slower when they weren't given an explicit end point. In another study, people performed boring mental tasks more slowly when they weren't told the task would run for ninety minutes. More important, they got stuck more often, taking more breaks from the task to replenish their mental resources.

There isn't a bright finish line when you're pursuing a career, parenting young kids, or trying to live a happier, healthier life. Many of these goals—the goals that matter most to the majority of us—are boundless, so the calculations we need to make are vastly more complex than the calculations Ulmer ascribed to migratory birds. When you add lifequakes to the mix—like, say, the COVID-19 pandemic—your physical, financial, and psychological resources are stretched further still. Alex Hutchinson, a writer who focuses on human endurance, described COVID-19 as "a marathon without a finish line." The solution, Hutchinson argued, was to treat the pandemic's open-ended format as a benefit rather than a weakness. "It turns out that, if you ask yourself 'Can I keep going?' rather than 'Can I make it to the finish?' you're far more likely to answer in the affirmative," Hutchinson suggested. French ultramarathon runner Guillaume Calmettes agreed: "[When there's no finish line,] you're never overwhelmed by what you have left to run because you simply don't know what you have left to run."

Calmettes' solution sounds a lot like the prescription for treating the friction you might encounter midway through an extended goal: break the goal down into its atomic components. Instead of focusing on the big picture, focus on the present. You won't find midpoint slumps if there's no midpoint, and the same logic applies to boundless goals. If you treat each step, minute, or unit of work as a discrete mini-goal, the absence of an end point is irrelevant. Put differently, Calmettes was advocating mindfulness in the context of goal pursuit.

Being mindful is akin to being profoundly present in the moment; paying attention to the task at hand and your relationship to that task. In being present, you're less likely to flail about for a finish line that doesn't actually exist.

———

Getting stuck is inevitable. During any extended experience, Clark Hull believed it happened early, his intellectual disciples believed it happened near the midpoint, and Hermann Ebbinghaus believed it happened late in the game. Between goal gradients, midpoint dips, and plateau effects, we're likely to get stuck somewhere along the way—and that's before we fold in Bruce Feiler's inevitable disruptions and lifequakes that strike as bolts from the blue. Even after completing 99 percent of the process, there's still a chance that, like Chandler Self at the Dallas Marathon finish line, we've underbudgeted by a fraction of a percent. Self poured too much of herself into that race, but the truth, for most of us most of the time, is that we tend to retreat too soon. At the first sign of friction, we despair that we'll perhaps never make progress again. The golden rule is that getting unstuck almost always takes longer than we expect—and too often we surrender just a few steps short of the finish line.

2

KEEP GOING

Hit pop songs are breezy by design, which hides the difficulty of turning catchy melodies into commercial gold. It takes time and talent to
shave away their rough edges, to "popify" them so listeners choose to
stream them dozens or even hundreds of times. This journey takes
incredible patience, often stretching across months or years. That was
the case for Magne Furuholmen, a young songwriter who was blessed
with an unusually deep well of persistence.

Furuholmen was fifteen when he composed a keyboard riff that
followed him from band to band for seven years. The catchy twenty-
seven-note melody was unpolished, but he eventually decided to spin
the hook into a complete song. His band was looking for a new singer,
and the top candidate thought the riff was dynamite. "Our new singer,
Morten Harket, said that he did not want to join the band if we did
not use it," Furuholmen remembered. Bowing to Harket's demand,
the band surrounded the riff with an intro, verses, and a bridge, and
the track was born. At first, the band struggled to name the tune. "It
started out being called 'Lesson One,'" Furuholmen recalled. "Then
we renamed the song 'All's Well That Ends Well and Moves with
the Sun.'"

Furuholmen's band was the Norwegian synth-pop trio a-ha, and the
track became "Take On Me." In October 1985, "Take On Me" reached
the number one spot on the *Billboard* charts in the United States and
stayed on the charts for twenty-seven weeks. It also topped the charts
in a dozen other countries, became an emblem for eighties synth pop,

and sold almost 10 million copies worldwide, making it one of the bestselling singles of all time.

Though it ultimately became a commercial hit, its journey was arduous. After Warner signed the band in 1984, its three young members recorded the first version of "Take On Me" in a London studio. The song was a commercial flop. This version, which is easy to find online, has the same genetic structure as the song's final version, but lacks much of its poppy charm. Warner's London office encouraged the band to record a music video of Harket moving to the song, but the video was forgettable amid a sea of similar mideighties pop videos. All three band members remember feeling stuck. Furuholmen's killer hook seemed to charm everyone who heard it, but the track was still undercooked. The unpredictable ups and downs of the music business seemed insurmountable. Just before their final tour, in 2009, the band remembered the frustrating process of refining the track. "To say that the boys were crushed is an understatement," the band wrote on its website. "The three idealists, who believed that talent alone would be enough to get them to the top, had now encountered so much adversity, wasted so much time, and been disappointed so often that they were on the point of giving up. They saw people's hopes, money and lives going to waste and decided to split up for a while."

Obviously the story didn't end there. A copy of the song reached Warner's main US office, and a group of influential execs decided to give the band one more chance to record a punchier mix in Warner's US studios. Critically, those same execs bankrolled a high-budget, semi-animated music video that took two months to produce, launched a-ha in the United States, and earned the band six MTV Video Music trophies in 1986. "I have no doubt that the video made the song a hit," Furuholmen said. "The song has a supercatchy riff, but it is a song that you have to hear a few times. And I don't think it would've been given the time of day without the enormous impact of the video."

The version of "Take On Me" that hit airwaves in 1985 was the product of an almost decade-long ascending creative spiral. Furuholmen's raw melody evolved more times than he could count, and the song continued to change even after it entered production. Each iteration became easier to digest for a-ha's commercial audience. But the song's path was tortuous. Success is lumpy, and most commercial triumphs are surrounded by discards and flops. Sometimes it takes years for the germ of an idea to become viable, and during that period there's a good chance its creators will consider abandoning the idea forever. a-ha were fortunate to get three bites at the pop music apple, and each time the product improved as Warner contributed a new chunk of resources, time, and commercial knowledge.

a-ha's frustration with the first version of its song reflects a common, naïve belief that creative products should arrive fully formed. The problem rests in how creativity is defined. Creativity requires using your imagination to produce something new. Most people can turn to their imagination at will, conjuring futures and worlds or events that may never exist. Using your imagination requires some effort, but not much, and the unspooling of an imagined idea happens over seconds or minutes more often than over years or decades. The quickness of our imaginations leads us to believe that creative products arrive quickly, or not at all. According to this belief, the best songs, artworks, films, and books are the products of distilled inspiration. If they aren't almost perfect early on, they're unlikely to improve later, and over time the quality of creative output generally declines. This idea is known as the creative cliff. As compelling as it seems, the cliff is an illusion. In truth, people tend to become more—not less—creative across time.

—

When psychologists Brian Lucas and Loran Nordgren first described the creative cliff illusion, they pointed out a paradox. On the one hand, we seem to recognize the value of persistence for other people. "Thomas Edison," they wrote, "experimented on over 1,600 filament materials—including hairs plucked from a friend's beard—before designing the electric light bulb." Stories of creativity through persistence are inspirational and hopeful, and we're taught from an early age that working hard is more effective than coasting. On the other hand, people also tend to doubt the value of persistence for their own sticking points. "If people do one round of a creativity task, and their brain feels fried, they're likely to disengage," Lucas told me. It's hard to train people to believe that mental difficulty is a sign of progress rather than stagnation.

In one experiment, Lucas and Nordgren asked people to spend ten minutes generating "as many original ideas for things to eat and drink at a Thanksgiving dinner as you can," then asked them to guess how many ideas they expected to generate during a second ten-minute period. Many of the participants felt stuck, imagining that their best ideas had already emerged, so expected to generate many fewer ideas during the second ten-minute block. In fact, they generated just as many ideas during that second block—66 percent more than they expected—and those ideas were rated *higher* in creativity by other people than the first crop of ideas.

Lucas and Nordgren found the same pattern over and over. People underestimated the value of persistence when trying to generate as many unusual uses for a cardboard box as they could, when coming up with ad slogans for a burger and fries, and when unscrambling letters to form words. Even experts weren't immune. Sketch comedians with years of training mistakenly believed their ability to write punch lines would decline over time, and professional comedians with decades of experience wrongly believed they would struggle to generate captions for blank cartoons as time passed. The pattern held across tasks that ran for a few minutes, but also across tasks that ran for many days. People were reliably more productive than they anticipated, and much of the time even the *quality* of their output improved across time. Lucas and Nordgren named this error the *creative cliff illusion* because it described the tendency for people to mistakenly believe their creative output would decline over time.

The problem with persistence, Lucas told me, is that it's *hard*, and we tend to equate mental difficulty with failure. If you're struggling to make sense of something, the solution feels remote. Being "in the zone" and "achieving flow" involve a sense of ease, whereas creativity, by definition, involves swimming upstream. You can't be creative if your creative output hews to your existing ideas, or to popular wisdom, and the experience of diverging from the path of least resistance is challenging. Lucas and Nordgren found that people generally confuse the difficulty of solving creative challenges for failure, and the people who are most confused are also more likely to underestimate the value of persistence. This matters a lot if you're trying to understand how to get unstuck. Being stuck feels hard—it takes energy to free yourself—which in turn makes it less likely that you'll persist in the face of friction. But Lucas and Nordgren showed this is a mistake. The quality of your ideas doesn't just remain constant over time—it's more likely to improve. The payoff that makes all that friction worthwhile is *more*—not less—likely to appear as time passes. If you're stuck, Lucas told me, the key is to remember that "you're more creative than you think you are." At the first sign of difficulty, persevere—and repeat that several times as you hit subsequent roadblocks.

Lucas was also careful to point out that persevering forever in the face of roadblocks doesn't make sense. You have to know when to redirect your energy. Every minute, dollar, and joule you devote to one sticking point might be better spent elsewhere. "People constantly engage in a cost-benefit analysis, deciding whether to continue or stop trying," he said. In some of his studies with groups, the groups would work hard to find solutions for a few minutes, then, having reached an acceptable or just-good-enough outcome, they'd relax for the rest of the session. The more important the problem, and the more valuable unsticking is, the more resources you should burn.

In deciding when to move on, one approach is to set audit markers, or waypoints, at which you'll reexamine whether to continue. For brief projects, those waypoints should be spaced at hourly or daily intervals;

for longer projects, at weekly, monthly, or yearly intervals. At each waypoint, you should zoom out to consider what progress you've made, the nature of the sticking points you still face, and whether to set a new audit marker or to fold and move on to a new venture altogether. The key, though, is not to fold too early. One useful rule of thumb is to give yourself 50 percent more time to work through the kinks than intuition suggests, and only then to seriously consider abandoning the venture.

Lucas' research is appealing in part because it's optimistic. If you're stuck or haven't yet succeeded, there's a good chance success lies ahead. Lucas explained to me that people perceive creativity through two contrasting lenses. The first is the *insight* lens, which suggests that creativity is the product of "Aha!" moments. These moments are hard to predict. They often arrive when you least expect them, and it's difficult to trace their origins. The second lens is the *production* lens, which instead sees creativity as the outcome of hard work. According to this model, creativity is more formulaic or algorithmic; more scientific than spiritual. Like an artist who paints religiously from sunrise to sunset, you're more likely to find creativity the more diligently you apply yourself. In some respects, these mental models of creativity oppose each other. Either creativity is ethereal or it's grounded; either good ideas emerge suddenly or they're the predictable outcome of long periods of hard work. In fact, though, both lenses suggest the same prescription: the more time, energy, and effort you pour into a creative pursuit, the more likely you are to succeed. That's true for both models, because the production models rest on hard work, and Aha! moments are more likely to arise the longer you spend immersed in the creative pursuit. You may not know *when* they'll arrive, but you have a better chance of stumbling on them if you give them time to flourish.

I asked Lucas why people are more likely to make a breakthrough the more time they spend on a task. "Obviously it's possible they'll eventually hit a wall," he said, "but before they do, there's good evidence that their ideas will improve over time." This is known as the serial order effect. "When you're generating ideas, the first thing that comes to mind for you is likely to be the most accessible thing, and if we all live in the same culture, and we're exposed to the same information, the most accessible thing for you is probably going to be the most accessible thing for me, meaning that the first thing we come up with is by definition not going to be very creative." Over time, though, your ideas improve. You discard strategies and approaches that don't work, so those dead ends interfere with your thinking less and less as time passes. Each dead end also pushes you to think beyond your default assumptions and strategies. As psychologists Roger Beaty and Paul Silvia explained the serial order effect, "If people first exhaust an obvious category and then stop and switch to new idea categories, their later responses will be better than their earlier responses." This isn't just true for lab experiments that run across minutes or days; it's also true across the life span of entrepreneurs and scientists.

———

In the tech world, it's good to be young. Peter Thiel's eponymous Thiel Fellowship awards $100,000 each to "young people who want to build things instead of sitting in the classroom." Entrepreneurs over the age of twenty-two, or those who want to complete their university degrees, need not apply. Vinod Khosla, who cofounded Sun Microsystems, believes that "people under the age of thirty-five are the people who make change happen," whereas "people over forty-five basically die in terms of new ideas." Venture capital firms prize youth over experience, fueled by the mythologies of twentysomething wunderkinder like Bill Gates, Steve Jobs, and Mark Zuckerberg. These stories are the water through which the tech world swims; it's a cultural truth that youth fuels billion-dollar businesses.

Only, this isn't true. The average age for successful entrepreneurs is forty-two—double the age of Peter Thiel's fellowship recipients. Many founders thrive in their forties, in part because they've *lived*. Many have families and children; many have held jobs across multiple sectors of the economy; and, importantly, many have failed not once but over and over before they find success. And the most successful of them are even older. The founders of the one-in-a-thousand most successful firms are on average forty-five years old, and those who successfully exit from their start-ups were on average forty-seven years old when they founded their start-ups. According to one study, "a founder at age 50 is approximately twice as likely to experience a successful exit compared to a founder at age 30." Founders in their twenties certainly launch successful companies, but the smart money flows to their parents and grandparents.

Scientific genius follows a similar pattern. In disciplines as varied as chemistry, economics, medicine, and physics, scientists tend to do their best work near age forty. Nobel Prize winners and inventors similarly do most of their best work between their late thirties and early forties. Precocity is fascinating because it's unusual. Instead, the richest advances come from getting stuck and then unstuck over and over; from learning what works and what doesn't; from persevering in the face of difficult lessons.

I'm neither a genius nor a Nobelist, but the research that makes me proudest emerged after the hardest period of my academic career. I spent my first semester as a graduate student working on a project that seemed new, exciting, and interesting. Then one day I opened my field's most popular journal and read a paper that said almost everything I'd been thinking for six months. This is known as being scooped, and it's a painful academic version of being stuck.

Being scooped early in your career can set you back months or even years, and some grad students despair to the point of reconsidering their careers. But it's an important rite of passage because it delivers a critical lesson in a concentrated package: diversify your interests so being scooped doesn't scuttle your entire research program. From that moment, I started several projects that were unrelated. One of those projects spawned a published paper, then several more, and became the presentation that opened the door to the academic position I still hold today. The same is true in creative pursuits more broadly. In one analysis of 3 million songs by seventy thousand artists, a creativity researcher showed that the biggest difference between one-hit wonders and sustained success across a career is a vibrant pipeline of "relatively creative" songs in the wings just waiting to be produced. The same lesson applies to other domains, too: make sure you have multiple productive threads in each area of your life so that losing a single thread isn't too painful. That's true for friendships, work endeavors, and recreation—any domain where obstacles are common and unpredictable. This approach borrows from the "don't put all your eggs in one basket" tradition, but it goes a step further. Not only should you spread your eggs across many baskets, but, to extend the metaphor, your various baskets should also contain hatchlings, older chicks, and mature chickens. In practice, that means having work products that range the full continuum from germ of an idea to almost complete. It means having a mix of mature and fledgling friendships, and hobbies and pastimes that are both new and established. The cost of spreading your resources, rather than being single-minded, is more than offset by the benefits of diversifying. Nothing sets you back or slows you down as reliably as watching your only egg tumble from your only basket.

Diversifying might slow you down, but slowing down has its perks. Take the business world, for example, where many entrepreneurs rush to enter young markets. Contrary to the entrepreneurial myth that you have to be first—that if you don't succeed early, you're doomed to fail—it's often best to enter a mature market whose kinks have been ironed out through early failures. Take the search-engine market. Sergey Brin and Larry Page revolutionized search with Google, which was the twenty-second entrant into that market. Before Google came Archie, VLib, Infoseek, AltaVista, Lycos, LookSmart, Excite, Ask Jeeves, and more than a dozen other also-rans. Google didn't just succeed because it was the best product; it also succeeded because Brin and Page had the luxury of learning from the products that preceded theirs. Part of succeeding is learning not just what works, but also what doesn't. In a Match.com study of two thousand people who said they'd met "the one," the average respondent had kissed fifteen people, begun and ended two or three long-term relationships, and had his or her heart broken at least twice. These early dress rehearsals, though many seemed like the main event at the time, were critical because they demonstrated not just what worked, but also what didn't.

Like Google, few of the largest tech companies today were first movers. Facebook (2004) came after Friendster (2002) and MySpace (2003); Instagram (2010) launched almost a year after Hipstamatic (2009), which offered the same photo-taking features without the built-in social network; Amazon was neither the first online bookseller when it launched in 1995 (Books.com launched in 1994), nor the first online marketplace when it expanded several years later; before Apple computers there were Olivettis, Altairs, and IBMs; Netflix improved on the dated distribution model of Blockbuster by delivering DVDs by mail, then introduced streaming in the wake of YouTube and other video-streaming services. Novelty is overrated; success often comes when you're second or third, or even twenty-second, to the party. The key is to keep pushing, because you're more likely to succeed with experience—and also because you're likelier to get lucky as time passes.

———

When smart people say, "You make your own luck," what they're really saying is that luck is less mystical than it seems. The best way to be lucky is to persevere, because luck overlaps with longevity. If luck is by definition unpredictable, you have a greater chance of being lucky the longer you push. "There is no such thing as luck," Robert Heinlein, an author and engineer, famously said. "There is only adequate or inadequate preparation to cope with a statistical universe." The universe is statistically lumpy, and luck rarely arrives on time. The key is to be receptive—to still be in the game—when it arrives.

In 2020, three European data scientists showed the importance of persevering by quantifying the role of luck across twenty-eight creative careers between 1902 and 2017. Their analysis suggested that the success of 4 million people in science, the movie industry, music, and art could be attributed to two components: skill and luck. They found plenty of variance even within industries:

> The film director with the highest [skill score is] Christopher Nolan, due to his many high impact movies like *Inception* and *Interstellar*. In contrast, one-hit wonders who achieved fame with a single song or movie, and whose success was neither anticipated nor repeated throughout their career with many high impact works, are typically characterized by lower [skill scores]. An example is Michael Curtiz (1886–1962), director of the all-time classic *Casablanca*, who has only a modest [skill score] as he did not direct any other movies with outstanding impact.

A director like Christopher Nolan doesn't need to rely on luck because, through skill, training, or opportunity, he's found the secret sauce for filmmaking success. His movies reliably attract interest and ticket sales (as measured, in this study, by how many ratings they attract on the Internet Movie Database). Curtiz—no less a genius—had a lumpier career. His biggest hits were colossal, and his misses were forgettable. Nolan's impact doesn't suffer much if you ignore his most successful film, but Curtiz's impact rests largely on one hit film. Perhaps it's too much to have expected a second *Casablanca* from Curtiz, but *Casablanca* dwarfed the other films in his catalog so much that it must to some extent reflect luck rather than predictability.

The authors considered specific geniuses—including Stanley Kubrick, Michael Jackson, and Agatha Christie—and then analyzed each of the twenty-eight careers in their database. They noticed that some careers turn more heavily on luck than do others. The most heavily luck-driven professions include astronomy, political science, book writing, biology, movie production, and physics. Somewhere in the middle falls rock music production, film-plot writing, zoology, mathematics, and movie direction. And the bottom of the pile—careers that turned very little on luck and almost entirely on skill—includes careers like jazz and pop music production, engineering, theoretical computer science, hip-hop artists, and classical musicians.

Some of these rankings make intuitive sense, and you can tell stories to explain them. Classical music and theoretical computer science, for example, rest on considerable skill, talent, and training, so a person who rises to the top of either career is likely to churn out consistent "hits." In contrast, astronomy and biology rest on breakthroughs, which makes success lumpier and therefore more susceptible to luck. Some of the patterns are puzzling, though. Book authors are prone to far more luck than, say, film-plot writers, and physicists, mathematicians, and engineers differ widely on the skill-to-luck spectrum.

Though luck matters more in some careers than others, the authors' major conclusion was that luck plays a huge role in success in all twenty-eight disciplines. Even hip-hop artists and classical musicians, who rely most heavily on skill, are at the mercy of luck and randomness. One mark of this randomness is that "the biggest hit of an individual occurs randomly within an individual's career." Michael Jackson and mathematician Paul Erdös achieved their biggest hits during the first third of their careers, whereas Stanley Kubrick and Agatha Christie had their biggest hits during the final third of their careers. The haphazardness of success across careers is known as the random impact rule, and it's one of the main reasons why persevering is so important. Had Agatha Christie or Stanley Kubrick retired during the spring or summer of their careers, their biggest hits would have gone uncreated.

Christie and Kubrick are rare talents, but the careers of everyday creatives are just as lumpy. In one study, researchers tracked the creative output of a sample of European adults across a twelve-day period. These were entrepreneurs who relied on their own ideas, and most of them were self-employed. The researchers discovered two things.

First, the entrepreneurs were far more creative following a good night's sleep, and after "nonjudgmentally" mulling over whatever roadblocks they'd faced a day earlier. For many of them, this meant running through the events of the previous day in their head while walking or driving—moments when they were lightly distracted. The nonjudgmental aspect was important, too. Those who ruminated by beating themselves up over whatever setbacks they'd experienced the day before were less likely to make progress. Among the most helpful techniques was to imagine the roadblocks were plaguing someone else who needed advice, which allowed the entrepreneurs to remain emotionally detached, and to explicitly "set their minds free" to consider the problem for several hours while continuing with the day. Much of the time, this form of light rumination produced breakthroughs more reliably than focusing deeply on the problem, or ignoring it altogether.

Second, as the researchers wrote, "most of the variation in entrepreneurs' creativity (77% of the total variation in creativity) resides within individuals (whereas 23% of the variation can be attributed to between-person differences, such as trait creativity)." We tend to think of people as more or less creative in the long run, but this result suggests that most of us are capable of great creativity under the right conditions. Most people, in the long run, score five or six on a ten-point creativity scale, but on the right day their score might rise briefly to a nine (and on the wrong day it might fall to a two). Another good argument for persevering, then, is that your capacity to get unstuck fluctuates. Some people are certainly more creative than others across time, but our best selves are *dramatically* more creative than our worst and even our average selves.

Whether or not you become the Agatha Christie of your field, your biggest personal hit could come at any time (and probably after a good night's sleep). It may come during the early part of your career, but there's a good chance it won't come till later. The creative cliff illusion shows that persevering *today* is critical, because your best ideas may come late in the day. The random impact rule suggests the same thing across careers: that persevering across weeks, months, and years matters because your greatest hits may arrive when you least expect them.

———

If you've ever missed an international flight by five minutes, or a train by ten seconds, spare a thought for Josh Harris. Harris is the king of the near miss, only his nearest miss happened in the opposite direction, and potentially cost him billions of dollars. Instead of being too late, Harris was too early. Imagine if Michael Curtiz had been born a hundred years earlier, before the development of motion picture technology, and had been forced to live with the idea of *Casablanca* in his head rather than turning it into a film. That's basically what happened to Josh Harris in the 1990s. His ideas were born a couple of years too soon, and he wasn't patient enough to shepherd them into reality.

Harris was an internet pioneer during the golden age of Internet 1.0—the earliest phase of the internet as we think of it now. Everything online was clunky. Ugly Web pages were crammed with text because dial-up modems struggled to cope with images and videos. When you did find a site that hosted videos or music, those files took hours or even days to download. When they did download, they were glitchy and grainy and sometimes laden with viruses and malware. Many Internet 1.0 evangelists tolerated these shortcomings because the internet's mere existence still seemed like a miracle, but there were chasms between what Web developers imagined in their heads and what they could achieve in practice.

This was the online world that faced Josh Harris in the early 1990s. Harris was wildly innovative in the mold of entrepreneurs like Elon Musk or Richard Branson. Harris founded a tech company called Pseudo Programs, a netcasting company that distributed radio stations and Web-based TV and video content. Andrew Smith, who wrote a biography of Harris, described Pseudo as "an amalgam of MySpace, YouTube, Facebook, and reality TV, but more subtle and sophisticated than any of those entities on their own." An entertainment exec called

Harris "one of the smartest people we've ever come across in the net-casting space," and another called him "one of the brightest guys in Silicon Alley."

Harris also imagined something like social networking before mo-dems and phone lines could shunt billions of likes, videos, photos, and updates from one computer to the next. His version existed on a smaller scale—an art installation called *We Live in Public* at a three-story loft on Broadway in New York City. One hundred people lived in the loft, and Harris filmed them twenty-four hours a day with 110 cameras that could be viewed by anyone inside the loft at any time. Harris had the prescience to see that people were hungry to share their lives while learning about the lives of others. As Andrew Smith noted, Harris had almost become Mark Zuckerberg five years before Zuck-erberg developed Facebook. "It's ironic," Jason Calacanis, an internet entrepreneur, told Smith, "because a lot of what people are trying to do today Josh did in 1996. He's one of the ten most important people in the history of the internet and nobody knows who he is."

Harris ultimately failed to invent early versions of Facebook, YouTube, and Twitter for two reasons. The first is that the Web's infrastructure in the 1990s was too immature to support his vision. Lis-teners were forced to download their favorite Pseudo shows overnight while they slept. Hobbled by bandwidth constraints, the average user listened to just one or two shows a month. (Today's broadband con-nections download information roughly forty thousand times quicker than dial-up modems did in the late 1990s. A video that takes one sec-ond to download today would have taken eleven hours to download in 1999.)

But Josh Harris also failed because he was impatient. Broadband was rumored to be around the corner, and Pseudo needed to marinate for a couple of years. Instead of biding his time, Harris spent millions of dollars on extravagant apartment renovations and chased investors with a half-baked product that wasn't quite ready for prime time. To turn Pseudo into a Facebook, a YouTube, or a Twitter, Harris needed to spend every spare dollar "professionalizing" the platform. Instead, tech commentators criticized him for becoming fixated on side projects and diversions. In an alternate universe where Harris succeeded, there would be no Facebook, YouTube, and Twitter. Instead, there would be Pseudo.com, or its successor, and billions of us would be downloading videos, sharing our thoughts, and posting about our lives on the platform that Harris imagined when Mark Zuckerberg was still in elementary school.

Impatience so often comes from being myopic—from focusing one's attention too narrowly. Instead of looking beyond Pseudo to examine how the Web's infrastructure was evolving, Harris poured more and more time and money into side projects. Meanwhile, broadband internet connections had arrived in the United States and Canada in 1996. Between 2000 and 2001, when Harris disbanded Pseudo, broadband subscriptions increased 50 percent. They continued to increase at a similar rate for several years, and by 2010, two-thirds of all US households had broadband connections. The broadband of 2000 was dramatically slower than it is today, but it was light-years quicker than dial-up connections and could soon transfer larger image and video files in seconds or minutes. Had Harris kept his finger on the internet's pulse, he might have spent his money differently, biding his time rather than spending Pseudo into the ground. The same lesson holds true in other contexts. To distinguish ideas that will never work from those that are held back by poor timing, zoom out and consider the context that cradles them. Are those ideas hindered by technological limitations, the political climate, unfavorable cultural mores, or an unfriendly economy? Or are they doomed to fail no matter the context? These are questions Harris seemed not to ask himself, or at least not to use as guides when choosing how, when, and whether to transform Pseudo from niche to behemoth.

By 2001, Pseudo declared bankruptcy. The company was purchased for parts, for just $2 million. Harris had been worth as much as $85 million, but was now broke. He purchased an apple farm in New York, then five years later moved to Ethiopia. I met Harris briefly, in 2009, at the Greenwich Village release of a film about his exploits during the 1990s called *We Live in Public*. He spoke, briefly and reluctantly, after the film ended with the same impatience that had hindered him a decade earlier. Patience makes the difference when bad timing conspires against you—and patience often steps in to salvage ideas that come too soon. That was true of a-ha, which needed a decade and several iterations to turn "Take On Me" into a megahit. It's also true of creatives everywhere, who, according to Lucas and Nordgren's creative cliff illusion, believe their best ideas will come early or not at all. And it's true of latecomers to hot industries—companies like Instagram, Amazon, and Google that built on the foundations of first movers to take their respective markets by storm. Patience and persistence solve poor timing and allow not-quite-ripe ideas to mature.

Sometimes getting unstuck means moving relentlessly onward, but at other times forward motion isn't enough. Breaking free sometimes means identifying and overcoming traps and lures that resist brute force. Often it's the subtlest traps that ensnare us most stubbornly.

TRAPS AND LURES

Traps come in hundreds of varieties, but the most effective ones share a common feature: they convince you that they aren't traps at all. These traps let you believe "this isn't a problem" until you're already stuck. You'll find these traps, among other contexts, when you're trying to stand out from the herd. When you're trying to be creative, for example, you can't just reproduce what other people are doing. By definition, you can't be creative without deviating from the herd. Often, though, people who believe they're deviating from the herd are actually hewing to convention far more than they recognize. These errors fall under the banner of unintentional herd behavior: failed attempts to behave differently from the majority.

Consider the naming of children. Just before I was born, in 1980, my parents scoured the cultural landscape for boys' names. They turned to newspapers and magazines and took suggestions from family members and friends. Their short list included names like Greg, Ryan, and David, and after whittling down the list, they settled on Adam. As far as they knew, Adam wasn't a common name. They knew of one other Adam, had listened to music by Adam Ant, and knew the story of Adam and Eve, but had otherwise never heard the name in the wild. This was an appealing sweet spot. In psychological terms, the name was *optimally distinctive*, or just different enough to be interesting, but not so different as to be jarring. The name wasn't so unusual that people might struggle to spell or pronounce it, but it also wasn't so popular that I might get lost in a sea of Adams.

As it turned out, I did get lost in a sea of Adams. When I graduated from high school, three of the twenty-five male students in my class were named Adam. Later, I shared a cubicle at a law firm with two other law students who were both named Adam. The name was vanishingly rare in the United States, Canada, Australia, New Zealand, and South Africa until the 1960s, then surged in popularity between 1980 and 1985. By the early 1980s, twenty-seven babies were given the name Adam for every baby given the name in the early 1960s. We were legion, and my parents were confused. How had they failed to evade the herd?

To begin, my parents encountered no Adams when they looked among their friends and acquaintances born largely during the 1940s and 1950s. The few Adams alive in the late 1970s were infants, toddlers, and preschoolers. Had my parents sampled from maternity wards and nursery schools, they may have encountered a handful of avant-garde Adams. But the more insidious force at play was an underlying shift in cultural norms and preferences that eluded my parents. The cultural waters through which they swam in the early 1980s were slowly becoming *Adamized*. The similar-sounding name Alan, for example, peaked in popularity between the 1940s and 1960s, so thousands of twenty- to forty-year-old Alans were now roaming the planet. They knew some of these Alans, including two of their closest friends. Similar names—like Alan and Adam—are important because they temper the strangeness of an unusual name without compromising its novelty. In one study supporting this idea, names that began with *K* were 9 percent more popular after Hurricane Katrina ravaged New Orleans. Another study showed that pairs of similar-sounding names like Aidan and Jayden, and Mia and Rhea, tend to become more popular or less at the same time. My parents had stumbled on the same name as thousands of other parents because they were all looking for a name that felt comfortable but special. In 1980, Adam was one of those names.

In art there's a huge difference between hitting and just missing this comfortable-but-special sweet spot. During the twentieth century, a swarm of artists known as color-field artists pioneered so-called monochrome paintings. Their canvases were covered with a single color and given titles like *White on White*, *International Klein Blue 191*, and *Black Square*. The characteristics that make most art valuable are absent from these works. They aren't awesome demonstrations of technical prowess; they aren't conventionally beautiful; and when you see them for the first time, they aren't blatantly innovative. But they did have two things going for them: they were different from other forms of art, and they were the first artworks to be different in this specific way. To a large extent art is about ideas, which is why aficionados who will pay millions for a genuine work will refuse to pay a cent for a perfect copy. They're paying for the work itself, but also for its provenance—where it comes from, how it was created, the story it tells, and its cultural significance. When Yves Klein, a pioneer of the color-field form, unveiled a series of identical blue canvases in the 1950s, he did something that no other artist was doing. He priced each identical canvas differently and argued that each viewer—and buyer— would experience something different when gazing at the very same work. His exhibitions were critical and commercial triumphs, and in 1992 Klein sold one of his blue canvases for £10 million.

You can't mimic Klein by selling an identical blue canvas for millions of pounds today. Klein achieved what my parents ever so slightly missed when they chose my name: his idea was novel, and it trailed similar, but not identical, ideas that gave it just the right degree of familiarity. Can you imagine an Italian artist presenting the Medicis with a plain blue canvas in the sixteenth century? Klein's audacious approach was built on a foundation laid by Impressionists and Expressionists half a century earlier. These artists had strayed from realism enough to be controversial, but as soon as art critics came to accept their deviance, a new round of works pushed the envelope further. Monet's impasto water lilies were scandalous, but next to Klein's plain blue canvases they're conformist. Klein succeeded because Monet had slowly moved the art world away from realism toward conceptualism.

It's surprisingly difficult to do what Klein did. Most of the time, people overestimate the novelty of their ideas. An Instagram account called @insta_repeat trawls the social network for repeated images. "Feet in a canoe" shows twelve almost identical images from twelve different accounts of people's feet as they lie in a canoe. These images were shot and posted as unique, but there are as many of them as there were Adams in the early 1980s. Other examples are "Small bird sitting on an outstretched hand" and "Single, centered tent, lit up, captured with a long exposure in front of the Milky Way." In each case dozens of nearly identical photos suggest their subjects are far more conventional than their creators intended.

Creativity is almost always elusive because we're all susceptible to the same cultural and biological forces. We share ideas about what makes something beautiful or valuable or desirable, and it's difficult to escape the constraints imposed by those ideas. To understand how this happens, it's useful to consider animal biology. Despite the diversity of animal life on Earth, true originality is rare. In a process known as convergent evolution, two species without recent common ancestors will sometimes evolve to become similar. Convergent evolution is strikingly common. For example, five completely distinct crustacean species have evolved to look like crabs—a process known as carcinization. Koalas, which are marsupials that diverged evolutionarily from mammals almost 100 million years ago, have evolved fingerprints that mimic the fingerprints of humans and other primates. Birds, bats, and butterflies have evolved similar wings and mechanisms of flight. The same copycat patterns are true of flying lemurs and sugar gliders, and of echidnas and hedgehogs. Some pairs of species are so similar that they're known as cryptic species—species that can only be distinguished by genetic analysis.

How can two species that have never come in contact, separated by tens of thousands of miles, come to have nearly identical wings or eyes or body shapes? The answer is that, despite the distance between them, they almost always inhabit parallel biomes that favor similar traits in the species they support. Many crustaceans come to mimic crabs because the temperature, gravity, and aquatic conditions that surround them favor crab-like animals—those with hard shells, similar vascular and nervous systems, and broad, flat bodies. The evolution of these convergent species mimics the evolution of ideas—and the term *meme* originally described ideas that developed and changed by evolution. Sometimes it's possible to transcend the cultural waters through which your ideas swim, but much of the time the pressures that leech originality are as compelling as those that unite two unrelated animal species.

These novelty traps even plague experts who are paid to be optimally distinctive. Film-poster designers are in hot demand because their posters are often the first marketing materials to reach potential filmgoers. They're plastered on huge city billboards, outside cinemas, and on platforms from Facebook to YouTube. You can't escape them. Here, too, you might imagine there's a sweet spot between jarring and derivative. An optimally distinctive film poster must draw on the tropes of its genre without being confusable. Yet a French film blogger named Christophe Courtois has done for film photography what @insta_repeat did for Instagram photos. Courtois noticed such templates as "a loner viewed from behind," "back-to-back viewed from the side," and "big eye." In each case, Courtois found dozens of nearly identical examples.

Some of this sameness is intentional. It might be important to show that you belong to a certain genre, and if your genre's films use big eyes in their posters, you might be wise to speak the same visual language. You might also mimic a successful film's marketing strategy, down to its visual imagery, but even so some of this copycatting must be unintentional. Some of the films in Courtois' collection are decades old;

others that use the same trope are from completely different genres. These posters fall far too close to the unoriginal end of the spectrum to be considered optimally distinctive.

Whether you're an artist, a filmmaker, or a soon-to-be parent—or anyone who equates success with optimal distinctiveness—it's all too easy to find yourself glued to the herd. Ask people to pick a random number from one to ten and around one-third of them will pick the number seven. Ask people to name the first vegetable that comes to mind, and the vast majority say carrot. It takes effort and skill to be optimally distinctive because your path of least resistance was shaped by many of the same forces that shape the decisions and preferences of other people who share your cultural background.

Optimal distinctiveness sets the perfect trap because it's hard to know you've ever been captured. Without stumbling on one of your posts on @insta_repeat's account, you'd never know you'd been un-original. My parents only realized several years later, when my pre-school was littered with Adams, that my name was more popular than they'd imagined. Optimal distinctiveness is the perfect "this isn't a problem" case study because it's difficult to detect your error.

Since the optimal distinctiveness trap is hard to recognize, you need to assume you're one step away from being ensnared (if you haven't already been captured). Every solution to the trap rests on the idea that you need to slow down and spend more time before reaching a decision. If you're trying to find an optimally distinctive name, film-poster image, or any other product of creative output, spend more time interrogating your ideas. If something comes to you quickly, it's likely to come to other people within your culture just as quickly. One rule of thumb is to question every decision three times, or to go through three separate rounds of brainstorming. Discard the ideas that pop up during rounds one and two—but recognize that they'll pave the way for the interesting, eccentric ideas that are likely to emerge during round three. If you fall in love with one of the ideas that pops up early, you'll need to spend more time and energy ensuring that the idea is truly novel. Parents might spend more time researching the recent popularity shifts in names, because there are usually signs that a name is about to rise in popularity. Adam, for example, started to become more popular in the late 1970s before its explosive rise in popularity in the early 1980s. If you're designing a piece of art or a film poster, say, devote more time to the brainstorming phase, and even more time to auditing the universe of film posters in your genre to ensure you aren't pursuing a Courtoisian cliché.

Genuine creativity is elusive because we so often fail to recognize that our ideas are shared by other people. Other traps reveal themselves earlier, but do their best to convince you that they're not worth worrying about. These are the "even if it's a problem, it's tiny" traps, and some of them are just as devilish as their "this isn't a problem" cousins.

—

The easiest way to understand the insidiousness of small traps is to think about what happens when two people miscommunicate. Miscommunication comes in two flavors. The first is to know that you're failing to communicate. If you speak only English and you're trying to explain an idea to someone who only speaks Spanish, you'll recognize the problem immediately. Your options are clear. You can try communicating with gestures or pictures, you can turn to a translator, or you can accept that you'll be unable to communicate. This is profound miscommunication, where the extent of the problem is unambiguous.

The second form of miscommunication arises when you don't know you've miscommunicated—when you think you've communicated perfectly, and both of you proceed under the mistaken belief that you're on the same page. Though you're *closer* to communicating perfectly than when you speak completely different languages, this is the more dangerous form of miscommunication. The two of you go on believing you agree when in fact you're now living in completely different mental universes. This is known as the pseudo-intelligibility trap, and it's both common and dangerous.

For example, here's how the problem plagues the legal system. If you don't understand what's happening in the courtroom, most legal systems assign you a translator. As a law student in Australia, I observed several criminal trials. Some of the defendants declared immediately that they struggled to understand or speak English, and the judge called in a translator before the trial began. This is an example of the first kind of miscommunication: the gulf between the parties is profound, and the problem is clear. The judge can't proceed without finding an immediate solution.

But what happens when miscommunication is harder to detect? English may be a single language, but it varies across 160 global dialects. You'll find Cockney in working-class London, Manx on the Isle of Man, Hiberno-English in Ireland, Scouse in Liverpool, Mancunian in Manchester—and those are just five of the more than sixty dialects across the British Isles. Some of the differences across those dialects are obvious, but others are subtle. The same word might have different meanings, more than one meaning, or a slightly different connotation.

Many Aboriginal Australians speak a dialect known as Australian Aboriginal English. It's deceptively similar to Euro-Australian English, but with important differences. The word *fire*, for example, has a single meaning in Euro-Australian English, but in Aboriginal English it refers to flames, matches, firewood, and even an electric heater. A judge who doesn't recognize this nuance might accuse an Aboriginal Australian defendant of arson when he says he "put a fire in the house," when the defendant actually turned on an electric heater. At other times the problem is a simple misunderstanding. In one hearing, an Aboriginal man who sought to claim his ancestors' land was almost accused of murder. "I belong to Rirmerr and Lakefield," the man said, explaining his origins. The stenographer believed the man had admitted to "murdering Lakefield" and a forensic translator had to be introduced to correct the record. Small communication gaps make for dangerous traps because they fail to ring your psychological alarm bells. Those alarm bells prevent you from miscommunicating—and getting stuck—and without them you continue to wade deeper into misunderstanding.

This same principle applies to other "even if it's a problem, it's tiny" traps. Matthew Fray, a relationship coach, has said, "The existence of love, trust, respect, and safety in a relationship is often dependent on moments you might write off as petty disagreements." These petty disagreements, like who does the dishes, might not be petty after all, a fact supported by Fray's suggestion that many marriages, including his own, dissolved because small disagreements went unsolved. "The things that destroy love and marriage often disguise themselves as unimportant," Fray said. "Many dangerous things neither appear nor feel dangerous as they're happening. They're not bombs and gunshots. They're pinpricks. They're paper cuts. And that is the danger. When we don't recognize something as threatening, then we're not on guard. These tiny wounds start to bleed, and the bleed-out is so gradual that many of us don't recognize the threat until it's too late to stop it."

Fray and his wife would routinely disagree about Fray's leaving a cup next to the sink. He preferred to leave it unwashed so he could reuse it later; she found his preference grating. Each time she saw the cup next to the sink, just inches from the dishwasher, she inched "incrementally closer to moving out and ending [their] marriage." Fray's mistake was failing to see that he had fallen into a trap. By refusing to put the glass in the sink, even with "sound" reasons, Fray showed his wife that his trivial preference was more important than taking her preferences into account. "It was about consideration," he explained. "About the pervasive sense that she was married to someone who did not respect or appreciate her. And if I didn't respect or appreciate her, then I didn't love her in a manner that felt trustworthy. She couldn't count on the adult who had promised to love her forever, because none of this dish-by-the-sink business felt anything like being loved." The trap for Fray was failing to see how a glass left on the countertop might symbolize a lack of trust, love, and respect. In hindsight, he'd have done it all differently, putting aside his mild preference for his wife's much deeper need to feel loved, considered, and respected. "I now understand that when I left that glass there, it hurt my wife—literally causing pain—because it felt to her as if I had just said, 'Hey. I don't respect you or value your thoughts and opinions. Not taking four seconds to put my glass in the dishwasher is more important to me than you are.'" To save his marriage, Fray believed, he needed to recognize that this tiny trap disguised a chasm that would swallow his relationship whole.

A similarly tragic trap ensnared the tallest man of all time. When Robert Wadlow was born in 1918, nothing indicated he would be especially tall. His parents, Addie and Harold, were of average height, and Wadlow was of average height and weight. Almost immediately, though, his pituitary gland began overproducing growth hormone, and Wadlow grew rapidly. By age one he was the size of an average five-year-old, and at age eight he was taller than his dad. At age sixteen he surpassed eight feet in height—a height reached by just twenty humans in recorded history—and at his peak, as a twenty-two-year-old, he was a shade under nine feet tall. On a trip to California, Robert stood among the giant sequoias. "Dad, this is the first time in all my life I ever felt small, and I like it," he said.

On July 4, 1940, Wadlow was the star attraction at a festival parade in Michigan, where he walked slowly past the crowd with the aid of leg braces. One of those braces was faulty, and Robert developed a small blister on his right ankle. Had he broken his leg or come down with pneumonia, doctors would have descended immediately, but the blister escaped their attention. It was irritating, and a bit painful, but Wadlow's psychological alarm bells were silent. It was the perfect "even if it's a problem, it's tiny" trap. Over several days, the blister became infected. Wadlow developed a fever and was admitted to a hospital, where his parents rushed to join him. Just eleven days after the festival parade, he died from septic shock.

Most blisters aren't fatal, so there's a reason our alarm bells don't ring every time we suffer a minor injury. Our coping resources are limited, so we're forced to conserve them except where they're essential. That makes sense—most of the time. But, every so often, large problems disguise themselves as irritations. What makes them so dangerous, and why they so often cause us to become stuck, is that we let them fester. They get worse, often slowly but sometimes quickly, while we believe we're saving our coping resources for bigger problems that may or may not arrive. Wadlow's death was almost certainly preventable. Had doctors tended to his blister immediately, chances are excellent he would have escaped infection and ultimately septic shock.

Another way to think about these below-the-radar traps is to consider how you decide whether to walk or drive when you travel. You'd walk to your mailbox, and you'd drive five miles to the grocery store, but somewhere between those distances is a point after which you'd drive instead of walk. Let's say for you that switching point is at one mile. If you're traveling farther than a mile, you'll drive; less than that and you'll walk. These shorter walking journeys of under a mile allow you to stretch your legs, but they're time sinks because they fail to ring your "I need to drive" alarm bells in the same way that Wadlow's blister failed to prompt medical attention. What happens, paradoxically, is that a journey of, say, three-quarters of a mile ends up taking much longer than a journey of three miles because you walk much slower than you drive. The shorter journey seems innocuous in the same way that smaller traps seem innocuous, and both end up causing a bigger dent in your resources.

The best way to break through the small-problem trap is to learn to separate today's small problems that will remain small from the ones that portend calamity. You need to prevent yourself from becoming paralyzed every time a small concern arises without assuming every small concern will remain small forever. The solution is to adopt an engineering technique known as preventive maintenance. Preventive maintenance is designed for just the problem posed by shortish journeys and blisters that turn septic. If you've flown on a passenger aircraft, chances are good you've been delayed for mechanical issues. Some of these delays are brief, but others ground the plane and cancel your flight. Airplanes comprise thousands of components from colossal metal fuselages to microscopic aluminum screws. Commercial planes fly almost nonstop, which makes maintenance both critically important and difficult to schedule. How do you keep planes in the air while also ensuring that they're airworthy? The answer is preventive maintenance.

Commercial aircraft undergo several levels of maintenance at different intervals. Every two days, they're grounded just long enough for a series of basic checks—visual checks, fluid-level checks, tire-pressure checks, and basic systems checks. These "daily" checks uncover major abnormalities that need immediate attention like leaks, missing or damaged parts, and electrical issues. Beyond these regular checks, engineers follow the so-called ABC check system. Levels A and B are relatively minor, whereas C and D are known as heavy maintenance. The A check happens every two to three hundred hours of flight (every ten days or so) and takes around fifty person-hours (for example, ten technicians working for five hours each). The B check happens every six to eight months and takes around 150 person hours. The plane is grounded for between one and three days for the B check, whereas it's grounded for only a few hours during the A check. The C check happens only every two or three years, and the D check—the heaviest form of maintenance—happens every six to ten years and grounds the aircraft for roughly two months.

The ABC check system is designed to balance two opposing aims: flying safely, and flying consistently. Aircraft with minor issues are sometimes put on a watch list and monitored, rather than being immediately grounded for repair. The safest course would be to inspect every aircraft intensively after every flight, but then you'd be removing those aircraft from service for several months every year. The most lucrative course for airlines and pilots would be to inspect aircraft cursorily and much less often, but then they'd be compromising safety. Large commercial aircraft, in particular, are incredibly safe, and the ABC check system generally keeps them that way while keeping them aloft.

Wadlow largely ignored his blister when it began to flare, and he continued to participate in parades as his fever worsened. When he turned to doctors, they were largely unconcerned. The night before he died, his biggest worry was missing his grandparents' fiftieth wedding anniversary party two weeks later. What Wadlow needed was a preventive maintenance system like the ABC check system. One symptom of his height was chronic numbness in his legs and feet, which were constantly suffering bruises and scrapes. Most healed without treatment, so could have been placed on a watch list and dismissed as soon as they improved. But some, like his fatal blister, became more than a nuisance, and these might have caught the attention of regular A and B checks. Today, the American Medical Association recommends annual physicals for adults over age fifty, which mimic the C check required by the Federal Aviation Administration. Less often, still, are routine mammograms, roughly every two years, and colonoscopies, every five to ten years, which are D checks.

The same preventive maintenance principle can be applied to any potential "even if it's a problem, it's tiny" traps. If the problem is truly tiny, it will resolve on its own or require minimal intervention. You can place those problems on the watch list. If it turns out to be a trap, though, a series of regular minor checks, and longer-term major checks, should catch those catastrophes disguised as minor irritations. You can apply the approach to, say, your finances, your relationships, your professional life—any domain where you might catch minor snags before they become major hindrances. In each case, the process begins with the creation of a checklist, the same way engineers check an airplane and doctors examine the human body. If you're concerned about financial sticking points, you might create a monthly preventive checklist, and a more detailed annual checklist. With the help of a budgeting app, you might check your account balances and overall spending by category once a month. Then, once a year, you might delve more deeply into the state of your retirement investments, and any other assets and liabilities you might have. The aim with both minor and major checks is to forecast sticking points before they arrive—to notice when you're flirting with overdraft fees, or if your investment portfolio isn't growing quickly enough to fund your postretirement lifestyle. You're better placed to avoid these sticking points if you spot them when they're months or years, rather than days, in the future.

ABC checks, whether physical, financial, or in any other domain, are designed to separate major from minor problems, but sometimes you need to know more than just the size of the problem. That's true when you encounter a third kind of trap that tells you, "Even if it's not tiny, it's far away"—that even if the problem is major, it's too remote to warrant your concern.

———

In the late 1950s, computer scientist Bob Bemer joined IBM. Bemer was a programming wizard, inventing the *escape* and *backslash* keys that ultimately became mainstays on every computer keyboard. One of his first tasks at IBM was to help the Mormon Church catalog its vast collection of genealogical records. Every bit of data was expensive, and computer punch cards typically had a limit of eighty characters each, so programmers trimmed the fat from every imaginable string of code. Instead of recording a year as 1923, they took to recording it as 23. Bemer had been entering dates that spanned two centuries, so he recognized immediately that trimming them to two characters introduced ambiguity. How could a computer distinguish between a member of the church born in 1840 and a member born in 1940 when both were entered as 40? This particular ambiguity had few follow-on consequences and could be fixed quite easily, but Bemer cast his mind forty years into the future, to the turn of the new millennium. As the calendar hit 2000, the digits 00 would suddenly mean both 1900 and 2000 (and perhaps other years ending in 00, too). Bemer imagined the world's major computing systems crashing. He shared his concerns with other programmers and ultimately published a series of papers on what would become known several decades later as the Y2K Bug.

As the clock ticked over from 1999 to 2000, it would have been fair to conclude that the Y2K Bug was overhyped. Planes didn't fall from the sky, and electrical grids didn't spontaneously combust. But that's largely because Bemer was an effective prophet for his cause. In late December 2019, journalists across a series of newspapers and magazines interviewed experts, who confirmed that the bug might have done immense damage. In *Time*, for example, Francine Uenuma published an article titled "Twenty Years Later the Y2K Bug Seems like a Joke—Because Those behind the Scenes Took It Seriously." Interviewing experts, Uenuma showed that the isolated problems that did arise on January 1, 2000, might have been a billionfold worse had engineers across the globe not acted. "The innumerable programmers who devoted months and years to implementing fixes received scant recognition," she wrote. "It was a tedious, unglamorous effort, hardly the stuff of heroic narratives—nor conducive to an outpouring of public gratitude, even though some of the fixes put in place in 1999 are still used today to keep the world's computer systems running smoothly." A technology forecaster and professor at Stanford University, Paul Saffo, told Uenuma, "The Y2K crisis didn't happen precisely because people started preparing for it over a decade in advance. And the general public who was busy stocking up on supplies and stuff just didn't have a sense that the programmers were on the job." Y2K wasn't much to write home about because Bemer had raised the alarm four decades earlier.

Cast your mind ahead forty years. It's difficult to imagine the world then—what has changed and what hasn't; who you are and whether you're largely the same person as you are today. If you're a computer programmer, it's hard to get worked up about a problem that won't arrive—if it isn't somehow remedied before then—for forty years. This was the problem that faced Bemer. He implored his colleagues to pay attention to the issue, and to consider solutions for the problem that wouldn't arrive for four decades. But here's where the "even if it's not small, it's far away" trap came in. These programmers were so busy with the demands of everyday life that they couldn't imagine spending time and energy on this remote problem with a strange name.

What ultimately happened, as often does with distant problems, is that a mad scramble to squash the Y2K Bug ensued shortly before the year 2000. The world had procrastinated for several decades, and the problem had not vanished. In fact, the bug had grown larger and more evasive. For decades following Bemer's warning, programmers continued to record years with two digits. What was a modest problem that required some undoing in the 1950s became a colossal problem that cost hundreds of millions of dollars to address in the late 1990s. Computers were mainstream and ubiquitous in 1999, while most people had never seen or used a computer in the 1950s. Many countries, including Italy and South Korea, decided the cost was too high and so chose not to address the bug at all. Others, like the United States, spent vast sums reprogramming and updating offending systems. The entire world was stuck because people had chosen not to solve the problem when it was still manageable. Governments were forced to overspend, or to hope that the problem was overblown.

Bemer was an oracle who recognized the value of sustaining small losses today to avoid massive losses tomorrow. There's a Bemer in all of our heads, but much of the time we ignore his voice just as computer programmers seemed to do between the 1960s and the 1980s. Most humans prefer to be lazy today even if they'll have to work twice as hard tomorrow. This finding is well-documented and applies to humans across the planet. Some people refuse to listen to the "even if it's tiny, it's far away" mantra, but the vast majority of us, most of the time, are shortsighted. According to one study, the average adult needs to be paid a 28 percent interest rate to wait a year to receive money. In other words, we'd prefer $1,000 today to anything less than $1,280 a year from now. Annual interest rates of 28 percent are impossible to find in the real world, so millions of us cling to what we have and refuse to give it up today for the prospect of more tomorrow.

There's a way to make people more Bemer-like—open to considering the long term as well as the here and now. About ten years ago I tested a kind of Bemerization intervention that seemed to help people focus on the long term. Our savings problems begin early. We make many important retirement-savings decisions in our twenties, when we first begin working. That's problematic because we're asking twenty-two-year-olds to deprive themselves for the benefit of their seventy-year-old future selves. It's hard to imagine being generous to your future self if you don't feel an emotional connection to that person, so one solution is to bridge the gulf between those two selves.

To Bemerize a group of twentysomethings, I worked with a trained hypnotist, who convinced them they had just retired. The hypnotist induced them to believe they were forty or fifty years older and asked them to imagine how they might spend this first day in retirement. Then he asked them to imagine that they hadn't saved enough money during their working years. Instead, they'd spent almost everything they earned the minute it hit their bank accounts. As you can imagine, they were crestfallen. They'd imagined world trips, rounds of golf, and cushy retirement living, and all of a sudden those dreams were scuttled by the reality that they were financially insecure. Afterward, the hypnotist woke each of them, one by one, and I asked them to reflect on their savings goals. The experience seemed to change them. Some reached for their phones to set reminders to change their retirement allocations. Almost all of them expressed a stronger desire to save, having both identified with their future selves and felt the consequences of saving too little. "It was surprising," one participant said, "because [my future retired self] was younger than I expected him to be." Another said her future "didn't feel like my future; it felt more tangible."

This was just a demonstration—hypnosis isn't a feasible solution to the "even if it's big, it's far away" trap—but it reveals the important truth that many sticking points that seem distant are much closer than we appreciate. Many of them can be avoided if we take small steps today, rather than allowing them time to grow in severity, as much of our planet did with the Y2K Bug.

It's also important to note that this trap doesn't just apply to money. It applies to any situation where a small step in the right direction today, and perhaps each day after that, would avoid a massive obstacle in the long run. Limit how much chocolate cake you eat today and you'll be healthier and slimmer tomorrow. Spend two minutes applying sunscreen every day and you'll avoid sun damage and skin cancer tomorrow. Exercise for twenty minutes several times a week and, all else being equal, you'll enjoy a longer and healthier life. This doesn't mean you have to become an ascetic monk. You don't have to save 50 percent of your income, swear off all desserts, and slavishly walk twenty thousand steps every day without fail. But taking small steps, and applying the ABC check system to your life, means you'll avoid many of the traps that ensnare non-Bemerites.

———

Many of the traps we encounter are avoidable as long as we adopt the right strategies: preventive maintenance, and a skeptical eye that questions whether major sticking points might be disguised as nonissues and trifles. But these intellectual approaches to trap avoidance tell only part of the story. Becoming stuck, then trying to unstick yourself, is laden with anxiety. It's not enough to manage your mental response to friction; you also have to manage your emotional response. Managing your emotions is an essential precursor to making breakthroughs, and it's almost impossible to formulate a coherent response to sticking points if you can't manage your emotions.

PART II

HEART

4

EXHALE

Your body is expertly designed to deal with physical entrapment. Every system delivers the same message: *Do something, and do it now*. Your heart and lungs accelerate, you develop tunnel vision, and your capacity for rational thought deserts you. You don't need to think; you need to *do*. In an emergency, some people even develop *hysterical strength*— the superhuman ability to move heavy objects. When artist Jack Kirby created the Incredible Hulk in the early 1960s, he told interviewers that he was inspired by watching a mother free her child from beneath a car. Every couple of years you'll see similar stories on local news broadcasts with teasers like "Superhero Woman Lifts Car off Dad."

The good news is that physical entrapment is vanishingly rare. The bad news is that its cousin, mental entrapment, happens all the time, and our bodies and brains struggle to tell the two apart. In both cases, we experience anxiety, a racing heart, tunnel vision, and the pressure to *do something, and do it now*. That rush of hormones can produce physical strength, but it inspires the opposite instinctive response when we're trapped mentally. Instead of hysterical strength, mental entrapment leaves most people disempowered. The trick to overcoming the paralysis of mental entrapment is to ignore the instinct to act immediately. Often, the best way to deal with being mentally stuck is to do less.

—

Miles Davis was two kinds of genius. His musical gift was obvious, but he was also a remarkable intuitive psychologist. He could be "vola-

62 ANATOMY OF A BREAKTHROUGH

tile," "arrogant," and "aloof," but he also knew that many musicians were overwhelmed by his brilliance. The only way to coax them to shine was to use a gentle touch. Gentleness wasn't natural to Davis. Sometimes he stalked offstage, refusing to return until seconds before his next solo. Still, he knew intuitively when to push harder, and when to ease up.

Herbie Hancock, himself a virtuoso, played piano with Davis for five years in the mid-1960s. In his own words, Hancock found playing with Davis "scary," but he saw Davis skate the line perfectly between tyrant and guardian. There's an incredible video of Davis and Hancock performing in Milan in 1964. Forty minutes into the performance, Davis is mid-solo when Hancock tinkles a couple of notes that disrupt Davis' flow. Davis pulls the trumpet away from his mouth, purses his lips, and scowls at Hancock across the stage. That gaze is one of the most withering expressions ever caught on film, but Hancock had been playing with Davis for about a year, and Davis knew that Hancock could handle the pressure.

Just one year earlier, though, Hancock was playing with Davis for the first time. Hancock was twenty-three years old, immensely talented, and absolutely terrified. Davis invited him to join several other musicians at Davis' house so they could jam. "I got to his house," Hancock remembered, "and Tony Williams was there—the great drummer. Ron Carter, the great bass player, was there. George Coleman, the great saxophonist, you know, he was there." Davis' living room held five of the greatest jazz musicians of all time. "Miles played just a little bit, and then he threw his trumpet on the couch and ran upstairs and kind of left the duties to Ron Carter, to have us go through a few tunes." Hancock assumed he was auditioning as the fifth member of Davis' ensemble, so Davis' departure seemed like a bad sign. On three consecutive days, Hancock returned to Davis' house and played with Carter, Williams, and Coleman, but Davis was conspicuously absent. Eventually, at the end of the third day, Davis returned and played a couple of songs with the band.

To Hancock's surprise, as that third day ended, Davis invited Hancock to meet the band at the Columbia recording studios the following week. Hancock was convinced he'd blown the audition when Davis had left the room for the better part of three days, but Davis' absence was carefully orchestrated. "What I learned, years later," Hancock recalled, "was that when Miles threw his horn down and ran upstairs, he went to his bedroom and was listening to us over the intercom. Because, like I said, I was scared. He knew we were going to be nervous with him around, so he wanted to hear us unencumbered by that kind of fear."

Davis knew that his presence inspired a response that mirrored hysterical strength. Young musicians like Herbie Hancock were dry mouthed, sweaty palmed, and breathless when they knew Davis was listening. Their bodies were preparing them to fight or flee, when what they really needed was a measure of calm. Sometimes, Davis knew, the only way to encourage them to perform was to leave the room altogether. The antidote to hysterical strength, and the key to Davis' collaborative success, was to dial the intensity down several notches.

Other collaborators had similar experiences with Davis. Guitarist John McLaughlin began playing with the band in 1969. During their first rehearsal together, McLaughlin was overwhelmed. "Forty-eight hours after arriving in New York," he remembered, "I was in the studio with Miles. I was sweating, my clothes were wet, I was nervous." Davis didn't like the band's rendition of a new song, so he asked the band to stop playing and told McLaughlin to play the piano melody on his guitar. McLaughlin was flooded with anxiety. He'd been tentatively following the piano's lead, but now he was forced to lead while the piano stayed silent. "I didn't know if I was ready. I was in a blue funk. And so he's waiting for me to do something. And all he says is 'Play it like you don't know how to play the guitar.'" Davis was known for these bizarre, mystical requests. He was saying the opposite of *do something, and do it now*. He was telling McLaughlin to stop thinking so hard, to rely on the instincts he'd developed over two decades as a guitarist. The band adjourned for ten minutes, and when they resumed, McLaughlin took Davis' command to heart. He played the melody without overthinking it, and Davis loved it. "I was in shock because he was able to pull something out of me that I didn't know I was capable of doing," McLaughlin said. "[Miles] was a very intelligent man. I'm sure he knew we had no idea what to do, but he would put us in the state of mind that we would play something other than what we knew. We had to, by necessity, move out of the box and do something we didn't know we could do. And this was masterful, in my opinion—how he was able to do this with his musicians."

Davis was a stunning soloist. He could shine with or without a backup band, but he knew that much of his best work was collaborative. To make those collaborations work, he had to coax greatness from his bandmates. What set Davis apart from other glittering talents was that he knew exactly when to take his foot off the gas.

When you strive to perform, whether musically or otherwise, part of the chatter inside your head mimics Miles Davis as he behaved in the presence of other musicians. Most of the time, your instinct is to mirror Miles as he was when Herbie Hancock offended his sensibilities onstage: to glower and slink away, to punish any performative shortcoming with disappointment. But the key is to license yourself to "play like you don't know how to play." Dial back the pressure; counteract the push to *do something, and do it now*, and allow your anxiety to wash over you as you fall back on intuition.

———

Dialing back the intensity contradicts modern folk wisdom. The order of the twenty-first century is boldness. If you don't love the hustle; if you aren't working a hundred hours a week; if you don't eat, breathe, and sleep triumph, you're destined for the minor leagues. If you don't want to get stuck, don't stop moving. In fact, don't slow down, because slowing down is stagnation's baby cousin.

Much of the time, this is terrible advice. We know this, in part, from the results of an experiment run in a laboratory aquarium in 1992. The experimenter was a biologist named Lee Dugatkin, who worked at the State University of New York, Binghamton. Dugatkin was studying boldness in the guppy, a species of tropical fish that grows to about an inch in length. As with humans, some guppies are go-getters. They live for the hustle. In their native streams in South America and the Caribbean, these bold guppies are the first to explore. They're quick to leave the safety of their schools, and they're curious about predators. They assume great risk for the potential of great reward. They learn more about their environments and find food more quickly, and their chutzpah convinces some predators to seek meeker prey. Timid guppies, in contrast, are second movers. They prefer to watch and wait. They miss out on some sources of food, but they tend to live to fight another day.

Dugatkin believed that boldness had its costs, so he ran an experiment to determine whether bold guppies tended to explore themselves into extinction. He began by sorting sixty male guppies based on how curious they were about a predator sunfish who was swimming in an adjacent tank. The bold guppies made a beeline for the sunfish, whereas the timid guppies shied away watchfully. Next, Dugatkin placed the guppies and sunfish in the same tank and left them to swim, eat, and explore for sixty hours. He wasn't sure what to expect when he returned to the tanks. Some of his colleagues believed that boldness was a virtue—that the hungry sunfish might prefer timid guppies who seemed more submissive than their bold shoalmates.

In fact, boldness was a disastrous strategy. Seventy percent of the timid guppies survived the first thirty-six hours, and 40 percent were still alive at the sixty-hour mark. In contrast, only 25 percent of the bold guppies survived the first thirty-six hours, and none of them were alive sixty hours after the experiment began. Dialing down the pressure—sitting back, watching, and waiting—was the key to survival.

The timid guppies in Dugatkin's tank were playing the long game. They seemed to prioritize survival, whereas impulsivity and curiosity were maladaptive. It's not that they weren't intrigued by the sunfish, or the strangeness of their situation, but rather that they wisely chose to bide their time as they gathered more information. Fish aren't known for playing the long game—they tend to live from moment to moment—but timidity in guppies is a proxy for long-term thinking.

When Herbie Hancock and John McLaughlin described Miles Davis, they seemed to recognize that he, too, was licensing them to play the long game. Instead of flooding his new bandmates with urgency, Davis took his foot off the gas and allowed them to be timid. He told them to fall back on what they knew and gave them plenty of space to explore musically without the press of anxiety. Sometimes, that meant leaving the room altogether, and other times it meant telling them to "play it like you don't know how to play."

I felt some of what Hancock and McLaughlin described when I started grad school almost twenty years ago. After thirty hours in cars, planes, trains, and buses, I arrived at Princeton University early one summer morning. Everything I owned was in two medium-size suitcases, which I lugged up the flight of stairs to my new apartment. After unpacking, I strolled ten minutes past collegiate Gothic dorm buildings, past maples, poplars, beeches, and elms, to the psychology department building, where I'd spend much of the next five years. That morning, and for many of those early months, I was overwhelmed by the weight of Princeton's reputation. I was an interloper who had somehow wriggled through the application process to find himself on a campus that had hosted Toni Morrison, F. Scott Fitzgerald, Richard Feynman, Joyce Carol Oates, John F. Kennedy, and John Nash.

I felt more comfortable as time passed, but I sensed similar anxieties in some of the undergrads I later came to teach. Like me, many of them hailed from unlikely origins. They had attended small public schools in remote parts of the United States (or outside the country altogether), or they were the first in their towns or families to attend college. They knew no one at Princeton, and they were minorities by ethnicity, wealth, nationality, or heritage. In contrast, some feeder schools send dozens of students to schools like Princeton every year. The nearby Lawrenceville School, for example, sent forty-seven students to Princeton between 2015 and 2017. You aren't guaranteed admission, but if you're a bright Lawrenceville student who wants to stay local, your chances are good. When you arrive as a freshman, you're not alone. Your family probably lives nearby, and you're joined by some of your high school classmates. Princeton is an extension of your high school years, rather than a completely new, completely different, entirely overwhelming leap from what you knew before.

Imagine two students who are equally bright, talented, and driven, but who come from very different backgrounds. One enrolls at Princeton after graduating from a small public high school in rural Wyoming, and the other joins a dozen of her Lawrenceville classmates who also drive the five miles from their nearby homes to Princeton's campus. I'm sure both students are nervous on the first day of college, but the student from Wyoming is saddled with all sorts of extra baggage. Do I belong here? Am I an impostor? Since there aren't many other Wyomingites here, do I stand out? Do people expect me to fail? It's easy to get stuck when you're paralyzed by questions like these, and they reminded me a lot of the questions that swam around my head when I first arrived at Princeton.

When I asked some of these "unlikely" students directly, they confirmed my suspicions. They weren't constantly preoccupied with their origins, but when asked which high school they had attended, or to name their hometown, for example, they started to ask the same questions I had asked a couple of years earlier.

I decided to run a small experiment to see whether they could be relieved of that burden the same way Miles Davis relieved Herbie Hancock and John McLaughlin of their anxieties. Each student completed a short math test that borrowed questions from the exam I had taken when I applied to Princeton. Here's an example:

Intellectual Ability Questionnaire

If Leah is 6 years older than her sister, Sue, and John is 5 years older than Leah, and the total of their ages is 41, then how old is Sue?

    (A)   6
    (B)   8
    (C)   10
    (D)   14

(With a bit of trial and error, or algebra, you'll find that Sue is 8 years old.)

One group of students who completed the test came from schools like Lawrenceville, and the other group came from schools that never, or rarely, send students to Princeton. Many of them, across both groups, did quite well on the test—apart from one group that did much more poorly. This group included students from underrepresented high schools who were asked, before taking the math test, how many students from their school generally attend Princeton each year. Answering this question before the test reminded them of their origins and inspired plenty of anxiety. (They also reported how anxious they were, and this group's anxiety scores were the highest.) As a result, their scores were about 20 percent lower than the scores of the students in the other groups—including those from underrepresented high schools who weren't asked about their origins before the test began. Being from an underrepresented school only hampers performance when you're reminded of that fact before the test.

Here's where the Miles Davis intervention comes in, though. Playing in front of Davis was, for a young Herbie Hancock, laden with anxiety. In psychological terms, Hancock was navigating a "threat"—a stressful experience that flooded his brain and robbed him of some of the valuable mental resources that he needed to play at his best. Davis restored those resources by dialing down the threat and turning it into a "challenge." Challenges demand a certain level of performance, but they're more forgiving. They're aspirational, rather than menacing. You can rise to a challenge, where you might succumb to a threat. This sounds like a small and perhaps trivial reframing, but it's critical. Where threats feel final and definitive, challenges can be attempted again tomorrow if they aren't conquered today.

For some of the students in my experiment, the test was described as an "Intellectual Ability Questionnaire," which they were to treat as "a reliable measure of basic quantitative ability." For those in the challenge group, though, the test was titled "Intellectual Challenge Questionnaire." They were asked to do as well as they possibly could, and to "treat the questionnaire as a challenge." The title and description made no difference to most of the students, but for the students from underrepresented high schools who were asked to report their backgrounds at the top of the test, it had a huge effect on performance. Whereas they struggled when the test was threateningly framed as a "reliable measure of basic quantitative ability," they sailed through the test when it was described as a challenge. The mental resources they needed to solve math problems were freed when they weren't threatened by the gravity of the test.

These results suggest two things. First, if you're in a position of power, recognize that your mere presence is a source of anxiety. Davis didn't flex his musical muscle when Herbie Hancock arrived at his home in 1963 because Davis was more interested in getting the true measure of Hancock's talent than in showing his own strength. Was Hancock worthy of a spot in Davis' band? The answer would never arrive if Hancock's anxiety prevented him from playing at his best. Though Davis naturally favored bluntness, he recognized that the only way to assess Hancock's ability was to leave the room altogether. If you can't leave the room, do what you can to reframe the interaction as a challenge rather than as a threat; license the timid guppies in your midst to hang back as they gather their bearings.

The second implication of the challenge study applies to performers themselves. Every now and then, you'll face an important test that can't be trivialized by a linguistic flourish. The bar exam doesn't mean less because you call it the bar challenge; the SATs aren't surmountable because you rechristen them the SACs. But if they seem daunting, there's value in lowering your emotional temperature. One way to do this is to buck the self-help trend of "visualizing your success." Instead, do the opposite. Spend some time focusing on the worst-case scenario. What if you fail the bar exam? What if your SAT score is lower than you hope? What if you don't get into the college of your choice? What if you have to take the bar exam a third time? Or a fourth? It hurts to follow that thread, but it's incredibly valuable because it shows you that there's life on the other side of disappointment. It also relieves you of the burden of obsessing over the prospect of failure, which makes failing more likely.

This strategy has its roots in an approach to getting unstuck known as radical acceptance—learning to accept and live with the prospect of failure. The term was coined by Tara Brach, a prominent clinical psychologist and practicing Buddhist. Brach describes the fear of failure as a universal affliction that plagues all of us from time to time. She describes it as a form of suffering that we can only overcome if we're kinder to ourselves and learn to lighten up. Brach has been touring the world for more than twenty years describing radical acceptance to audiences large and small, and her central suggestions are that we learn to appreciate our lives as they are currently, and that we train ourselves to accept failure. Brach is careful to say that radically accepting the prospect of failure isn't easy. It requires practice, and particularly in the individualistic cultures of the West, it goes against the grain. "In individualistic cultures," Brach says, "there's not an innate sense of belonging as there is in collectivist cultures," so we hitch our social currency to success. If we don't ace the SATs or the bar exam, we don't belong.

Reframing threats as challenges is an important tool of radical acceptance. It shrinks the overwhelming prospect of failure into something manageable. Instead of treating every day as the last word, as Lee Dugatkin's bold guppies did, you can find value in holding back. As long as you live to fight another day, life can and does go on, and you'll have the chance to master your challenges tomorrow.

I am a scientist, and a part of me finds this kind of advice woolly and imprecise. For a while, I struggled to embrace radical acceptance. But it *works*. You can only marshal so many mental resources as you strive, and if those resources are constantly occupied with the threat of failure, you're more likely to get stuck. I've used this approach—visualizing the worst-case consequences of failure—for almost twenty years, and it continues to liberate me the way Miles Davis liberated Herbie Hancock and John McLaughlin.

———

If you aren't ready to embrace failure, you can try relaxing your definition of success. This approach traces its roots to the concept of *satisficing*. The word is a combination of *satisfy* and *sacrifice*. In 1956, the cognitive scientist and economist Herb Simon suggested that there were two approaches to decision-making: maximizing and satisficing. Maximizing requires an exhaustive search of the environment for the best outcome, whereas in satisficing you search until you land on an option that's just good enough. Satisficing made a lot of sense to Simon. He recognized that maximizing consumed a lot of time and energy, whereas satisficing was conservative and sensible. In practice, it's almost impossible to encounter and examine every option, so setting an acceptable threshold makes more sense.

Almost fifty years later, psychologist Barry Schwartz and several of his colleagues suggested that maximizing and satisficing were more than strategies: they described enduring personality styles.

Some people tend to maximize, while others tend to satisfice. To an arch-maximizer, anything less than the best outcome is a failure. If you buy the second-best car or house or earn slightly less than your potential, you've failed to maximize. As you can imagine, maximizing is laced with anxiety. In a world with millions of cars and jobs, how can you possibly confirm that you've found the best option? Most of your life exists in a state of failure, and when you do succeed, you're exhausted by the quest. Maximizers tend to earn more money than satisficers, but at the cost of higher rates of regret and depression, and diminished happiness. In contrast to maximizers, satisficers are more forgiving. Instead of searching for the best car, for example, they distinguish between essential features and optional bonuses. They buy the first car they encounter with every essential feature, and if it has some of the optional bonuses, too, that's a windfall.

The difference between maximizer and satisficer mindsets is, for me, visceral. When I think about making important decisions as a maximizer, my chest constricts. I'm laced with anxiety. I'm the bold guppy that can't rest until I know more about the predator in my midst. But my chest loosens as soon as I reframe the decision as a satisficer might. In almost every imaginable context, satisficing is good enough. It's also an excellent mindset for unsticking yourself when you're frozen in place. Whereas maximizing is inherently stubborn, satisficing is flexible, nimble, accommodating, and—most important—forward focused. Maximizers look backward, reconsidering decisions over and over once they're made. Satisficers leave the decision behind and move on with their lives. Satisficing is also different from "settling" or giving up too soon, both of which happen when the process ends before you've found a truly acceptable outcome. Between settling and the maximizing option lies a sweet spot: the first option that genuinely meets your threshold of acceptability.

Though satisficing is an innate personality style, even maximizers can learn to satisfice in contexts where they're willing to relax their standards. The first step is to assign each domain an importance rating. Consider buying a car, for example. Many people might maximize when choosing a car. We spend a lot of money on cars, buy them only every few years, use them daily, and drive them for hundreds of hours. Earlier this year, when buying a car, my first instinct was to maximize. With unlimited time, I'd comb every imaginable review, report, and data source on every car before making a decision. Short on time, though, and pressured by necessity, I decided to try a satisficer mindset. I decided that only three things matter when I buy a car: safety, cost, and space. I set aside a morning and spent several hours looking for an SUV with an excellent safety rating, three rows of seats, and a reasonable monthly cost. By that same afternoon, I'd leased the car. It's safe, affordable, and roomy, and this is the first time I've reconsidered it since making the decision.

Apart from actively deciding to satisfice, and considering which aspects of a particular decision are nonnegotiable, you can also impose artificial time constraints. I allocated a morning to the car research phase, which made maximizing impossible. Paradoxically, imposing constraints can be liberating because they relax your definition of success. They dilute whatever anxiety you may have had about the decision, allowing you to accept a satisfactory outcome where you might otherwise have tried to maximize. Self-imposed decision and action deadlines have similar benefits. By giving yourself permission to spend a certain amount of time on a task, guilt-free, you move forward without being preoccupied with time. These meta-questions—"Am I spending too long on this task?" "Should I have decided already?"—eat up limited mental resources, making it more difficult to act and decide competently. By saying "I'll take the morning to choose" or "I'll decide two weeks from today," you allow yourself to be occupied only by the task at hand, while implicitly suggesting how much effort and energy you should be devoting to the task. It's a win-win that quells anxiety and improves outcomes.

Maximizing overlaps substantially with perfectionism, which is the often paralyzing, anxiety-provoking drive for flawlessness. Though perfectionists can be driven and successful, they're also hypervigilant and self-critical. You can't be a perfectionist without magnifying and identifying every blemish, no matter how trivial, so students who score A-minuses, and adults who fail to achieve workplace promotions, can become mired in destructive loops of rumination. Your permanent state, according to Paul Hewitt, a clinical psychologist who specializes in perfectionism, is the sense of being flawed or imperfect. "One way you try to correct that," Hewitt says, "is by being perfect." A large survey of 284 studies found that perfectionism is associated with depression, anxiety, eating disorders, headaches, insomnia, deliberate self-harm, and obsessive-compulsive disorder. Perfectionism is also on the rise. Another troubling study found that the proportion of high school students who identified as perfectionists doubled between 1989 and 2016.

Perfectionism causes friction because it sets paralyzing goals. Students must score A-pluses on every assessment; adults must achieve fast-tracked promotions, towering salaries, rom-com–worthy relationships, and sitcom-worthy friendships. How do you even begin to tackle a goal as daunting as perfection in every sphere of life?

One solution is to strive for excellence instead of perfection. Psychologists have shown that striving for perfection is often debilitating, whereas striving for excellence improves both your performance and your well-being. Excellence is less stringent than perfection. You can be excellent without being perfect, but perfection surpasses excellence and demands an often unattainable standard of performance. In one study, researchers showed that people who tended to be perfectionists performed significantly more poorly on a range of creative tasks than those who prioritized excellence. Perfectionism is stifling, whereas excellence is mobilizing.

If even excellence seems like too daunting a standard, an alternative solution is to atomize, or shrink, every goal to its tiniest elements. Computer programmers call this approach granularity, which dismantles behemoth coding chores into manageable, line-by-line tasks. There's a version of atomizing for every imaginable sticking point—and almost anyone can manage tiny doses of almost any task. Struggling to write a book? Write a single word and then several words to form a single sentence. Struggling to write a sentence? Spend sixty low-stakes seconds writing and see what follows. Runners sometimes describe the difference between running easy and running hard. When you run easy, your body moves fluidly, you bounce from step to step, and the miles accumulate mindlessly. Your mind wanders, and you focus less on the mechanical act of running than on the scenery. When you run hard, though, every step seems insurmountable. Your heart, lungs, and legs burn to achieve the same pace that felt easy an hour earlier. Sometimes, in these moments, atomizing is the only trick that coaxes you forward. Each step is elemental, but combined they form the molecules of a quarter mile, then a mile, and eventually five or ten miles. You don't have the time or energy to overthink, or to be paralyzed, when your mental resources are occupied with tallying the atoms as they accumulate toward your goal. Atomization works, in part, because it forces you to focus intently on the mechanics of the task, rather than on the emotional baggage that surrounds the task. Instead of wrestling with the task, you become intensely focused on the nuts and bolts of its components.

The value of "letting go," or choosing not to fight, is central to Eastern philosophy. One fable suggests that Chinese emperor Lao Tzu ensnared potential members of his court in so-called Chinese finger traps, which captured their index fingers in a small cylinder made of woven bamboo. Most animals instinctively fight when trapped, and the finger trap capitalizes on this instinct by tightening when pulled and loosening when the two fingers are pushed closer together. The only way to free yourself from the trap is to relax—to work with the trap rather than trying to work against it. The emperor watched as the applicants to his court tugged against the trap and rejected those who were unable to free themselves as they continued to fight. Lao Tzu saw wisdom in the applicants who relaxed, stopped fighting the trap, and ultimately freed themselves. Not only could they override their faulty intuitions, they could relax in the face of acute anxiety. The story may be apocryphal, but a kernel of wisdom lies in Lao Tzu's fabled approach. When people face crises and important decisions, their instincts to tighten up and become inflexible are generally counterproductive. Relaxing conserves energy and forces us to pause as we consider our options.

—

Despite Lao Tzu's preference for yielding, the idea of giving way isn't popular. Giving way is, by definition, a lowering of standards, and you can't give way if you aren't compromising on a position you held just seconds earlier. Literally thousands of quotes from self-help gurus, scientists, artists, actors, athletes, and anonymous sources suggest that lowered standards are the beginning of the proverbial end. "Don't lower your standards for anyone or anything," begins one such quote. "Self-respect is everything." Another declares, "To raise the quality of your life, set higher standards." Guy Kawasaki has suggested, "You're not doing anyone any favors by lowering your standards."

This view is popular, but for getting unstuck, it's unhelpful. Stratospheric standards are paralyzing, often unrealistic, and almost always hollow. We're taught to aim for the best in every imaginable domain, but this advice assumes that we're more likely to succeed because we can imagine the epitome of success. This fetish for striving and goal setting is central to why so many of us are plagued with the kind of anxiety that causes us to stop making progress in the first place.

These motivational quotes fall short for a number of reasons. First, they assume success is binary: you either succeed or you fail. In fact, many goals are continuous, and lowered standards often land at what a satisficer might call a "good enough" outcome. You may long for a $100,000 salary, to run a sub-twenty-minute 5K race, or to attract more than ten thousand followers on Instagram, but these standards are illusory. They fetishize whole numbers, when in fact a salary of

$99,999, a 5K time of 20:05, and 9,999 followers are barely different outcomes. (Another way to consider this is to ask if $100,001, a 5K time of 19:55, and 10,001 followers are materially better than the original benchmarks. Assuming they aren't, falling short by the same margin isn't materially worse than the original goal.)

Second, these quotes turn standards into a moral issue. Some standards are certainly moral. Jonathan Safran Foer, in the first chapter of *Eating Animals*, recounts a conversation he once had with his grandmother in which she described the combination of fear and hunger that haunted her in Eastern Europe as World War II drew to a close. When she became so hungry that she couldn't imagine living through another day, a kind Russian farmer gave her a piece of meat:

"He saved your life."

"I didn't eat it."

"You didn't eat it?"

"It was pork. I wouldn't eat pork."

"Why?"

"What do you mean why?"

"What, because it wasn't kosher?"

"Of course."

"But not even to save your life?"

"If nothing matters, there's nothing to save."

Foer's grandmother believed this particular standard was so central to her moral identity that she preferred to die rather than compromise. That sort of standard, though, is rare, and in fact most benchmarks are amoral. They have nothing to do with your goodness as a human. You can go on being a terrific person after you've accepted an outcome that falls just shy of your original target. An idea, salary, or instance of creative output that doesn't meet your most stringent standards paves the way for progress, whereas clinging to the original standard mires you in the present.

These quotes also fall short for a third reason: because they conflate standards and self-respect. They assume that you've lost respect for yourself because you revise your standards downward. Standards that underpin your identity or a core belief might be immovable, but you can and should update others without feeling that you've compromised your self-respect. Finding yourself stuck because you're stubbornly clinging to a standard that no longer makes sense is far more degrading than accepting that you'll have to settle for evolution rather than the revolution you'd originally planned.

This is the heart of why lowering your standards makes sense: you open up the possibility of evolution as soon as you part with the idea that revolution is the only way forward. Whether you're making music or art, completing math quizzes or college entrance exams, asking for a higher salary or a promotion, there's almost always a "tomorrow." Evolution takes time, but most forms of progress play out over weeks, months, years, or decades. Treating these outcomes as acts of revolution when an acceptable path forward is paralyzingly unrealistic is the best way to guarantee you won't move an inch. Sometimes, paradoxically, pausing completely while you get your bearings is the best way forward.

PAUSE BEFORE YOU PLAY

What separates the very best in the world from the remaining 7 billion of us? Exceptional talent often looks like an act of revolution—a person doing something in a way no one has ever done it before—but many revolutionary talents are actually built on a foundation of evolutionary tweaks. These tweaks develop over time, often compensating for weaknesses and anxieties that might derail a lesser talent.

Take the world's best soccer player, an Argentinean named Lionel Messi. Messi has won more Ballon d'Or trophies, awarded to the best soccer player of the year, than any other player. He has scored more goals in a calendar year than any other living player, is the top all-time scorer in Spain's La Liga, and has the highest goal ratio in the sport today, scoring almost once every match. When Messi left his longtime Spanish club, Barcelona, in August 2021, the club's TV channel broadcast every goal Messi had scored for the club. The broadcast started at 11:15 p.m. and concluded at 4:30 a.m.—five hours featuring hundreds of goals that each lasted only seconds. (Some argue that Portugal's Cristiano Ronaldo is today's best player, but of the two only Messi has won the World Cup, and Messi has won more awards, has the best of the head-to-head matches between their teams, and is the selection of most of the world's best players and match commentators.)

Messi is a soccer genius for many reasons. He scores effortlessly, is almost impossible to dispossess when he has the ball, and is unbelievably quick. In a sport known for diving, Messi abhors going to ground and instead uses his speed to dart around the stray legs that fell lesser players. But what makes Messi most impressive is his ability to "see" the game. He's diminutive, at five feet, seven inches, but when he plays, Messi seems to tower high above the field, enjoying a tactical bird's-eye view that allows him to see the game more sharply than the other twenty-one players on the field.

For all his brilliance, though, he's famously anxious. For several years, Messi habitually vomited on the field before big matches. Argentina's coach at the time, Alejandro Sabella, explained, "In these moments, it's anxiety more than anything." Messi admits to being anxious on the field. When Argentina defeated Ecuador, 1–0, in its first match after COVID-19 restrictions were lifted, in October 2020, he attributed his and the team's slow start to "nervousness." After a string of disappointing national-team losses, another former Argentinean coach and giant of the game, the late Diego Maradona, uncharitably criticized Messi by suggesting that it was "useless trying to make a leader out of a man who goes to the toilet twenty times before a game." Being incredibly talented doesn't immunize you against anxiety, and many of the world's best grapple with anxiety precisely because they expect so much from themselves. But Messi hasn't allowed his anxiety to diminish his brilliance because he's mastered a coping mechanism that also doubles as the secret behind his tactical brilliance.

A soccer match runs for ninety minutes (plus a few minutes for "injury time"), and most players are active in the game from the first minute. As soon as the whistle blows, they implore their teammates to pass the ball, and pursue the tactics their coaches laid out before the game.

But Messi is famous for *not* playing the game during its opening minutes. This is his evolutionary tweak, which developed as he played the game at progressively higher levels. For the opening minutes, Messi ambles back and forth near the middle of the field and almost never engages with his teammates. Whereas other players run and sometimes sprint, Messi spends much of his time walking, rarely breaking into more than a slow jog. "Messi shows little interest in the ball during the game's opening exchanges," one soccer writer observed. "Instead, he prowls about, barely leaving indents on the turf, watching closely for weaknesses and vulnerabilities." A small handful of players have scored at least one goal during every minute of play (from the first to the ninetieth), with many others missing a goal or two during random minutes scattered throughout the game. In contrast, Messi has scored during every minute of the game—except minutes one and two.

Messi does two things during these first few minutes. First, he calms himself. Easing into the game is Messi's way of ensuring he's fully engaged for the remainder of the game. This is how he deals with the anxieties that crippled him earlier in his career. His on-field vomiting has resolved itself, in part perhaps because he's found a more effective way to calm his nerves. Second, he spends this time scoping out the opposition. His legs move slowly, but his eyes dart from player to player, assessing his opponents' strengths, weaknesses, and tactics, and monitoring his own team's movement with and around the ball. Messi is less valuable to his team early in the game, but this tactical pause elevates his value for the remaining 95 percent of the game. Messi's coaches at Spanish club Barcelona, where he spent the first eighteen years of his professional career, accepted his early idleness for the benefits it produced later. "Right, left, left, right. He smells who is the weak point of the back four," recalled former Barcelona coach Pep Guardiola. "After five, ten minutes, he has the map. He knows if I move here, I will have more space to attack." According to another Barcelona coach, Ernesto Valverde, Messi watches every movement of the opposition's play during those early minutes, looking in particular for weaknesses that he might exploit later. Some players study hard before the game, learning the strengths and weaknesses of their opponents from recorded footage or by reading expert analyses. Messi prefers to form his opinions on the day because strengths and weaknesses change from day to day, and players react differently as their team lineups evolve.

If you split soccer game play into "preparatory" and "engaged" components, Messi leans heavily on preparation. During one classic game between Messi's Barcelona and archrivals Real Madrid, in 2017, Messi ran for just four minutes and walked for more than eighty of the game's ninety minutes. When he was engaged, though, he was dynamic, creating nine chances, scoring one goal, and feeding the ball to a teammate who scored another goal. That pattern isn't unusual for Messi, and it's often in the biggest games that he accentuates his in-game preparation. That preparation also explains his ability to find himself in the right place at the right time, over and over. Though his positional play appears otherworldly, it isn't a miracle; it's that he's learned, minute by minute, that a particular defender leaves a particular square of pitch uncovered, or that two midfielders leave a small corner of the pitch open when they gravitate to the middle of the field. "Surely it must mean something," mused Irish soccer commentator Ken Early, "that the best player in the fastest era of football hardly ever runs at all."

Messi's assiduous preparation, even in the midst of competition, isn't unique. In contrast to Messi's consistency, the career of tennis star Andre Agassi was patchy. Between bouts of brilliance, Agassi contended with drug use, extended injuries, and high-profile romantic entanglements. At age twenty, early in his career, Agassi lost an important match because, in his telling, he was worried that his long-haired wig might fall off during the match.

When Agassi did succeed, though, he succeeded big. By the time his long career ended, he was the only male tennis player to have achieved the so-called Super Slam, winning all six of the biggest tennis tournaments: Australian Open, Roland-Garros (French Open), Wimbledon, US Open, ATP Finals, and Olympic Games. Agassi was a talented striker of the ball, but his biggest weapon was cerebral. He planned, analyzed, and interpreted the game meticulously.

One of Agassi's notable rivals was Boris Becker, a German star who was famous for his tremendous serve. "Boris Becker beat me the first three times we played," Agassi remembered, "because his service motion was something the game had never seen before." Becker's service motion was indeed unique, combining a deep knee bend and a whipping follow-through at full extension to produce one of the game's fastest serves. Agassi was stuck, unsure of how to combat Becker's serve, and he admitted publicly to avoiding games against Becker whenever possible. The rivalry left him anxious, so he turned to a different tactic that mirrored Messi's approach: paying close attention to every aspect of Becker's service motion. Was there a key, Agassi wondered, to returning Becker's serves more reliably?

The breakthrough lay in a barely perceptible movement that preceded each of Becker's serves. In an interview nearly thirty years later, Agassi explained the insight that turned their rivalry upside down:

> I watched tape after tape of him and stood across the net from him three different times, and I started to realize he had this weird tic with his tongue. He would go on his rocking motion, his same routine, and just as he was about to toss the ball, he would stick his tongue out, and it would either be right in the middle of his lip or to the left corner of his lip. So, if he's serving in the deuce court, and he put his tongue in the middle of his lip, he was either serving up the middle or to the body. But if he put it to the side, he was going to serve out wide.

Becker had played hundreds of matches against dozens of elite players, but only Agassi had spotted this "tell." It's easy to understand why. Becker's tongue appeared for milliseconds before each serve at a moment when his opponents were preoccupied with their own preparation. They were focusing inward, readying their bodies to return Becker's serve, when Agassi had the presence of mind to focus on the tiniest, most fleeting of cues more than eighty feet away. Agassi turned to videotapes of Becker's matches to confirm his hunch and discovered that Becker's tongue was a perfect guide to the position of his serve. After losing their first three matches, Agassi won nine of their next eleven. Becker was puzzled by the turnaround, as Agassi recalled:

> I told Boris about this after he retired. I couldn't help but say, "By the way, did you know that you used to do this when you served?" He about fell off the chair, and he said, "I used to go home all the time and just tell my wife, 'It's like he reads my mind,'" and he said to me, "Little did I know you were just reading my tongue."

Messi and Agassi were anxious for different reasons—one temperamentally, and the other in the face of overwhelming opposition—but both broke through by deliberately preparing and pausing. The very best athletes in any sport create the illusion of ease—the sense that they're achieving great heights without exerting much effort. In the moment that may be true, but the illusion of ease requires considerable planning.

The lesson for the rest of us is clear: when you're anxious, whether in athletics or in life more broadly, pause. Slow down. Prepare. Messi sacrifices the first few minutes of each game, and Agassi sacrificed a couple of service returns, to glean information that repaid them both many times over. Sometimes getting unstuck is about slowing down, rather than speeding up.

———

Tara Brach, whose "radical acceptance" approach to managing anxiety I described in chapter 4, also believes that slowing down is critical to overcoming anxiety. In fact, Brach doesn't just advocate slowing down; she advocates pausing completely. She believes, paradoxically, that the best way to move forward when anxiety fixes you in place is to stop moving entirely.

Brach's presence is disarming. If you search for her on YouTube, you'll find hours of footage in which she charms large audiences in churches, halls, and auditoriums. She speaks quietly, sibilantly, and deliberately, emphasizing each word as though she herself is pausing between thoughts.

In one story, she illustrates the importance of knowing when to pause, or to do nothing, when barriers arise. The anecdote, first described by Tom Wolfe, centers on a group of US test pilots in the 1950s. The highly trained pilots were asked to fly at dizzying altitudes, where the ordinary laws governing aerodynamics ceased to apply. At these altitudes, "the plane could skid into a flat spin, like a cereal bowl on a waxed Formica counter, and then start tumbling—not spinning and diving but tumbling end over end." Most pilots became frantic, handling their controls wildly and attempting one correction after another. Some plummeted to the earth as they pleaded with ground control for help. One of these test pilots was Chuck Yeager, best known as the first pilot to fly faster than the speed of sound. Yeager, like the pilots before him, struggled to control his plane at high altitude, and the plane moved with such violence that he was knocked unconscious. For several minutes, his plane plunged toward the ground, losing fifty thousand feet of altitude, as he sat motionless in his seat. Eventually, as the plane descended to denser air, he came to, steadied the craft, and landed safely. He had inadvertently learned the secret to surviving these moments of terror: do nothing—pause—until it was time to reengage.

For Brach, Yeager's experience captures an important lesson. In the face of barriers, most of us struggle. Survival instinct suggests we do more rather than less when times are hard, and often doing more is counterproductive. Yeager survived because he was prevented from acting until acting was once again valuable. On later flights, he and other pilots learned to resist their instincts to act, sitting immobile as their planes heaved violently toward the ground. Brach, with her spiritual lens, calls this moment "the sacred pause." It readies you to act when acting is most valuable and prevents you from acting too rashly, when anything you do might entrench you further.

Brach suggests pausing in the midst of all sorts of sticky moments—during difficult conversations, when we should be listening but instead feel the need to speak; when anxiety makes it difficult for us to think, speak, or write; and when we're overwhelmed by our responsibilities. What makes her sacred pause radical is that she suggests we stop everything we're doing, from walking and talking to eating and worrying, until we're calmer and prepared to reengage with the world.

Radical pauses, as Brach sees them, are largely spiritual, but they're also supported by scientific studies. In one study, a team of psychologists investigated the value of pauses during negotiations. They asked sixty pairs of university students to negotiate over a job package, in which one of the students was the recruiter, and the other was the job candidate. The researchers recorded the conversations as the recruiter and the candidate negotiated the terms of the candidate's new job package. The researchers focused on how much value was created in total during the negotiation—not just on whether one party or the other dominated the discussion. Conversations tend to flow quickly, in part because we're averse to silence. We prefer noise, even if it's counterproductive, because it masks awkwardness and anxiety. Most of the pairs paused occasionally for one or two seconds, but longer pauses were rare. Fewer than half the groups experienced a pause that lasted more than five seconds. Yet pausing was valuable, particularly when those pauses lasted between three and twelve seconds. With long pauses, the two parties enjoyed more positive outcomes, collectively, than when the negotiations progressed smoothly, without an extended period of contemplative silence.

In a second study, the researchers directed some groups to pause, whereas they allowed others to communicate naturally. Pauses were again valuable. They inspired superior outcomes for both parties and encouraged negotiators to see that some issues could be negotiated to the benefit of both parties, rather than competitively. This tendency to view negotiations as zero-sum competitions often deprives both parties of value, and silent pauses seemed to inspire valuable cooperation.

Silence quells anxiety, and it inspires deliberation. Performance artists know this. Paul Simon has said of his music that some lines are difficult for the listener to digest. They are complex or unexpected, and the listener needs a grace period of downtime to absorb them. "I try to leave a space after a difficult line," Simon has written. "Either a silence or a lyrical cliché that gives the ear a chance to 'catch up' with the song before the next thought arrives and the listener is lost." Gifted comedians use a similar approach, managing the emotional states of their audiences with strategic periods of silence. The "beat," or pause, that comes between a comedic setup and its punch line is precisely timed. Most novice comedians find silence awkward so they rush the punch line. That's a mistake. If the beat is too brief, the audience is so busy trying to grasp the joke's setup that the punch line loses its oomph.

Some comedic giants don't just pause; they employ pregnant pauses. They extend beats to the point where the audience is hungry for the joke's punch line. Gene Wilder, known as the "master of the comedic pause," delivered his punch lines glacially, punctuating each word with a second or two of silence. In 1974's *Blazing Saddles*, Wilder's character, the Waco Kid, tries to console Cleavon Little's character, a small frontier town's newly appointed Black sheriff dealing with the town's white residents. "These are just people of the land," Wilder says slowly. "The common clay of the West. You know . . . . morons." Wilder spends sixteen seconds uttering those sixteen words, pausing for several seconds before releasing the punch line. The line is funny, but it also alleviates the anxious tension that builds as Little's sheriff grapples with the town's racism.

Like Chuck Yeager, Wilder time and again resisted the urge to act. Both recognized that sometimes the smartest thing is to pause. These pauses don't need to last long. Even a few seconds makes a difference. But Tara Brach also explains that the sacred pause sometimes lasts longer: "The pause can occur in the midst of almost any activity and can last for an instant, for hours, or for seasons of our life." The cost of pausing is modest, and it more than pays for itself later. For Yeager and his fellow test pilots, pausing ensured survival; for Lionel Messi and Andre Agassi, pausing distracted them from competition for a short time, but calmed their nerves and made them more effective in the long run. "By disrupting our habitual behaviors," Brach says, "we open the possibility of new and creative ways of responding to our wants and fears."

———

As you might imagine, pausing is harder than it sounds. In the face of silence and anxiety, our instinct is to act. Chuck Yeager did nothing as his plane dived, but only because he was briefly unconscious. Other pilots were less fortunate because they were incapable of doing nothing. They saw the ground approaching and impulsively grabbed at their controls. Over time, though, Yeager taught himself to do nothing, and doing nothing is largely a matter of practice.

Judson Brewer, a psychiatrist and neuroscientist, has spent much of his career thinking about how to do nothing. About fifteen years ago, Brewer developed a mindfulness-based treatment for addiction. His approach instructs addicts to resist the waves of anxiety during moments of craving by following the four steps of an approach that goes by the acronym RAIN:

Recognize what is arising.
Allow it to be there.
Investigate your emotions and thoughts (e.g., "What is
     happening in my body now?")
Note what is happening from moment to moment.

This sounds a lot like something Tara Brach might suggest, and Brewer has said that his approach was inspired by Brach's. To test the approach, Brewer worked with smokers who were struggling to quit. Nicotine addiction is notoriously stubborn—more so than many harder drugs that produce stronger immediate responses in users. This is because nicotine is an upper that can be taken at any time of the day, under any situation (it doesn't dull you as, say, alcohol and heroin do); it's more socially acceptable than other substances; and though it is delivered efficiently through tiny capillaries throughout our bodies, it harms us more slowly than other substances do, so it can be used for decades without pause.

Before unleashing the program on smokers, Brewer wanted to test the system on himself. This approach is popular among clinicians because it reveals which aspects of the approach do and don't work and gives them credibility when skeptical patients ask probing questions. The problem was "I was a nonsmoker," Brewer wrote, "who needed to be able to relate to patients who felt as though their heads were going to explode unless they smoked. I couldn't be pulling any I'm-the-doctor-do-as-I-say nonsense. They had to trust me. They had to believe I knew what I was talking about."

Nicotine has a half-life of around two hours, so to begin smokers need to resist the urge to light up for two hours at a time. (If you pay attention, you'll see that smokers tend to have smoke breaks every couple of hours or so.) Brewer reasoned that smokers who could last two hours without a cigarette would cultivate new nonsmoking habits, extending those stretches till they no longer felt the urge to smoke at all. He simulated these periods of resistance by learning to meditate for two-hour stretches without moving. During moments of restlessness, he followed the RAIN steps—recognize, allow, investigate, note—and if he moved his body, the clock would reset, and he'd have to start again.

This might sound easy, but two hours is a long time to sit still without entertainment. (Imagine sitting down to watch your favorite movie, discovering that your TV isn't working, and instead sitting silently with your eyes closed for the entire length of the movie.) "Surprisingly it wasn't the physical pain of not shifting for a long time that got me," Brewer wrote. "It was the restlessness. . . . Those cravings shouted, 'Get up!'"

For many months, Brewer would get close. He'd make it to an hour and forty-five minutes, then restlessness would defeat him. "Then one day," he wrote, "I did it. I sat for the full two hours. . . . Each subsequent sit got easier and easier because I had the confidence that it could be done. And I knew that my patients could quit smoking. They simply needed the proper tools."

Brewer was right. His patients were stuck, incapable of quitting one of the most addictive substances on earth. But when he ran study after study, pitting his RAIN mindfulness method against the most effective addiction treatment approaches of the day, his approach was more than twice as effective. Months later, when most of the patients on other treatment plans had relapsed, his mindfulness group stayed clean. They were more than *five times* as likely to have shaken their addictions using an approach that essentially taught them to pause at the moment their bodies were most urgently driving them to act.

Of the four steps in Brewer's RAIN model, the second—allowing— is perhaps the most critical. Allowing an experience to wash over you sounds disarmingly easy because it doesn't require you to *do* anything. But that's exactly the point. It's difficult because you're forced to do nothing despite the urge to act.

A famous experiment illustrates how strongly people are driven to act. In the 1970s, social psychologist Stanley Milgram was studying the power of social norms. He wanted to understand what it feels like to swim upstream against the current of a strongly held norm. In one experiment, he asked a group of students to board the subway in New York City and ask twenty random subway riders for their seats. This simple request breached the norm of keeping to yourself on the subway, and few of his students completed the task. Hearing their reports, Milgram tried the task himself and found it just as difficult. He boarded the subway, approached the first seated subway rider, and froze completely. "The words seemed lodged in my trachea and would simply not emerge," he said in an interview. He took a few steps back and wondered, "What kind of craven coward are you?" Completing the task required Milgram and his students to *allow* the discomfort of the experience to wash over them.

Years later, I asked some of my students to violate an even simpler norm that didn't require them to act or interact with anyone else. Their assignment was to face the rear of an elevator, rather than turning to face the doors as almost all elevator riders do. Try it sometime. It's incredibly awkward. The other passengers assume you're unhinged. I've tried this myself, and the urge to *do something* is almost irresistible. Many of my students told me they blurted out an apology as the elevator ride ended: "Sorry! This is an experiment my professor made me do!" Gritting your teeth through the experience, though, is strangely liberating. You feel stronger, more confident, and more capable for having resisted the urge to explain yourself or flee altogether. That's true about friction more generally, too. The only way to strengthen your resistance to hardships is to engage with small doses of hardship from time to time. Judson Brewer learned this as he taught himself to meditate for minutes, then an hour, and finally two hours. The longer you can resist the urge to act, the more likely you are to triumph over friction.

—

In the back of his mind, Milgram worried about how the subway riders might respond as he asked for their seats. New Yorkers aren't known for being warm and fuzzy, and engaging with them on the subway, where personal space is limited, seemed risky. Would a particularly volatile passenger stand up and take a swing? Would he curse and shout? Neither of these things happened because, as Milgram discovered, the passengers he approached were more scared of him than he was of them. "What kind of maniac would ask for my seat?" they asked themselves. The norm he was violating was so strongly held that only someone truly dangerous would ignore it.

For all the danger Milgram perceived in his request, the worst-case scenario was modest compared to what Alex Honnold faces in his line of work. You may know Honnold's name. He was the subject of a 2018 documentary called *Free Solo*, and he's famous for what's known as "free soloing" a rock face known as El Capitan—climbing it alone, and without a rope.

Honnold has been stuck many times. That's the nature of rock climbing, even for the very best. If the rock face is unyielding, or slippery, or the foothold looks as if it might crumble under your weight, you turn back and concede defeat. You don't survive years as a free soloist by taking needless risks. This is the paradox in Honnold's character: he leads one of the most dangerous lifestyles imaginable, while abhorring risk. "I hate gambling," Honnold said in an interview with NPR's Guy Raz. "A lot of people when they talk about risk, it's like it's okay to fail. Particularly with financial risk, people take financial risk because the upside outweighs the downside. But with free soloing it's not like that because the downside is infinite, basically. I'm really making sure that that chance is a zero, you know?"

Honnold's combination of traits is vanishingly rare. How many people are fearless in the face of imminent death, while doing everything in their power to avoid risk? This is what makes him so successful. He pauses and prepares for months or years before a big climb, but attacks the climb without a shred of fear once he decides he's ready to begin.

Honnold's aversion to risk, and preference for meticulous planning, were inspired in large part by an experience he had in 2008. That year, he completed one of his first major free solo climbs, of a granite edifice in Yosemite National Park called Half Dome. Honnold free soloed Half Dome a couple of days after completing the climb with ropes and a partner. This practice climb allowed him to plan his free solo attack of Half Dome with clarity about each component of the route. But on the day of his free solo, he decided to deviate from the route he'd practiced earlier. Part of that earlier route was tricky, so he chose to take a slightly different, but unpracticed, route that bypassed the most precarious part of the climb.

As he rounded a curve on the granite slab, Honnold was confronted by a slab of blank granite. No obvious footholds or handholds. This is a free soloist's worst nightmare. He tested several footholds, none of which seemed safe. "I started to panic," he recalled. "I knew what I had to do, but I was just too afraid to do it. I just had to stand up on my right foot. And so after what felt like an eternity, I accepted what I had to do, and it didn't slip, and so I didn't die. And that move marked the end of the hardest climbing. And so I charged from there towards the summit."

Everything worked out that day, but Honnold was rattled. "I was disappointed in my performance because I knew that I'd gotten away with something. I actually took the next year or so off from free soloing because I knew that I shouldn't make a habit of relying on luck. I didn't want to be a lucky climber. I wanted to be a great climber." Honnold spent that year off coming to terms with how close he'd come to the ultimate disaster. In free soloing, he was temporarily stuck. To his credit, he spent that year forming new, more careful habits, readying himself for the even greater free soloing challenges that lay ahead.

A decade later, after dozens of climbs alone and with ropes and partners, Honnold decided he was ready to free solo El Capitan. His preparation was immense. He spent two seasons training and aborted more than one attempt because he just didn't feel prepared or ready on that particular day. Apart from developing general physical fitness, he had to learn to complete each of the thirty-three pitches, or separate moves, that constituted the three-thousand-foot climb. Some required brute strength; others required acrobatic leaps; and others relied on uncommon flexibility. Honnold practiced each with ropes, some dozens of times, but the bulk of his prep was mental. He rehearsed each pitch in his mind, over and over, until he was sure he could master it unaided.

When he woke up the day of his successful climb, everything just felt right. "On that particular day, I didn't feel like there was any risk," he said. "You know, I mean, the day that I free soloed El Cap was the culmination of years of effort. And I think that practice always desensitizes you to things. I mean, I think that's kind of the only real way to broaden your comfort zone—is to just slowly push—you know, just to keep on pushing at the edge of it until, eventually, you're pretty comfortable with things that you weren't before." Three hours and fifty-six minutes after beginning his ascent, Honnold pulled himself up over the lip of El Capitan's peak, achieving the world's tallest free solo climb in history.

Preparation made Lionel Messi and Andre Agassi better sportsmen, but for Alex Honnold, preparation ensured he got stuck at the "right" time—during practice climbs—and remained unencumbered when his life was at stake. Honnold knows that the right time for being stuck is in planning and anticipation of the main event, whether physical or mental. Being stuck when you have ropes and climbing partners is very different from being stuck when you're free soloing. Since we're all going to be stuck at some point, we may as well try to be stuck during low-stakes moments that matter less and teach us more. These moments are followed by a second chance, or they come before higher-stakes tests with meaningful consequences. It's okay to be stuck during these moments because they're instructive, and they make you more effective when the main event arrives.

We can also learn from Honnold the value of pausing, preparing, and, above all, knowing when to abandon a venture partway through. Honnold isn't afraid to turn back if he feels unprepared or mentally unmoored. This same embrace of pausing and preparing explains Andre Agassi's mastery of Boris Becker's serve, Lionel Messi's otherworldly insights about his soccer opponents, and Judson Brewer's ability to coax longtime nicotine addicts to quit smoking.

For all the benefits of pausing and preparing, though, sometimes the main event doesn't go to plan. Honnold has abandoned dozens of free solo attempts, Agassi and Messi have lost countless matches, and not all of Brewer's nicotine addicts stayed quit weeks or months after his experiments ended. Mastering the anxiety and discomfort that follow these failures is essential—and it's one of the major differences between people who achieve breakthroughs, and those who stay mired indefinitely.

FAILING WELL

Anxiety is an all-purpose warning system that tells you something's wrong. Maybe your body's moving too fast through space, or you've bitten off more than you can chew at work, or your reptilian brain has detected a dangerous situation that hasn't yet tickled your forebrain. Sometimes that warning system is productive, driving you to fix immediate problems that might otherwise escape your notice. At other times, though, anxiety freezes you in place, or swells wildly even in the face of minor concerns. At these times anxiety entrenches rather than frees you.

Much of the anxiety you feel when you're stuck is of this unhelpful kind. It flourishes in the face of friction when you misinterpret a modest or brief setback as a profound or extended threat. Anxiety is a natural response to resistance, but some people, through experience, strategy, or personality, marshal or move beyond this form of anxiety. It's worth asking what separates them from the rest of us.

——

What would happen if you rolled over early one Monday morning, refused to turn on your phone, and went back to sleep for twelve hours? Is there a job you'd be neglecting? Children who expect you to make breakfast and take them to school? Someone else you care for who would be lost without you, even for a single day? How much will you lose for embracing a single day of gross and unplanned inefficiency?

Your answer to this question is an important measure of your personal wealth. If you have billions of dollars, but your decision to sleep late one day topples multinational organizations or governments, by this measure you're a pauper. If you're comfortably middle-class, but have vast tracts of temporal freedom, by this measure you're immensely wealthy.

Most of the time we don't equate wealth with freedom. Instead, we treat people as ongoing balance sheets. The Forbes 400 list exemplifies this approach. In 1981, Malcolm Forbes asked his editor in chief to compile a list of the four hundred wealthiest people in America. Forbes, like his father, who founded the magazine in 1917, was a fan of capitalism and free markets. He collected Fabergé eggs, yachts, airplanes, and motorcycles and was himself worth hundreds of millions of dollars. Forbes chose the number four hundred because rumor had it that Caroline Astor's famous ballroom held four hundred people. A small team of *Forbes* writers traversed the country for leads. They walked up and down New York's fabled Park and Fifth Avenues looking for names that appeared on more than one building cornerstone and conducted hundreds of interviews with bankers, journalists, and fundraisers. To make the first list, moguls needed to demonstrate a net worth of around $100 million (today it's closer to $2 billion). The members of that inaugural class were a mix of delighted and irritated. Media giant Malcolm Borg complained, "Every goddamn stockbroker in the country has called me," whereas real estate baron William Horvitz said his inclusion made him "feel pretty good deep inside."

When you dig into the list, though, you'll find hundreds of people who have huge sums of money, but relatively little time. The complex financial lives that bring them billions leave them almost none of what researchers call "time slack," or temporal freedom. These are not people who can easily go quiet for days or even hours.

Beneath these four hundred multibillionaires are hundreds of thousands of Forbes 400 wannabes. I know this because some of my students have similar aspirations. The gulf between student debt and billions in the black comes down to arch-efficiency. If they don't "love the hustle," if they're incapable of rising to the top of a multinational behemoth or finding a start-up that will "change everything," they've lost. That view of the world imposes colossal pressure. It leaves no margin for inefficiency. No slack. The hustle requires that you sacrifice relationships, weekends, and, above all, happiness today as you stumble toward the mirage of happiness tomorrow.

If this is your outlook, you'll feel near-constant setbacks, and those setbacks will provoke piercing anxiety. I say "feel" because many of those setbacks will exist only in your mind. If "the hustle" is your proxy for progress, you'll interpret slowing down to tie your shoelaces as a failure. Missing a workout, a high-fiber protein shake, or a scheduled hour of networking is also a failure. If you adopt a razor-thin definition of success, you'll fail all the time. Humans aren't machines, and treating ourselves as efficient automatons is the first mile on the highway to burnout.

If you want to succeed really, really badly, the paradoxical solution proposed by many successful people is to ease up. Albert Einstein was obscenely productive, but his productivity came in bursts. Between those bursts, he was gentle with himself. "If my work isn't going well," he said, "I lie down in the middle of a workday and gaze at the ceiling while I listen and visualize what goes on in my imagination." Try to imagine Einstein, white mane and all, lying on his back and staring at the blank ceiling at two in the afternoon. This isn't the Einstein of myth, but it's central to what made him great. Rather than fighting friction, Einstein allowed it to wash over him like a wave, using it as an opportunity to take two or three mental steps backward so he could "listen" to his imagination. Instead of fighting friction, he allowed it to defeat him—and, in doing so, learned to fail well.

The same was true of Mozart, who allowed himself to slow down between bursts of productivity. Mozart found the best of his compositions arrived when he was most placid. "When I am, as it were, completely myself," he wrote, "entirely alone, and of good cheer—say, traveling in a carriage or walking after a good meal or during the night when I cannot sleep—it is on such occasions that my ideas flow best and most abundantly." Mozart may have experienced fevered bursts of productivity, but those bursts are hard to sustain. You don't make a string of breakthroughs, composing six hundred symphonies and concertos, by wrestling your demons every time your productivity hits a wall. Like Einstein, Mozart recognized that the quickest way to guide a derailed mind toward productivity is not to exert brute force, but to seek space and solitude—and to accept that some failure is necessary.

Einstein and Mozart were one-in-a-billion talents, which is why it's surprising to learn they were in some ways type B personalities. Neither one stood atop a metaphorical mountain proclaiming his love for the hustle. Instead, both retreated inward, embraced quiet, and allowed their ideas to land in good time.

One of the benefits of this laid-back approach to friction is that it makes room for failure. It accepts that we can't always produce at peak productivity, and that highs will be separated by lows. Modern theories of learning and development acknowledge that progress is impossible without challenge, which in turn means you'll have to fail before you can succeed.

Several years ago, a team of psychologists and neuroscientists sought to identify the perfect success-to-failure ratio. At one end of the spectrum, you have perfect success, and at the other you have abject failure. Both poles are demotivating, but for different reasons. Perfect success is boring and uninspiring, and abject failure is exhausting and demoralizing. Somewhere between these extremes is a sweet spot that maximizes long-term progress. "When we learn something new, like a language or musical instrument," the authors wrote, "we often seek challenges at the edge of our competence—not so hard that we are discouraged, but not so easy that we get bored. This simple intuition, that there is a sweet spot of difficulty, a 'Goldilocks zone,' for motivation and learning is at the heart of modern teaching methods."

According to the researchers, the optimal error rate is 15.87 percent. Obviously the true rate varies more than that disarmingly precise number suggests. On good days you might tolerate a higher error rate, and on days when you're discouraged or tired, you might prefer to avoid error altogether. Some tasks probably demand higher failure rates than others, and perhaps you need to embrace more failure if you're in a hurry to learn. Personality probably matters, too. Einstein and Mozart, with their laid-back approach to friction, may have been more willing to tolerate error than most people are, and that may explain a part of their ongoing success.

What makes the mere existence of this optimal failure rate valuable is that it does two things for you. First, it gives you an objective benchmark for optimal difficulty. If you're failing much more than once in every five or six attempts, you're probably failing too often; and if you almost never fail or fail rarely, you're probably not failing often enough. Second, though, from an emotional perspective, the optimal error rate licenses you to fail. Not only is failing okay, but it's *necessary*. Without those moments staring at their literal and metaphorical ceilings, Einstein and Mozart may have been less productive and less successful across time. Those blips and troughs weren't glitches but rather essential components of the process.

This one-in-five-or-six failure metric is a useful guide when you're learning a new skill, particularly as technology makes it easier to quantify success. Whether you're learning a new language, learning to code, learning a new soccer technique, training to run a particular distance at a particular pace, or trying to meditate for a certain duration uninterrupted, you'll be able to quantify your success. At first, your failure rate may be higher than one in six, but if it isn't declining to that level, you'll know you're failing too often to be productive.

The same rules apply to organizations, which also do best when they tolerate some failure. In the late 1990s, a decade before the rise of smartphones, Motorola launched a satellite phone provider called Iridium. The company's name referred to the seventy-seventh element in the periodic table because Iridium's original plans required a network of seventy-seven satellites that orbited the Earth, just as Iridium's seventy-seven electrons orbit its nucleus. The company's promise was spectacular: a global phone network that offered perfect reception anywhere on the planet, and a vanishingly small dropped-call rate. Even today's most sophisticated smartphones can't compete with Iridium's decades-old technology. Wall Street experts were enamored with Iridium as its stock hit the market, but the company's focus on perfect clarity and perfect connections made the phones prohibitively expensive. Iridium's executives adopted a zero-tolerance approach to product flaws, but that was not what phone users wanted. They were willing to accept a small drop in clarity and a small rise in dropped calls in exchange for significantly cheaper phones and service plans. The surest way to get stuck is to rigidly pursue perfection.

Assuming that setbacks are to some extent necessary, the next question is how to manage them. How do you deal with the roughly 15.87 percent of occasions when things don't go to plan? The answer is not just to fail, but to fail *well*, and some people fail better than others.

—

Failing well is critical because it's rarely the last thing you do. It's almost always a waypoint on an extended journey, the remainder of which is shaped by how you respond to that failure. What's critical is that you respond to failure productively, and one of the major differences between successes and setbacks is that most people respond to successes similarly, whereas failures invoke a diverse array of responses. Most people know how to celebrate victory, and to celebrate it well. We're taught not to gloat as children, and for most of us the lesson takes quite early. Oscar winners, Grammy recipients, and Olympic gold medalists are groomed to win gracefully, and so from a young age we see them behaving respectably over and over when they win. It's easy to be gracious in victory, but it's rarer to see grace in defeat.

Much of what determines whether you respond to setbacks with grace is how you interpret those experiences. In "Failing and Flying," American poet Jack Gilbert suggested that we tend to ignore successes and train our attention on failure. Gilbert illustrates this idea by re-framing the legend of Icarus. "Everyone forgets that Icarus also flew," he begins, noting that we universally remember Icarus for plunging to the earth after straying too close to the sun. Gilbert concludes the poem with the lines "I believe Icarus was not failing as he fell, / but just coming to the end of his triumph." What Gilbert wrote is true about humans in general. Most of the time, when we focus our attention on losses, failures, and mistakes, we're protected from repeating our mistakes and from making risky decisions. But when we're trying to unstick ourselves, focusing on negatives entrenches us more deeply.

Gilbert's answer is to train our attention on the successes that brought us to where we became stuck. In many cases, being stuck is a sign of progress—of having moved beyond a place of comfort and mastery to a place where you're challenged. The key is to remember that straying to more difficult terrain invites setbacks, but those setbacks are essential for progress in the long run.

—

Setbacks may be inevitable, but the anxiety that follows them is sur-mountable. One way to ensure you don't respond to every setback with anxiety is to expose yourself to stress tests that steel you against setbacks. This approach is popular among athletes. Elite golfers know that transient losses of focus threaten otherwise impeccable scores. If you're expecting to hit seventy-two shots during a round of golf, just one lapse—on, say, the fiftieth shot—might add two, three, or four extra strokes to your round. A full round of eighteen holes might last four or more hours, so distraction and fatigue are almost inevitable. When American golfer Phil Mickelson isn't playing championship golf, he taxes his attentional skills by playing at least two rounds a day. "I'm making more and more progress by trying to elongate my focus," Mick-elson has said. "I might try to play thirty-six, forty-five holes in a day and try to focus on each shot so that when I go out and play eighteen, it doesn't feel like it's that much." If Mickelson trains himself to hit two hundred shots without losing focus, he should be able to hit the seventy-odd shots during a standard day of championship golf. "I'm trying to use my mind like a muscle and just expand it," he said. This approach rests on the idea that humans are tremendously flexible. For most golfers, focusing for eighteen straight holes is a significant challenge, but eighteen holes constitutes just 40 percent of Mickelson's training diet.

Mickelson's overtraining technique worked to delay his physical and mental fatigue on the course, and the same approach also drives emotional resilience. To test this idea, three of my colleagues and I examined the performance of college basketball teams across a ten-year period. Before each season's competitive games begin, college teams play a series of noncompetitive preseason games. These are "friendly" games, which means the stakes are low. They're designed to ready each team for the rigors of competition, and the results aren't officially tallied. What's important about these preseason games is that they're randomly drawn. Some years, a team might play a collection of formidable opponents, and other years the same team might play a string of weaker opponents. We wondered whether teams do better during the competitive season when they play weaker opponents or when they play stronger opponents during the preseason.

The answer isn't obvious. We interviewed coaching experts and elite college athletes across a range of sports, and their opinions varied. Some said they preferred light preseason schedules, which would instill confidence ahead of the competitive season. What could be better, heading into a new season, than winning your entire slate of preseason games? You might also experience fewer injuries, and you'd be able to rest your strongest players for competition.

Other coaches and players believed the opposite: that challenging preseasons were critical for team preparation. If you're playing weaker teams, you won't have an opportunity to refine the strategies you'll need when you meet elite teams during the competitive season. Some told us, too, that it's important to learn how to lose. Losing is inevitable—even strong teams usually lose a game or two each season or tournament—so learning how to rebound from loss is an essential skill. Some coaches worried that their teams might head into a tailspin following a loss, which might turn that single loss into two or three before the team regained its balance. The best way to deal with that concern is to lose when losing doesn't matter quite so much.

This latter approach is known as hardship inoculation. The term, borrowed from the treatment of infectious diseases, suggests that our bodies and minds become more resilient to formidable challenges when they've been inoculated against those challenges. The best way to inoculate your body against a disease is to expose it to small or inert doses of the disease before the real disease arrives. Hardship inoculation applies to setbacks, too. Across ten seasons, we found that college basketball teams performed better during competitive games following challenging preseason schedules. The effect was large, too. Our model suggests that teams with the easiest preconference schedules might have reached a round or even two rounds deeper into the postseason knockout tournament had they drawn one of the most difficult preconference schedules.

Hardship inoculation works in intellectual domains, as well. Humans have been playing the complex Chinese board game of Go for thousands of years, and though performance has improved across time, it has to a large extent stagnated over the past several decades. That was true until sometime between 2016 and 2017, when a new artificially intelligent Go engine surpassed the ability of all human Go players. The best human players in the world routinely lost to the Go AI, but these losses paved the way for a new era in the game. For years, human skills had seemed to hit a ceiling, but after the AI's introduction, the entire field of Go players seemed to improve. They made better moves and achieved higher scores on the most commonly used rating scale. The hardship of facing a superior machine liberated a reservoir of ability that most Go players failed to tap earlier in their careers.

Beyond sports and intellectual pursuits, you can also inoculate yourself against emotional challenges. One person who knows this firsthand is Michelle Poler, a brand strategist and founder of the Hello Fears movement. Poler was an anxious child, raised in an anxious family. Her ancestors had fled Nazism during World War II for a new life in Venezuela, and many of their anxieties remained half a century later as Poler was growing up in Caracas. "My mom was raised with lots of fears, and so was I," she says. "And while our fears may not overlap, we both had the same attitude toward fear: if it's there, don't bother!"

In 2014, Poler overcame a basket of fears to move to New York City, where she began a master's in branding at the School of Visual Arts. During the first day of class, her professor asked her two questions that changed her life. First, the teacher asked where Poler imagined herself ten years in the future. Poler's list included becoming a successful entrepreneur, traveling with her husband, speaking at companies around the world, and buying an apartment in Manhattan. Second, the teacher asked whether one crucial obstacle might prevent Poler from achieving those outcomes. The answer arrived in capital letters: FEAR. "Fear was the one obstacle that could prevent me from achieving my ten-year plan," Poler realized. "How could I apply to the best companies in NYC if I was so afraid of rejection? How could I then become an entrepreneur if I couldn't deal with uncertainty? How would I ever be able to speak at conferences about my 'accomplishments' if I was terribly scared of public speaking? I wanted all of those things, but I was dreadfully afraid of them."

Poler had never heard the term *hardship inoculation*, but she recognized that her dreams might elude her unless she learned to tolerate her anxiety. Her choice was either to do nothing and to remain insulated from fear, or to learn to manage her fears in the service of that ten-year plan. She chose the path of inoculation, and so began her "one hundred days without fear" campaign.

Each day, for one hundred days, Poler did something that scared her. Some of those fears revolved around pain and danger, others around embarrassment, rejection, and loneliness, and others around control and disgust. She began by eating three oysters at her parents' anniversary dinner at New York's Balthazar restaurant. "I'm afraid of eating things that look, feel or smell disgusting," she explained on her website. "In an effort to stay away from that uncomfortable situation, I embrace my safe food area which includes: pizza, mac'n'cheese, crunchy tuna roll, arepas, cereal and delicious looking things without eyes, tentacles or shells." Poler captured the experience on video. It didn't go well. She gagged a couple of times, spat out the first oyster, and had to steel herself before washing down another oyster with a slurp of red wine.

Poler still detests oysters, and she doesn't believe that eating oysters, specifically, has anything to do with her ten-year plan. Embracing her fears, though, inoculated her against the legitimate challenges she might face as she tackled that plan. Eating oysters was her preseason, and she had begun with a particularly difficult assignment.

Poler's list of fears was diverse. On day fourteen she drove alone through the streets of Miami at night. On day twenty-six she took a helicopter ride. On day thirty-five she spoke in front of a crowd, and on day thirty-nine she donated blood. Later, she crowd-surfed, crashed a wedding, did stand-up comedy, flew a plane, rappelled down a cliff, and—on day one hundred—delivered a TEDx Talk in front of almost five hundred people. The experiences changed her. After the project ended, Spanish-language broadcaster Telemundo invited her to its Miami studios for an interview. She was incredibly nervous. She was still afraid of public speaking, and particularly afraid of live TV—and her worst fears were realized when the interview went horribly wrong. "I suddenly forgot how to speak Spanish (my first language)," she recalled. "I started using many words in English, which I shouldn't have. I was just so nervous that I couldn't think well." When her interviewer revealed that Poler would be taking a surprise trip to Poland, to take part in the International March of the Living (a march between concentration camps Auschwitz and Birkenau to commemorate the Holocaust), she froze and struggled to regain her composure. But—and this is critical—she not only survived the embarrassment of that interview but used it to gird her against future challenges. This was her new philosophy. Each time she was anxious or faced a barrier, she remembered the hundred-plus barriers she'd faced and overcome during the inoculation journey.

Fear is such an elemental component of stuckness that Poler's approach applies to more than just acute phobias. Whether a sticking point involves a difficult conversation, a leap from one career path to another, or anxiety about attempting a new skill, Poler's twist on exposure therapy is a valuable tool. On one level, it shows the value of taking on manageable doses of anxiety on the way to growing past a roadblock. On another, more profound level, it suggests that we become globally more resilient to roadblocks when we adopt Poler's philosophy. Once you take on a couple of your fears, you become the kind of person who faces rather than runs from fear. When a new roadblock-driven anxiety arrives, you're primed to meet its challenge.

As time passes, Poler continues to expose herself to new fears, in part to ensure she's still inoculated. Extending the inoculation metaphor further, these new exposures are like antibody tests that confirm her immunity. That's an important part of the process, too—ensuring that you know whether and to what extent you can manage the anxiety of new setbacks.

Living constantly in fear isn't for everyone, but there's another way to determine whether you've been inoculated. This technique draws on a psychological phenomenon known as the illusion of explanatory depth. The illusion works like this: Ask yourself right now how well you can explain how a bicycle works and give yourself a rating. A rating of one means you have no idea how a bicycle works (and may not even know what a bicycle is), and a rating of ten means you could explain its operation perfectly. Most people give themselves a score of six or seven, which means they believe they can do a reasonable job of explaining how a bicycle works. Now try, in words, to explain how a bicycle works. Really try.

Most people know that a bike has handlebars, wheels, a chain, gears, and pedals, but in explaining how the bike works, they falter. They're not sure how those components interact with one another, how they produce movement, whether and how the chain is connected to the pedals and the gears, and so on. This is the illusion. Unquestioned, we assume we know how a bicycle works, but when pushed to *unpack* our knowledge, we struggle. The same is true of many other mechanical devices, like ballpoint pens and zippers, and even of the policy positions held by prominent politicians. Most of the time these shortcomings are hidden from view. We mistake our superficial understanding of *what* a bike is for *how* a bike works. The only way to reveal this deficit is to interrogate it—to ask ourselves the way a child might to unpack our knowledge. Only when you're forced to fully express your knowledge do you realize what you don't know.

Coping with setbacks is similar in that we rarely question how we'd manage the anxiety of friction before that friction is real. Michelle Poler's campaign was effective because it showed her precisely what she could and couldn't manage and made her more resilient. As she progressed through the hundred days, she recorded how she felt before, during, and after each challenge. While eating the oysters, her fear rose to a ten on her ten-point scale, but afterward receded to a six. In contrast, going to a dog park scared her in anticipation (an eight), but was less scary in the moment (a six), and not at all scary in retrospect (a three). These numbers matter because they told Poler two different stories about these two specific fears: she continues to fear oysters and has no plans to eat one again, but can imagine spending time among dogs. "I don't think you overcome such fear in so little time," she wrote, "but I do believe this helped me understand that dogs don't want to hurt me, they just want to have fun."

There's something to this approach for the rest of us, even if we aren't embracing a trial by fear. One technique for treating aerophobia, or fear of flying, is to slowly expose aerophobes to the experience of flying. This exposure therapy gives them progressively larger doses of fear so that they learn to cope with the stresses of actually flying. At first they might be shown images of the inside of a plane or asked to sit in a plane seat that isn't inside a real plane. Then they might actually walk onto a plane, sit down, then leave before the plane takes off. They might also sit inside a virtual reality simulator that makes them feel as though they're flying, with the knowledge that the experience isn't real. Once they've completed each of these steps, they might actually take a short flight, then perhaps a longer flight.

The same approach works, though, with any sticking point, whether or not it involves acute fears. The key is to imagine how you might manage the anxiety of being stuck, with progressively more detail, to the point where you've become inoculated against the obstacle should it materialize. This technique works particularly well if you're frozen by the fear of failure. Trying something new, from a job to a new business venture, is threatening because it requires embracing the unknown. Many people who choose not to move forward are paralyzed by the prospect of failing. That fear remains abstract and unformed because they don't engage with it deeply enough to imagine how failing might actually affect their lives. It makes sense to reconsider launching a new business if its failure will leave you penniless and homeless, but as long as you've saved enough for a financial safety net, failure is more personally distressing than ruinous. You can work through the potential hit to your self-esteem and social standing the same way an aerophobe might work through the fear of flying—by imagining ahead of time how you'll feel if the business fails. How will you explain its failure to friends and family? What concrete steps will you take next? Do you have a follow-up business in mind? Will you abandon entrepreneurship temporarily? Answering questions like these is the best way to test how you'll cope with failure—and the best way to move forward despite the fear that you might not succeed.

These techniques, from hardship inoculation to exposure therapy, work at the individual level, but they're difficult to scale. It's almost impossible to deal with the anxiety of getting stuck in an organization or among a collection of people with solutions that don't change the structure of the organization or the collection at large. To do that you need to give people within the collective room to fail.

———

The rule of thumb in classrooms goes something like this: praise students three times more often than you reprimand them. This ratio implies that you can spoil students with too much praise. Several years ago, a team of education experts put this ratio to the test. They followed teachers and students for three years across nineteen elementary schools across the United States. Some of the teachers were taught to praise their students more freely, whereas others were left to manage their classrooms as they always had. The researchers monitored the behavior of the students in each classroom.

As the data trickled in, it became clear that the students thrived on praise. The three-to-one ratio ceiling was a fiction. In some classrooms teachers offered nine times more praise than criticism, and those were the classrooms in which the students did best. They were more likely to remain on task the more praise and the less criticism they received. (The researchers were careful to minimize the possibility that better-behaved students required fewer reprimands, which might have suggested that better-behaved students get more praise.)

This effect isn't confined to children in classrooms. One study examined the extent to which abusive NBA coaches shaped the careers of the young players on their teams. The study tracked the performance of hundreds of players coached by fifty-seven coaches across six years. The results were unambiguous. Players with abusive coaches were less efficient and committed more technical fouls even ten years after escaping those coaches. It's no surprise, perhaps, that abuse is counterproductive, but what is surprising is that it continues to damage athletes for the remainder of their careers. This result is concerning, too, because a second study found that between one-sixth and one-third of all college basketball coaches are abusive, implying that the damage might be done even before young athletes fully mature.

Praise in the classroom and on the basketball court is effective because it counteracts the anxiety that students and athletes might otherwise feel as they develop. It licenses them to fail, and to take risks, both of which tend to provoke anxiety, but both of which are critical for the breakthroughs that follow periods of learning and development. Praise is a buffer that protects budding students and athletes from self-esteem threats.

Praise and support change the lens through which people experience the world by changing how they perceive anxiety. Though stress and anxiety feel unpleasant in the moment, it's almost impossible to succeed without experiencing them from time to time. Both too little and too much stress can hamper performance. What's critical is interpreting anxiety and stress as drivers of rather than detractors from success.

Psychologist Alia Crum and her colleagues have shown, across dozens of experiments, that seeing stress as beneficial boosts performance dramatically. For example, in one study, Crum followed 174 Navy SEALs as they navigated a series of training exercises. The tasks were physically demanding and stress inducing, so Crum wondered whether the SEALs who perceived stress as performance-enhancing might do better than those who believed stress was a liability. Indeed, the SEALs who believed stress predicted achievement were more likely to persist through training, to complete obstacle courses more quickly, and to receive fewer negative evaluations from their peers and instructors. In other studies, Crum and her colleagues trained people to see stress as beneficial, and they, too, performed better on a range of mental and physical tasks.

Perhaps the most striking example of an intervention that changes how people experience anxiety and stress is the introduction of a universal basic income, or UBI. UBIs are negative taxes that are paid to every member of a region or country—say, $1,000 a month with no strings attached. One of the strongest arguments in favor of UBIs is that they liberate people to take entrepreneurial risks that they might otherwise avoid. If you want to start a new business, for example, and you know you won't be earning an income for several months or longer as the business grows, the UBI frees you to take that risk, whereas the absence of an income would prevent you from embarking on the venture. One of the most consistent findings from UBI trials, over many decades, is that they reduce anxiety and liberate people to focus on more than putting food on the table each week.

Before writing the first book in the Harry Potter series, J. K. Rowling was destitute. What saved her was a guaranteed income from government benefits. In an interview with Jon Stewart, she explained the importance of this: "I couldn't have written this book if I hadn't been as poor as it's possible to go in the UK without being homeless. We were on what you would call welfare, what I would call benefits, for a couple of years." Stewart asked Rowling whether the government had ever made a better investment than supporting her during those years. Rowling replied, "Absolutely, my country helped me, and there are places in the world where I would have starved."

A similar UBI policy in Nigeria has been wildly successful. In 2011, the Nigerian government gave $60 million to twelve hundred entrepreneurs who were launching new ventures—a total of roughly $50,000 per venture. Three years after the program launched, 54 percent of a group of unfunded entrepreneurs were still running their businesses, whereas 93 percent of those in the program had thriving businesses. Those businesses were also more than three times as likely to have grown beyond ten employees. The money helps in part because it simply gives people the resources to start new ventures, but it also helps because it's freeing. Most acts of entrepreneurship and innovation are risky, and risk-taking is less intimidating to the privileged. If a risk exposes you to financial ruin, it's far more daunting than if you have a financial cushion beneath you. One recipient of UBI explained that a regular paycheck emboldened her to be more entrepreneurial: "It gave me the security to start my own business." Dozens of other recipients have made similar claims, some likening the experience to "winning the lottery."

Perhaps the most compelling argument for the unsticking effects of UBI programs comes from the New Leaf program in British Columbia, Canada. The program, founded by the University of British Columbia and a charitable organization called Foundations for Social Change, paid fifty homeless residents of Vancouver a onetime sum of $7,500 and tracked their behavior for one year. Recipients spent their money on a combination of food, rent, clothes, transportation, and medical bills, and the vast majority managed to retain more than $1,000 across the year, despite Vancouver's high cost of living. A number of the recipients also felt liberated to pursue employment, signing up for classes and applying for new jobs. "My goal is to better myself," one recipient named Ray told New Leaf. "I want to go into the front line for alcohol and drug abuse; to give back where I came from. I just started computer training, so I'm advancing myself." Ray's unsticking would be impossible had the program not taken care of his basic needs and, in turn, the anxiety he experienced being homeless.

Mastering your emotional response to friction is critical, but taming your anxiety is just the first step in getting unstuck. The next step is learning how to think about the problem so you're less likely to become stuck in the first place, and less likely to remain stuck for long when you do. Thinking about the problem intelligently begins, paradoxically, when you realize that breakthroughs often come when you limit rather than expand your options.

PART III

HEAD

FRICTION AUDITS AND THE ART OF SIMPLIFICATION

In the 1980s, an architect named Bill Hillier traipsed around London to measure the "maze-iness" of the city's neighborhoods. Some neighborhoods were open and plotted on grids, whereas others, like the Barbican Estate, were so serpentine that tourists could only navigate them by following yellow road markings. Hillier devised the mathematical term *intelligibility* to capture the complexity of each neighborhood. Intelligibility scores ranged from zero to one, where "unintelligible" neighborhoods with low scores were more likely to ensnare newcomers. Hillier's intelligibility score applies to other domains of complexity, too. For example, every maze you've ever encountered has an intelligibility score that captures its difficulty. Hillier's key insight was that the same complexity that caused people to get stuck when they were navigating neighborhoods and mazes also described the complexity of life more broadly.

The best way to get unstuck, according to Hillier, is to simplify the unintelligible. Strip away complexity, and you carve a straighter path from beginning to end. That's especially true when the concept is inherently complex. Take the domain of diagnostic medicine. The human body combines dozens of bones, hundreds of miles of hair, tens of thousands of miles of blood vessels, and trillions of cells. Humans are susceptible to more than ten thousand identified diseases, many of them so rare that doctors have only ever identified a handful of cases. Doctors navigate this web of ailments with a total of several hundred treatments and cures, leaving many diseases difficult to diagnose and even more difficult to treat.

For the most complex cases, expert diagnosticians like New York City's Thomas Bolte are called for a fresh opinion. "In mainstream medicine there's an expression: 'When you hear hooves, don't initially look for zebras,'" says Robert Scully, who has worked alongside Bolte. "As a result, zebras are missed all the time. Tom's a zebra hunter." Bolte's focus on complex diagnostics has earned him the title the Real Dr. House, recalling the TV doctor played by Hugh Laurie, who diagnosed exceptionally complex cases that eluded his colleagues. Bolte shines when the proverbial hoofbeats of disease belong to zebras rather than horses.

Bolte has a boyish crop of thick hair, and Rollerblades between his office and the apartments of his homebound patients. He's a man of science, but also a spiritualist who favors Jungian psychology and the importance of keeping an open mind. He spends an unusually long time listening to his patients, asking them dozens or even hundreds of questions before settling on a diagnosis. Though he treats these patients with humanity, he recognizes their ailing bodies for the machines they are: mechanical, governed by certain laws of science, and prone to a finite set of afflictions.

Bolte learned to diagnose as a child, but his first patients were houses rather than people. His father succumbed to melanoma when Bolte was a boy, and his mother, Rosemarie, supported her two children by renovating and renting out dilapidated homes by the sea on Long Island. Rosemarie's tenants tended to trash those houses, so she employed a team of handymen to repair them from one lease to the next. Tom watched those men work, and soon he could manage basic plumbing, carpentry, drywall hanging, and electrical jobs. Later, he graduated to fixing appliances, cars, and computers and came to believe that even the most complex repairs were to some extent formulaic. Understand the formula and you could make the repair. That was true of simple home repairs, appliance overhauls, and even fixing sick people.

As a young diagnostician, Bolte learned the importance of simplifying the task. In Hillier's language, Bolte approaches the unintelligible maze of the human body with an algorithm that almost always ends in a successful diagnosis. Bolte's algorithm is a questionnaire that runs for thirty-two pages. Every patient completes the questionnaire, which covers, among other topics, family medical history, social behavior, habits and hobbies, employment, exposure to household chemicals, and foreign travel. Most patients spend between two and four hours completing the questionnaire, and for Bolte their responses are the first step in making them well. He has refined the questionnaire over time, pouring all the intricacy of diagnosis into this simplifying mold.

Bolte isn't the quickest diagnostician—but he is among the most likely to make a breakthrough. He moves forward, slowly and methodically, and, more often than the vast majority of his colleagues, finds his way to the solution. He has worked in traditional medical practices, but their emphasis on speed doesn't work for him. Insurance companies rank physicians according to how many patients they see per hour—a sort of "batting average"—and by this metric, at most of his practices he finished dead last. "There was a time in this country when doctors made house calls, and when they were done," he says, "they sat down to dinner with the family. That's how they got to know you. The next time someone in your family took sick, the doctor knew their context. He knew what their home life was like, knew what they did for a living, and so on. Today you're lucky if your doctor sees you for twelve minutes. How can you possibly find out all you need to know about a patient in twelve minutes?" Bolte doesn't have dinner with his patients, but his exhaustive questionnaire does much of the information gathering that those ongoing social relationships achieved before modern medicine became a commodity. He has reduced his process to an algorithm because he knows that the complexity of medical diagnosis is paralyzing. Without simplification, identifying a zebra among horses is next to impossible.

Bolte's story reminded me of an experience I had more than twenty years ago as a young law student. Between classes, I worked part-time at a large commercial law firm in the heart of Sydney, a forty-five-minute bus ride from my home in the city's northern suburbs. I spent many of those bus rides reading legal cases in preparation for law classes. Over the years I read hundreds, maybe thousands, of judgments, hoovering a mountain of criminal law, contracts, property law, torts, and cases from many other branches of the law. Cases are often exhausting to read. Judges aren't known for writing beautifully or simply, and many older judgments are written in impenetrable legalese. Every few minutes my mind would wander, and I'd have to go back and reread large chunks of text. Sometimes I fell asleep midcase, and when I woke up, I'd start again.

On some of those bus rides, I shared my seat with a prominent lawyer who'd been in practice for thirty years. In Australia, the profession is divided between solicitors, who largely prepare cases, and barristers, who largely argue cases in court, in front of judges. About 10 to 15 percent of the most senior barristers are honorifically known as Senior Counsel. My seatmate was a Senior Counsel, one of the top barristers in the country. He was (and still is) brilliant—impossibly knowledgeable about the law, and quick on his feet during an oral argument. During some of our shared bus rides, he was accompanied by a stack of ring-bound folders jammed with legal documents. When there were too many to carry, he would use a small hand trolley to lug them onto the bus.

If you gave me a week alone, without interruption, I couldn't possibly read through and process the information in one bus ride's worth of that lawyer's folders. But he did just that. We would talk for ten minutes, then he would apologize and begin reading. He picked up each of the folders, one after the other, and leafed through them quickly, and then sometimes slowly. He would pause on some pages for a couple of minutes, then largely ignore hundreds of other pages, before stopping again at another critical page. These bus rides began around seven thirty in the morning, and I knew he would be in court a couple of hours later, delivering oral arguments for five or six hours based on what he had read during our shared ride.

One morning, incredulous, I asked, "How can you possibly go into the courtroom for hours with so little preparation?" The process was unintelligible to me, but for this lawyer, as with Thomas Bolte, the algorithm was simple. "I've been doing this for a long time," he told me (I'm paraphrasing here). "Each of the cases rests on a few subtle pieces of information—critical evidence or a crucial fact. Understand that, and combine it with a lifetime of legal knowledge, and you can argue your case for days on end."

I couldn't match his legal knowledge, but I took seriously the importance of learning to simplify thousands of bits of information into their essential components. You don't learn by reading everything, but by figuring out which parts you don't need to read. I wasn't reading thousands of cases during law school because I'd need to apply the ideas from those old cases to new cases. I was reading them to learn to simplify—to recognize the difference between essentials and distractions. The same was true for Bolte, whose thirty-two-page questionnaire was the written version of his essentials. Decades of medical knowledge for Bolte, and legal knowledge for the lawyer on my bus, were distilled into a series of steps that made complex tasks simple.

Turning unintelligible mazes into streamlined algorithms has a meta flavor to it because the process itself requires the use of an algorithm. The algorithm's first step requires that you become a taxonomist. Taxonomy is the science of naming or classifying, and the first step in simplifying is to name or classify every aspect of the complex process you're trying to streamline. For diagnosticians like Bolte this might involve listing every symptom, and pairing it with potential diagnoses. For example, most of the time a cough signals bronchitis or an upper respiratory tract infection—but then there are the zebras: occasionally, a cough signals an allergic reaction to medicine, asthma, lung cancer, or whooping cough. For lawyers, the taxonomy might identify the key issues on which a case is likely to rest—the legal rules that are most likely to be debated in the courtroom.

With the ingredients labeled, the next step is to organize them. Do some tend to go together more often than others? Do constellations of medical symptoms or legal issues tend to occur together? In medical terms, do symptoms cluster together to form syndromes that in turn inspire diagnoses? From the outside, Bolte can appear rambling or nonchalant, but in his head he's examining a list of potential leads to determine whether they're dead ends or open paths to elusive zebras. Bolte's list, though long, is *finite*. One of the problems with complexity is that it can seem unbounded. If you don't know where the world ends, it's impossible to gain a sense of control, so you're far more likely to get stuck. But once you've identified the boundaries, regardless of how expansive the territory you need to cover, you've turned an impossibly complex web into an intelligible algorithm. That's what labeling and organizing does—it provides the ingredients that become, for example, a thirty-two-page questionnaire that guides you from darkness to light.

—

What Bolte does for diagnosis, I have been trying to do for companies and individuals around the world for the past several years. I call this simplifying of the complex a *friction audit*. Just as an auditor might examine a company's financial books, I examine processes and businesses for friction points. Say, for example, you run a small online store that sells sports shoes. Potential customers take a journey that begins when they discover your store and ends—ideally—when they buy a pair of shoes. Today it's possible to trace these customer journeys. You can track how a customer finds your store, which links she clicks on, which pages she visits and for how long, whether she leaves the site, and how long it takes her to buy. In the best case, a customer says, "I need a pair of Nike running shoes." Over, say, fifteen minutes, she searches Google for *Nike running shoes*, discovers your store, browses your inventory of women's Nike running shoes, chooses a pair, adds it to the shopping cart, and checks out.

This sort of friction-free journey is rare. Instead, most customers experience multiple friction points along the way, some of which may lead them away from your store. They may find your home page confusing, they may click the wrong button when shopping, your website may not work properly, they may struggle to choose among an overwhelming array of shoes, and so on. Each of these friction points shows up in the data you collect through your website's server. Bottlenecks appear in the form of time spent on each page. You might see, for example, that hundreds of visitors to your site sail through the first few pages easily, but routinely struggle to navigate the shopping cart interface. They might spend an average of ten minutes trying to check out, and many may return to the cart and your website two or three times before completing the purchase. Worse still, many might not purchase the shoes they've placed in the shopping cart. A friction audit is designed to achieve three ends: to locate these sticking points; to remedy them by simplifying the complex or smoothing the inelegant; and to check later that the remedies have worked. That's it. Three steps that, completed correctly, make a huge difference to how businesses perform and people live their lives.

A few years ago I worked with a number of commercial real estate companies. Some of them specialized in shopping malls. They noticed that some customers came to their malls, spent hours wandering through stores and along walkways, but seemed to leave suddenly after purchasing none of the items they intended to buy. This was a puzzle. Why would people waste hours of their lives only to leave in a hurry? The answer, which comes as no surprise to me because I have two small kids, is that their children demand a rapid exit. Most kids don't mind shopping for a little while, but stay too long and their—and therefore your—world ends. Some of these malls were losing hundreds of thousands of dollars in revenue a month because parents couldn't complete the shopping trips they'd begun. This was the first step of the friction audit: locating the friction point.

The second step was figuring out a solution. How do you pacify kids who've hit their limit? The answer turns out to be fairly simple and inexpensive: invest a modest sum of several thousand dollars in a decent kids' play area. Add a jungle gym to the middle of your mall, and you've created a waypoint for grumpy kids and their exasperated parents. Instead of leaving, parents know to break midway through their shopping trips. IKEA stores have known this for a while. Many have a kids' play area called Småland, which functions as a free day care center. "IKEA Småland coworkers will take care of your children for free for an hour," the IKEA website explains. Shopping centers and stores in Germany, China, and India have introduced a version of Småland for another traditional sticking point: husbands who prefer not to be shopping. These "husband storage facilities," as one Chinese mall calls them, are stocked with beers, gaming consoles, and TVs playing wall-to-wall sports. Whatever you think of these solutions, they work. They keep shoppers in stores for longer than they might otherwise stay, and the cost of running a Småland or a "husband storage facility" is dwarfed by the extra revenue these stores and malls enjoy because shoppers can complete intended purchases.

This friction audit process isn't just about streamlining sales; you can apply it to life at large. Friction is at the heart of being stuck, and the friction audit gives you an algorithmic tool for both finding and weeding out unwanted friction points, and for inserting friction points to prevent unwanted behaviors. If you're eating poorly, or stuck at a punishing job, or struggling to find time to exercise, a friction audit spotlights the problem, which in turn tells you where you need to intervene.

Take the case of eating more chocolate than you'd like, which is a weakness of mine. Many people eat poorly because too little friction separates them from the unhealthy food they're trying to avoid. For several reasons, eating chocolate is, for me, a frictionless experience. There's often chocolate somewhere in my house, so I don't have to go far to find it. It's usually in the same place in my pantry, so I know where to look. Each time I eat it, I feel good and don't immediately see the downsides of eating too much chocolate over time. (I imagine people would eat healthier foods if each bite automatically showed itself as a small, visible change on our bodies.) In the past, I've used a kind of friction audit to trim my chocolate consumption. Taking each of the three issues I mentioned above: I stop buying chocolate; when I do have it at home, I store it in places where I'm less likely to stumble on it automatically (so I have to be mindful about eating it); and—the key—I make the negative consequences of eating it perceptible. One trick some experts recommend is putting chocolate in a small cupboard near a mirror where you're forced to watch yourself—to look into your eyes—as you retrieve the chocolate. If you're trying to avoid it, answering to your reflection as you pull the chocolate from the cupboard is a surprisingly effective friction point.

—

Friction audits are tools for simplification that can be applied by almost anyone, though there's an art and science to applying them well. This is true of most simplification aids. If they're truly formulaic, why can't just anyone use them effectively? Why, if Bolte's approach to medical diagnosis is formulaic, can't other doctors use the same formula for getting unstuck when faced with tricky diagnoses? If legal briefs turn on a few key nuggets, why can't every lawyer digest thousands of pages of evidence on a thirty-minute bus ride? Something must distinguish these giants from the doctors and lawyers who got stuck before them and were unable to find a solution.

These formulas are incredibly powerful, and if other doctors and lawyers applied them, they'd find themselves, say, 80 percent of the way toward the same outcomes. A lot of education works like this. Give people the frameworks and tools to master a new skill, and they'll develop a serviceable version of that skill. They may not move mountains, but they'll succeed, and they'll often get unstuck when they encounter boundaries.

To see the power of these formulas, you just have to ask experts how they simplify the complex. Consider storytelling and narrative. Stories well told are the foundations of empires. Disney's success is built on great storytelling. Without the intellectual property of compelling stories, Disney's technical prowess as an animation and production company means nothing. In theory, there's no limit to the number of different narrative arcs that might define a good story. Stories could zig and zag unpredictably, splintering into as many different narrative maps as there are lives lived by Earth's billions of inhabitants. No two lives are exactly the same, but stories adhere to a narrow set of paradigms and principles.

For a month and a half, in 2011, a story artist at Pixar—a Disney subsidiary—named Emma Coats published twenty-two tweets summarizing Pixar's approach to storytelling. Each tweet described a "rule of storytelling" that Coats and her colleagues turned to when constructing film narratives. She explained that she'd learned these basics from some of her more senior colleagues. The list attracted considerable attention, because Coats specifically, and Pixar broadly, are storytelling experts. Pixar revolutionized the animated film industry with franchises like *Toy Story*, *Monsters, Inc.*, *The Incredibles*, and *Finding Nemo*, and Coats worked on, among other films, Pixar's *Up*, *Brave*, and *Monsters University*.

Among other items, the list included:

4. Once upon a time there was ___. Every day, ___. One day ___. Because of that, ___. Because of that, ___. Until finally ___.

This fourth rule is nothing if not formulaic. It boils down storytelling to the idea that change—deviations from the past, and the results of those deviations—is the stuff of interesting narrative.

Coats' sixth rule is similarly formulaic:

6. What is your character good at, comfortable with? Throw the polar opposite at them. Challenge them. How do they deal?

This rule advocates challenging characters with hardship—and, combining rules 4 and 6, suggests that narratives leap forward with opposites and contrasts. A story becomes interesting when consistency and strength meet their opposites in change and weakness.

Many of the rules deal with getting stuck. Coats knows that writing stories is hard, and storytellers sometimes meet proverbial brick walls:

5. Simplify. Focus. Combine characters. Hop over detours. You'll feel like you're losing valuable stuff but it sets you free.
9. When you're stuck, make a list of what *wouldn't* happen next. Lots of times the material to get you unstuck will show up.
11. Putting it on paper lets you start fixing it. If it stays in your head, a perfect idea, you'll never share it with anyone.

These twenty-two rules are formulas for getting unstuck. That's not exactly how Coats described them, but that's how they work. And they aren't the only rules for getting unstuck, or getting started, in narrative writing. Screenwriter Ken Miyamoto has published a list of ten narrative structures that describe some of the greatest films of the last hundred years. "Screenplay structure has nothing to do with mythology or saving a cat," Miyamoto begins. "It's all about basic choices a screenwriter can make to determine how they want to tell their story. It's actually pretty easy: you just have to know what structures you can play with." Among the options, Miyamoto describes the three-act structure (the setup; the conflict; the resolution), which describes action plots including *Star Wars*, *Raiders of the Lost Ark*, and *Die Hard*. In contrast, the real-time structure follows an event in the moment, as in *12 Angry Men* and the TV series *24*. Other structures include multiple timelines, reverse chronology, and circularity, in which the end of the film returns to its beginning.

Other rules from other writers are holistic and overarching, rather than structural. When Trey Parker and Matt Stone, the creators of *South Park*, visited a group of New York University film students, they explained their narrative process. "We found out this really simple rule," Parker says. "We can take these beats, which are basically the beats of your outline, and if the words *and then* belong between those beats, you're fucked, basically. You've got something pretty boring." Parker explains, "What should happen between every beat you've written down is either the word *therefore* or *but*." He sketches the structure using a more concrete example: "You come up with an idea, and it's like 'this happens' and then 'this happens. . . .' No, no, no. It should be, this happens, and therefore this happens, but this happens, therefore this happens. We'll write it out to make sure we're doing it." Stone continues, "There are so many scripts we see from new writers, where it's like 'this happens, and then this happens, and then this happens . . . ,' and that's when you're, like, 'What the fuck am I watching this for?'"

Though simplification is effective, people often fail to pursue it because it's completely counterintuitive. For whatever reason, people are more likely to add to or complicate a situation before they even consider subtracting from or simplifying it. A couple of years ago, Leidy Klotz, an engineer and expert in behavioral design, watched as his son, Ezra, played with LEGO bricks. "My son was about two and a half at the time, and we were building a LEGO bridge," Klotz said. "One column on the bridge was longer than the other, so to make the bridge level, I turned around to grab a block to add to the shorter column. By the time I turned back, Ezra had removed a block from the longer column." Removing an element often leads to better design, Klotz realized, but he was struck by his instinct to add to rather than to subtract from the structure. "One example we love," he said, "is balance bikes—the pedal-less, miniature bikes that allow two-year-olds to ride. If you've seen a two-year-old move on these things, it just makes you disappointed that you didn't have them when you were a kid. The breakthrough was just taking away the pedals." For decades, engineers had added training wheels, but removing the pedals is a far more effective way of teaching small kids to balance—the primary skill involved in riding.

Klotz moved his observation to the lab, where he presented two hundred people with a puzzle. He gave them a small, unstable LEGO structure in which a figurine stood beneath a ceiling of LEGO bricks. The ceiling balances on a single, small piece that in turn sits on a more stable, larger set of blocks. The task is to make sure the structure doesn't collapse when a standard brick is placed on the ceiling. To achieve this, you can add towers of bricks to the structure, which steadies the roof, or remove that one single small piece, which allows the ceiling to rest directly on the stable set of larger blocks. Klotz told the people completing his task that they would earn a small sum of money for completing the task, but that they would pay ten cents for each brick they added to the structure. Only 41 percent subtracted the single stand-alone brick; the remainder added bricks despite their cost, suggesting the intuitive appeal of adding rather than subtracting. (When Klotz also said, "Subtracting bricks is free," 61 percent subtracted the single brick, suggesting that this intuitive error could be partially solved with a gentle nudge.) Klotz and his colleagues showed the same effect across eight experiments: unless encouraged to subtract, people tend to solve problems by adding complexity rather than subtracting and simplifying.

Klotz's work is fascinating, but it's also practically important. Adding is expensive and time-consuming. In Klotz's work as an engineer, it also costs physical materials, and it's more likely to entrench you when you're stuck, where simplifying, removing, and streamlining are unsticking agents. They're more likely to lead you around or over an obstacle, and to cost you less.

Simplification is a good place to begin, but there's more to progress than applying algorithms and formulas alone. If those were enough, every lawyer, doctor, screenwriter, and engineer would hew to an identical, canonical playbook. Obviously the very best do something different. They inject their work with a secret sauce that transcends prefabricated structures. Emma Coats, the Pixar storyteller, recognized this. Though her list was celebrated as a set of "rules," she was quick to revise the term. On her Twitter bio, she writes, "ex-Pixar . . . wrote '22 Story Rules,' should have called them guidelines." For Coats, the guidelines were a launchpad. They were valuable, but they were also optional. The best writers know when to obey them, and when to abandon them, and exactly how to combine orthodoxy and iconoclasm. Rules, guidelines, formulas, and algorithms—whatever you call them in the discipline that matters to you—are valuable aids, but adhering to them all the time doesn't work, either. The key is learning when to obey, and when to defy, and the easiest way to experiment with defiance, paradoxically, is to limit yourself by imposing constraints.

———

For many years, painter Phil Hansen practiced pointillism. He'd use his brush to stab at a page or canvas over and over, laying down a series of dots at varying distances from one another so from afar they looked like something identifiable. Thousands of dots would come to look like Bruce Lee, or Michelangelo's *David*. Hansen was immensely skilled, so much so that he went to art school and began attracting a reputation as an innovative young talent.

One day, Hansen noticed that his pointillist dots had begun to resemble tadpoles. Whereas the dots were once tight and perfectly round, now they were followed by an unmistakable wavy line. He had developed a tremor, and since his art required arch-precision, he was devastated. "This was the destruction of my dream of becoming an artist," he told an audience at the TED2013 conference in Long Beach, California.

At first, he fought his new ailment. He'd hold the brush tighter and tighter, attempting to overcome the tremor by force of will. This only made the problem worse. He developed joint pain and repetitive-stress injuries that aggravated his tremor. As the issue worsened, he was unable to hold not just pens and paintbrushes but any object at all. Dejected, he abandoned art school, and then the art world, completely.

Hansen missed his art, though. He longed to exercise his artistic muscles again, but struggled to imagine how he could paint tiny dots on the canvas while his hand refused to be still. He arranged to see a neurologist, and the news was devastating. The tremor was likely to remain forever, and rubbing salt into Hansen's wound, the neurologist explained that years of applying dots to the canvas had left Hansen with chronic nerve damage. As he was leaving the neurologist's office, the doctor said to him, "Well, why don't you just embrace the shake?"

Hansen had been saddled with an unchosen constraint—a limiting factor that prevented him from painting the way he longed to paint. It's hard to think of many limiting factors as profound as a chronic tremor for a painter who relies on precision. But "embracing the shake" had the strange, paradoxical effect of training Hansen's attention on what he *could* do. So much of being an artist is vision. You have to be able to see in your mind's eye what you hope to represent on the canvas. You have to distinguish between the one image you hope to create and the infinite images you're trying to avoid. Hansen's ability to see the world crisply, and to translate his vision into art, were central to his talent as an artist. And, more important, those abilities were intact.

He returned home after his appointment and grabbed a pencil. "I just started letting my hand shake and shake," he recalled. "I was making all these scribble pictures. And even though it wasn't the kind of art that I was ultimately passionate about, it felt great. And more importantly, once I embraced the shake, I realized I could still make art. I just had to find a different approach to making the art that I wanted."

The art Hansen wanted to make still drew on the fragmentation of pointillism. He loved "seeing tiny dots coming together to make a unified whole." So instead of using his hands, he stepped in black paint and applied the dots with the soles of his feet. Then he used two-by-fours to apply the paint. He even used a blowtorch to singe the canvas. His works were larger now because his methods of applying paint had changed, but they retained the same fragmentation and vision that made his earlier work great.

For a while, Hansen was overjoyed to be painting again, but once the initial thrill passed, he hit a creative wall. He decided the problem was inferior tools, since he had been using the same old paint supplies he'd had in high school and college. Now, with a paycheck, he could afford better supplies, so he headed to his art store and "went nuts." He bought every imaginable piece of equipment he could find—but remained just as stuck as he had before. He had tried to give himself more options by acquiring new tools, but had only entrenched himself further. Complication wasn't the answer; constraint was the key:

> I realized I was actually paralyzed by all of the choices that I never had before. And it was then that I thought back to my jittery hands. "Embrace the shake." And I realized, if I ever wanted my creativity back, I had to quit trying so hard to think outside of the box and get back into it. I wondered, Could you become more creative, then, by looking for limitations? What if I could only create with a dollar's worth of supplies?

One evening, Hansen visited his local Starbucks, where he asked for not one but fifty free extra cups. To his surprise, he was handed the fifty cups, no questions asked, and so Hansen made a project for just eight cents. "It really became a moment of clarification for me that we need to first be limited in order to become limitless."

Soon, Hansen became known not for pointillism but for the artificial constraints he imposed on his artworks. "I took this approach of thinking inside the box to my canvas," he remembered, "and wondered what if, instead of painting on a canvas, I could only paint on my chest? So I painted thirty images, one layer at a time, one on top of another, with each picture representing an influence in my life. Or what if, instead of painting with a brush, I could only paint with karate chops? So I'd dip my hands in paint, and I just attacked the canvas, and I actually hit so hard that I bruised a joint in my pinkie and it was stuck straight for a couple of weeks."

With the onset of his disability, Phil Hansen discovered that even unwanted constraints are agents of simplification. In another universe, he might have pursued a long and happy career as a pointillist, but in this universe he was forced to work within his newly acquired constraints. The result was an eccentric, creative, genuinely new way of painting that sets him apart from every other artist on the planet. There have been countless pointillists since Impressionists Georges Seurat and Paul Signac developed the technique in 1886, but only one artist, today or ever, paints like Phil Hansen.

As Hansen's case shows, constraints are breakthrough agents in part because they force people to abandon the obvious in favor of novelty. The same insight applies to people on teams. Many professional basketball teams, for example, are dominated by one or maybe two star players who spend almost every minute of the season on the court, while their lesser teammates rotate on and off the bench. These stars are involved in almost every play, acting as default options whenever their teammates look to make a pass. But what happens when these stars are injured?

To examine the effect of injuries on performance, a group of researchers analyzed twenty-eight thousand basketball games between 1992 and 2016, focusing on periods when star players were temporarily sidelined. Say you call the five players on the court at any one time A, B, C, D, and S for the star player. What usually happens is that the ball flows something like this: A → S → B → S → C → S → D → S. The star player acts as a consistent node, touching the ball twice or three times more often than peripheral players A, B, C, and D. Those players learn to pass to and receive from the star player, but not to work with one another. Over time, opponents pick up on this trend, and it makes the team predictable. If the star player is having an off night, the team suffers greatly—and, critically, if the star player is injured for several games, the team is forced to adopt a completely new strategy. Now the court includes players A, B, C, D, and E—who replaces the star player temporarily—and since none of the players is a star, the ball flows more equitably among the players. Now the ball follows the path: A → B → C → D → E → C → A → E → D → B, and so on.

As hard as it is for teams to overhaul their strategies, this constraint is *good* for them in the long run. It makes them more versatile, less predictable, and ultimately better than they were before their star was injured. The best evidence for this? When the star player returns, he's immediately put back on the court, but he sees less of the ball than he used to, and the team wins more games and generally does better than it did before his injury. The constraint "we can't rely on S to solve our problems" unsticks the team and reveals a whole new menu of strategic options that were hidden by complacency.

Removing star options works in other contexts, too. For forty-eight hours, from February 5 to 6, 2014, the London Underground was crippled by union strikes that closed 63 percent of the system's stations. For many people, these closed stations were their "star players"—hubs in the journeys they took between their homes and workplaces. During the strike, millions of Londoners were forced to experiment with new commutes, beginning their journeys at whichever nearby stations were unaffected by the strike. If you've seen the London Underground map, you'll know it's a series of artificially straightened colored lines that only loosely resemble the zigzagging tube lines they represent. The map is designed for clarity rather than to accurately show the distances between each station, so unless commuters experiment with multiple routes, many adopt and then stick to a route that may add unnecessary time to their commutes.

A team of economists wondered whether the strike might have unintended benefits. They examined how many commuters stuck to the new route they discovered once the strike had ended and estimated how much time this new route saved. They found that the strike led around 5 percent of commuters to adopt a new route, and those commuters collectively saved around fifteen hundred hours of commuting time each workday. Taking the obvious solution out of play was a surprisingly effective unsticking agent for commuters who had been mired in suboptimal travel routes.

The constraints in these examples—neurological damage, sporting injuries, and transportation strikes—were uninvited, but every now and then you'll find people who impose artificial constraints on themselves. This takes insight, because you have to embrace the paradox that restriction can be liberating. One well-known example is business titan Warren Buffett's "twenty-slot rule." Buffett's right-hand man, Charlie Munger, explained the idea during a business school commencement speech almost thirty years ago: "[Warren says he can] improve your ultimate financial welfare by giving you a ticket with only twenty slots in it so that you had twenty punches representing all the investments that you got to make in a lifetime. Once you'd punched through the card, you couldn't make any more investments at all. Under those rules, you'd really think carefully about what you did, and you'd be forced to load up on what you'd really thought about. So you'd do so much better."

Buffett's strategy is immediately clarifying because it forces traders to focus on what matters most. If they're restricted to twenty investments across their life span, they can't get bogged down in marginal strategies, or in forecasting notoriously volatile short-term stock price movements. As Buffett knows better than anyone else, the key to making (a lot of) money is to do nothing—to sit on sound investments for days, weeks, months, and decades as the "miracle of compound interest" does its work.

The same rules apply to the domain of creativity. Since 1979, French artist Pierre Soulages has painted exclusively using black paint. By simplifying his color palette, Soulages, who turned one hundred years old in 2019, says his work relies on the emotional experience of seeing the light play with differently textured black pigment. "I'm not a believer in the myth of the chaotic artist, with paint everywhere," he has said. Color choice is for many artists a major decision. It formed the foundation of the French Impressionist movement, which reached its peak shortly before Soulages was born, and painters like Claude Monet would slather their canvases with impasto waves of every imaginable color. By hewing to black, Soulages was free to spend his artistic energy on other decisions.

Similarly, some writers work under the strictures of formal haiku, with its five-seven-five-syllable, three-line structure, or under the rhythmic constraints of poetic forms from relatively common pentameters to the rarer cinquains, nonets, and even Fibonacci-structured poems. For a real challenge, try composing a six-word memoir, which forces you to focus on the essential components of what it means to be you. These approaches are artistically limiting, but they're also paradoxically quite liberating. Once your field of options shrinks, you're free to be creative with the options that remain.

You can apply this simplification-by-restriction philosophy more broadly by automating as much of your life as possible. Automation restricts your options by eradicating decision points. Instead of choosing between a set of options, for example, you pursue a default option. This adaptable tool works in almost any context. Do you regularly lose your phone? Choose one or two default locations where it remains throughout the day. Do you find yourself watching more TV episodes than you intend? Adopt a no-more-than-two-episodes default, which you enforce by setting an alarm, or using an app that intervenes when you spend too long on your device. Do you struggle to decide what to eat for lunch or dinner, or what to wear? Automatic defaults that tether these decisions to particular days of the week free your limited decision-making resources for more consequential decisions. This is the philosophy that led Barack Obama to famously cycle through the same revolving set of suits, and Steve Jobs to wear the same signature black turtlenecks on repeat—a philosophy that freed Obama and Jobs to preserve their mental energy for more important tasks.

Simplifying is a flexible, powerful tool, and it's a strong first step toward getting unstuck. The next step, though, is figuring out the best way to combine the options that remain. This combining and configuring is far more important than most people imagine. It's the beating heart of human ingenuity, and almost every instance of creativity requires combining two or more existing ideas to form a new and different product.

RECOMBINATION AND PIVOTING

There's an important difference between being genuinely stuck and feeling stuck because you're demanding too much of yourself. When creatives tell you they have creative block, for example, what they're really saying is that they're failing to meet their high standards. A painter can always apply brush to canvas, and a writer can always string words together, even if the resulting images and sentences aren't world-changing. That might seem like a trivial distinction for an expert with high standards, but it matters because lowering your threshold, even temporarily, is often the best way to generate truly great ideas and products. That's particularly true if you measure success by originality, because in many domains genuine originality is vanishingly rare. Often, the best way to get unstuck on the quest for originality is to combine two old ideas to form a new one, rather than searching for a single, novel creative nugget. That was certainly true for a young singer at the dawn of his colossal career in the 1960s.

Robert Zimmerman was a freshman at the University of Minnesota as the 1950s gave way to the 1960s. Soon after arriving, Zimmerman began singing and playing guitar at a local coffeehouse. Occasionally he would introduce himself as Bob Dylan, but he remained Robert Zimmerman officially until 1962. Zimmerman was toying with different musical identities when he heard a record that nudged him away from rock 'n' roll toward folk—and therefore changed the course of popular Western music. Browsing a local record store, Zimmerman bought a copy of folk singer Odetta's 1957 *Ballads and Blues*. He later remembered that the first time he heard her, "I went out and traded my electric guitar and amplifier for an acoustical guitar, a flat-top Gibson. . . . I learned almost every song off the record, right then and there, even borrowing the hammering-on style." Odetta passed through Minnesota that year, and she and Zimmerman met briefly—but long enough for her to praise the young musician who was a decade her junior.

Zimmerman reported "falling in love" with Odetta. He dropped out of college at the end of that first year and moved to New York City to find his musical fortune. He saw Odetta again, in 1961, this time when she was performing the antislavery hymn "No More Auction Block for Me." Black soldiers had sung the hymn while marching during the Civil War, lamenting their former lives as slaves, and vowing never to return to "the auction block," where their enslavement began. Zimmerman was so moved by the song that it lodged itself in his memory. It lay dormant for a couple of years as he released his first studio album, formally changed his name to Bob Dylan, and grew to become a commercial star. Then, in anticipation of his second album, Dylan recorded one of his first big hits, "Blowin' in the Wind."

The one description you'll read of Bob Dylan, over and over, is that he's unique. Regardless of how people feel about his music, they seem to believe there is no one else quite like Dylan. Filmmaker David Lynch—an original himself—said of Dylan, "He tapped into some kind of vein, and it keeps on keeping on. There's no one like him. He's unique, and just . . . way cool." Rock & Roll Hall of Famer Jackson Browne said, "The biggest influence? I've had several at different times, but the biggest for me was Bob Dylan, who was a guy that came along when I was twelve or thirteen and just changed all the rules about what it meant to write songs." Likewise, John Mellencamp called Dylan "the ultimate songwriter. . . . Nobody could ever write a song as good as him, and nobody ever has written a song as good as him."

What's striking is that for all these claims of originality, "Blowin' in the Wind" sounds *a lot* like "No More Auction Block for Me." They begin with the same melody and follow the same structure throughout. Dylan knows this, and Odetta knew it, too. She was good-humored about it, but she recognized the two songs overlapped to an extent that could not be attributed to chance. On her death, in 2008, the *New York Times* published a recently taped video interview with Odetta:

Interviewer: "'Cause he stole liberally from you. . . ."

Odetta, chuckling: "No, no, no, no. We call it . . . in folk music . . . we don't call it stealin' or appropriation. . . . It's 'passing on the folk tradition.' It ain't what you say, it's the way you say it, right? That influence was just like a key that opened up something that was his own stuff . . . so I can't even take credit for how he heard something."

Even true originals like Dylan are prone to appropriation, borrowing, or "passing on the folk tradition."

———

From least to most charitable, here are three ways to explain cases of blatant similarity. The first is to argue that creative people cheat, lie, and steal all the time, and that it's naïve to believe that creatives strive for originality. According to this view, musicians, artists, writers, and other people who produce creative output are expedient by nature, mining past successes for nuggets they might lightly reshape for themselves. I think this is rare—that few creatives actively seek to plagiarize the work of other people (if for no other reason than that the penalties are severe, and many plagiarists are caught).

The second explanation is that people are naturally cryptomnesic. Cryptomnesia occurs when we mistake a forgotten memory for a new idea, and it's one of the primary explanations for inadvertent plagiarism. Say you hear the song "Happy Birthday" a couple of times as a child, and then it pops into your head decades later when you're an adult. Having forgotten hearing it as a child, you might imagine you created it from thin air—and so, if you were writing a new melody, you might inadvertently copy "Happy Birthday." We encounter new ideas like this all the time, and sometimes we remember the content of those ideas longer than we remember where, when, or how we encountered them. As our memory for their sources decays, we often forget having encountered those ideas at all, believing instead that they've miraculously made their way to our heads as unexplained flashes of invention. The difference between this explanation and the first one is that cryptomnesia is unintentional and so isn't as dishonest as willfully stealing. I believe cryptomnesia is relatively common, explaining many obvious similarities between pairs of nearly identical songs, books, and artworks.

The third explanation for blatant overlap among creatives—my preferred explanation, and the most important if you're on the hunt for a breakthrough—is that *there's no such thing as genuine originality; there are only degrees of overlap*. Put simply, everything is a remix of something else. Dylan remixed Odetta, and Odetta remixed the thousands of artists she'd encountered during her life. Some remixing is more blatant than other remixing, but every creative work stands on the shoulders of earlier works.

Many of today's most prominent creatives know that borrowing is endemic. When listeners accused teen artist Olivia Rodrigo of plagiarizing Elvis Costello's "Pump It Up," Costello said, "It's fine! It's how it works. You take the broken pieces of another thrill and make a brand-new toy." Nirvana's drummer Dave Grohl was responsible for the thumping beats that drove "Smells Like Teen Spirit," the band's breakout hit in 1991. Grohl was disarmingly open about borrowing ideas from the unlikeliest of places, including disco bands that couldn't have been more different in tone and style from early 1990s Seattle grunge. "I pulled so much stuff from [disco bands] the Gap Band and Cameo, and [disco drummer] Tony Thompson on every one of those songs," Grohl admitted in an interview. Questlove is a polymath—an author, a musician who plays six or seven instruments, the backbone of seven or eight bands—and he, too, has admitted that his apparent originality obscured liberal borrowing. "The DNA of every song lies in another song," he says. "All creative ideas are derivative of another."

Here's why this watered-down interpretation of originality matters:

it's incredibly liberating. Trying to do something *completely new* is a recipe for paralysis. I've advised dozens of start-ups, and dozens of entrepreneurs who were searching for something new and different, and one of the commonest roadblocks they encounter is the drive to be profoundly original. Instead of searching for an incremental innovation that people actually need, they search for a radical innovation that no one wants. Most of the time, success comes from a well-placed tweak, a novel combination of two or more existing elements, or the better version of an idea or product not yet perfected.

If you aren't convinced, just look at many of the most successful products and ideas today. I challenge you to find more than a few that are truly, profoundly original—products and ideas that owe nothing to inventors and creatives of the past. In chapter 2, I mentioned that Google was the twenty-second entrant into the search engine market. Google did a much better job than the search engines that came before it, but it was far from radically new. Amazon wasn't the first online store, or the first online bookseller, but on Jeff Bezos' watch, the company became the finest product-distribution machine in the world. Products that once took weeks to move from one part of the globe to another took just hours or days when purchased through Amazon. Apple and Microsoft weren't the first computer companies, and their products, from operating systems to tablets, phones, and laptops, weren't first to market, either. But Apple and Microsoft triumphed over earlier entrants by borrowing their strengths and jettisoning their weaknesses. And if you say, "But if you trace those products and companies back far enough, you'll find the original source!" you'll embark on a losing game. You may find the original computer, but peer inside its creator's head and you'll see a host of influences from nearby and not-so-nearby fields. The extreme version of originality we associate with genius is a fiction; in practice, reality is just borrowing ideas more effectively than others have done before.

This form of originality is called recombination because it requires finding novel combinations of two or more existing—and therefore *unoriginal*—concepts. It's Dave Grohl marrying punk and disco to form Nirvana's grungy drum sound, or Apple marrying smartphones and laptops to form the iPad tablet.

One of my favorite examples of recombination was the brainchild of Arlene Harris, a then fifty-seven-year-old tech entrepreneur who went on to become the first woman inducted into the Wireless Hall of Fame. Many tech entrepreneurs are in their twenties and thirties, training their attention on segments of the market that they naturally understand: other twenty- and thirtysomethings. The outcome of this demographic quirk is a tech marketplace flooded with products designed for young adults—but few designed for older adults. This doesn't make much sense because older adults have more money to spend than younger adults, and when you ask them, they'll tell you they're hungry for products that meet their needs.

While much of the industry ignored older people, Arlene Harris paid attention. What she heard was that mainstream phones were too complicated and their buttons too small, and there was no one to help older adults when they ran into trouble. Listening to these overlooked customers wasn't an act of charity, but an act of shrewd entrepreneurship. "The [people] working out at the edge of innovation are far too focused on trying to create things people want," Harris has said, "rather than looking in their rearview mirror and saying, 'What have we left behind that needs to be done better now that we have got better technology to do it?' And that's where there's this big difference between financing cool stuff and financing needed lifestyle-improving stuff that will help build a better human culture."

To build her version of this "better human culture," in 2005 Harris and wireless industry pioneer Martin Cooper formed a cell phone company called GreatCall, and designed a phone called the Jitterbug. The Jitterbug was anything but new and original. It was a traditional flip phone with large rubbery buttons and a big bright screen. The phone's TV ad showed young people dancing the World War II–era jitterbug and explained that Jitterbug users had access to personal service through a dedicated hotline. "I'll be happy to place that call for you, Mrs. Kelly," an agent says into her headset. I show the Jitterbug ad to my twenty- and thirtysomething MBA students, and they laugh, at first, then go quiet when they realize Harris made millions and millions of dollars from the phone. She combined two elements—a traditional cell phone and an overlooked segment of the market—in an original way. Instead of competing in the overheated cell phone market, dominated by huge companies like Apple and Samsung, Harris' Jitterbug lived in a niche of its own. Soon, Harris began designing new products, from screen-based smartphones to personal emergency alarms, and the company was ultimately acquired by electronics giant Best Buy for almost a billion dollars.

Recombination, whether in business, art, music, or any other pursuit, is disarmingly simple: take two or more existing concepts and blend them in a way that's new. Harris took a product that was designed for young people and adapted it for an audience of older adults who were underserved and looking to spend their considerable disposable income. Bob Dylan's career flourished when he found a new way to combine blues, poetry, and acoustic folk. The principle that Harris and Dylan used to unstick their respective industries works just as well in other contexts. The trick is finding two existing concepts that can be combined to create something new and useful.

One valuable way to use this understanding of originality to unstick yourself is to keep and draw from a journal of great ideas and observations. I've been doing this for so many years now that it's become automatic. Every time I see a good idea—a product, a piece of art, a solution to a problem, a piece of writing—I store it in an all-purpose document. This document is almost twenty years old now, and it houses thousands of great ideas. A few years ago, I decided to organize them to make the document more useful, and now they're loosely arranged by theme. When I'm stuck trying to write a thorny paragraph, or devising solutions for a client's business problem, I'll randomly choose two ideas from the document. Here's an example featuring two ideas from the "technology" theme:

Idea #487: An alarm clock mat that you have to stand on to deactivate the alarm, thereby preventing you from hitting the snooze button and oversleeping.

Idea #522: Netflix's "postplay" feature, which changed the default setting on the platform from "you must hit play to start the next episode in a season" to "the next episode in the season will automatically start playing in fifteen seconds."

In the book I wrote before this one, *Irresistible*, I explored why people spend so much time glued to screens. Since 2012, when Netflix introduced postplay (Idea #522), much of that time has been spent binge-watching TV shows on the platform. (The term *binge-watching* barely existed before 2012—we can thank Netflix for introducing it to the world.) Postplay short-circuits a person's ability to stop watching TV by automatically cuing another episode, and once that new episode begins, it's usually only seconds or minutes before a new plot point begins that won't be resolved till later that episode or season. Shows are written to grab us early because without these early hooks we'd stop watching sooner than we actually do.

The alarm clock mat (Idea #487) has no obvious relationship to Netflix, but it suggests an easy solution to the lure of postplay. The alarm clock mat forces people who are deep in sleep to move their bodies to turn off the alarm, which has two important consequences: it prevents them from hitting the snooze button or oversleeping, and it forces them to stand up, which encourages their bodies to stir. Postplay short-circuits exactly this process in Netflix viewers: it keeps them in a stupor between episodes, effectively allowing them to hit snooze as they watch "just one more episode," which, by four in the morning, has become six more episodes. The solution: decide how many episodes of a show you want to watch, set an alarm to ring at a time that coincides with the conclusion of those episodes, and—here's the kicker—place that alarm in another room or far enough away from the TV that you're forced to walk to turn it off. You can't continue watching mindlessly while the alarm blares in the background, and standing up to turn off the alarm breaks the show's hold on you. It's a simple analog solution to a digital problem, and it marries an unhelpful idea in postplay, and a helpful idea in an alarm clock mat, to generate a not-truly-original-but-effective innovation.

—

When you combine two ideas to form a new one, you need to relax the boundaries that surround those preexisting ideas. If you think of them too rigidly, only in terms of their original purpose, you'll overlook how they might interact. The easiest way to understand this mental nimbleness is to borrow a metaphor from the world of golf.

I play golf seldom (and poorly), but the one piece of advice that made the biggest difference to my game comes from Sam Snead. Snead was an American golfer who dominated the game for several decades, between the 1930s and 1970s. Snead's swing was a sublime combination of grace and power. Jack Nicklaus described it as "perfect," and Gary Player said it was "the greatest golf swing of any human who ever lived." When asked for his secret, Snead said it was all in the grip: "You should be holding the golf club with the same pressure you would hold a small bird. Tight enough so it doesn't fly away, but soft enough so you don't crush it." I've never held a small bird in my hand, but I imagine one sitting there every time I swing a golf club, and my game, such as it is, has improved for that image.

Snead's advice isn't just useful in the domain of golf. It's also valuable if you're trying to get unstuck. When Arlene Harris decided to sell technology to older adults, and Bob Dylan left behind his electric guitar for an acoustic Gibson, both were showing the kind of nimbleness that comes from cradling your ideas as you might a small bird—firmly, but gently. In continuing to design and sell tech products, Harris stuck to what she knew, but in abandoning the dogma that tech was for the young, she was holding that knowledge lightly. She was willing to be flexible in the face of fresh insights, just as Dylan was willing to try something new after sampling from the new world of acoustic folk.

Put broadly, cradling a small bird gently prepares you to *pivot*. Pivoting is a critical cognitive skill when you're trying to avoid inertia. To pivot you have to be willing to sacrifice moving forward today for the possibility of making great leaps in a new direction tomorrow. To find that new direction, you have to be open to the idea that the path you've been treading may not be the best path forward.

One of the most striking examples of pivoting—of holding beloved ideas like a small bird—comes from chemist David Brown. In the early 1990s, Brown worked at a large drug company. For eight years, his team searched for a new heart drug. Eight years is a long time to work toward a single outcome, but for a chemist like Brown little is more important than discovering a drug that saves thousands of lives. Unfortunately, the search was going nowhere. Brown knew one of two things was about to happen: his team would either produce a breakthrough or be disbanded.

Brown's team tested hundreds of different formulations, but none hit the mark. "I stood up in front of the clinical development committee and, as in previous quarters, got crucified for wasting money," Brown recalled. "And I was given an ultimatum, basically: 'Come back in September. If you've not got good data then, we're closing it.'" Anticipating the project's demise, Brown's team put together a final desperate trial. "It was so close to failure that people weren't coming to the meetings," Brown remembered. "I mean, you know how people sort of smell failure and disappear? It was that close."

This was an inflection point for Brown and his team. He had one remaining hope: a drug code-named UK-92480, a formulation designed to treat pressure and tightness in the chest. Its trial began in 1993, when a battery of Welsh miners agreed to test the drug. Ten days later, the miners assembled in small focus groups at the research team's headquarters. Brown attended one of the earliest focus groups. He was disappointed because the drug still wasn't working. As the focus group ended, Brown decided to ask the men if they'd noticed or wanted to report anything else. One of the men put up his hand and said, "Well, I seemed to have more erections during the night than normal." Brown remembers the others smiling and saying, "So did we."

Brown's presence of mind in ad-libbing that extra question turned out to be worth tens of billions of dollars. He and his team had unwittingly discovered Viagra.

Many of Brown's team members were despondent. Ian Osterloh, Brown's colleague at Pfizer, believed the team had failed. "At the time, no one really thought, 'This is fantastic, this is great news, we're really onto something here. We must switch the direction of the program.'" Brown, though, was receptive to a new direction. Instead of equating this latest roadblock with failure, he recognized that one person's embarrassing side effect might be another's godsend.

Brown implored his managers to fund a follow-up study. "I need one hundred and fifty thousand pounds to do an impotence study," Brown told the head of research and development, "and I'm not leaving your office till you give me the money." The first trials commenced in Bristol in late 1993, and subsequent trials followed in France, Norway, and Sweden.

Brown's insight earned Pfizer almost $40 billion from the drug between 1998 and 2018, and branded and generic competitors flooded the world market.

From the ashes of a failed heart drug emerged a lucrative solution to erectile dysfunction. Brown's pivot from heart drug to impotence treatment is a popular business fable. When I discuss it with my MBA students, they tend to see themselves in David Brown. They believe they, too, would see the glint of opportunity in a "failed" trial. In truth, Brown's skill is rare, and for most people unintuitive. The rest of his team acknowledge that Viagra only exists today because Brown pivoted instead of folding. He had a suite of skills that were essential to the drug's success: the ability to recognize opportunity amid failure; the

drive to campaign for further trials in the wake of dozens of failed pre-
liminary trials; and the wherewithal to tamp down disappointment long
enough to ask the right questions and pay attention to their answers.

Brown's skills are, to a large extent, learnable. They're grounded in
knowing when to ask the right questions, and asking those questions
habitually. Every time you sniff failure or some other barrier approaching, ask these classic pivot questions: First, is there any aspect of this
attempt worth bottling, or is it a complete failure? Put differently,
though this attempt isn't going to plan, what's the best thing about
it? Is there a silver lining? The second question is whether some small
or moderate tweak might have changed the outcome. What could you
have done differently? Among pharmaceuticals, Viagra is hardly alone
in turning failure for one application to success in another, so asking
follow-up questions when a trial goes awry is critical. Brown knew this
and pounced on the idea that the drug might have an unintended, but
potentially lucrative, alternative use.

This approach to pivoting isn't restricted to the pharmaceutical industry. A century before Brown's triumphant pivot, William Wrigley
Jr. traveled from Philadelphia to Chicago to sell soap. "He began with
nothing," a *New York Times* obituary said of Wrigley, "unless $32 can be
considered as capital. He had no protectors and no influence. What he
did have was nerve and enterprise and an optimistic spirit which never
failed him." Wrigley's father had been a soap merchant, so selling soap
was the natural path for William Jr. The soap business was competitive
because soap was reasonably easy to make. As long as you obeyed some
basic laws of chemistry and stirred in the right ingredients in the right
proportions, you'd have a bar of the scouring soap that Wrigley and
many other soap merchants were selling in the 1890s. Scouring soap
was a commodity—each brand was as good as the next—so Wrigley
introduced a differentiator that set his product apart. "Competition
was keen," the *New York Times* suggested, "but Wrigley did fairly well
by giving premiums to his customers." With each bar of soap, he threw
in a small packet of baking powder.

As freebies go, baking powder was a smart choice. Baking was becoming a popular pastime as the 1800s gave way to the 1900s, so Wrigley's bonus became his company's main attraction. Soon, customers were asking more questions about the baking powder than the soap. Like David Brown at Pfizer, Wrigley was sensitive to these cues, so the Wrigley Soap Company became the Wrigley Baking Powder Company.

Wrigley continued to offer bonuses with each sale, this time including two packs of chewing gum with each large package of baking powder. The first sticks of chewing gum—first licorice-, then tutti-frutti-flavored—had entered the marketplace in the 1870s and 1880s, so Wrigley decided that the product's combination of novelty and cheapness made it the perfect add-on. He was right. In a case of déjà vu, the gum was soon more popular than the baking powder, and Wrigley pivoted a second time. He was no longer selling soap or baking powder, but rather Spearmint and Juicy Fruit chewing gum.

Wrigley's talent for sales didn't end with product pivots. At first, he conceived of gum as an impulse product—the sort of thing you might buy without much thought as you line up to pay for the groceries that brought you to the supermarket in the first place. But impulse buying was limited. Wrigley wanted people to seek out his gum rather than buying it because they lacked self-control at the end of a shopping spree. He sent samples to thousands of American homes and took out a mortgage on his home to pay for an extensive ad campaign. In the wake of this campaign, the *New York Times* explained, "What had been a bad habit became a general custom." Wrigley argued that chewing his gum after meals meant fresher breath; cleaner, healthier teeth; and less bloating and discomfort after overeating. During World War I, he convinced the armed forces that gum staved off thirst and calmed the nerves. These weren't the properties of an impulse product—they were the hallmarks of a staple. So the value of his product skyrocketed, and in 1929 he found himself on the cover of *Time*.

—

The way Brown and Wrigley pivoted is impressive, but not unusual. To avoid pivoting, you'd have to be right the first time, every time, whether in business or in other areas of life. If you think back, you'll see that your past is littered with redirection. Avoiding pivots means never changing your mind—marrying the first person you date; pursuing the first career you dream of as a child; living in the same town your entire life; and so on. Humans develop and mature across the life span, and our preferences and attitudes shift as well. We learn and grow, so change is inevitable.

In their nimbleness, Brown and Wrigley exemplify Sam Snead's mantra, as long as you replace "golf club" with "idea": "You should be holding the *idea* with the same pressure you would hold a small bird. Tightly enough so it doesn't fly away, but softly enough so you don't crush it." What that means, in practice, is knowing which aspects of an idea to hold tightly, and which ones to hold gently so they have room to shift and grow. Brown didn't decide to become an artist or an accountant overnight; he remained a chemist, but a chemist who applied his skills to a new goal. Wrigley sold three very different products, but each time recognized the value of "giving premiums to his customers," while remaining receptive to what those customers were telling him.

These ideas matter even if you aren't manufacturing pharmaceuticals or chewing gum, and they're easy to apply to any situation. There are only three steps, and they overlap with the friction audit I described in the previous chapter: isolating the problem, listing potential solutions or paths forward, and then choosing the best solution from the resulting menu.

This is the approach that Ties Carlier, the cofounder of a Dutch bicycle company called VanMoof, took in 2015 when his company's expensive bicycles were arriving at American homes bent and damaged. "In 2015 we began shipping our bikes to the USA," the company's blog explains. "The only problem was that a lot of them were arriving to their new customers damaged. Annoying for them and expensive for us. We couldn't say for certain, but US handlers didn't seem to take as much care as we'd hoped." The problem was clear, so Carlier considered his options. He tried a range of shipping companies, but the results were similar. Next, he and his team sketched a range of new packaging options. They considered heavier, more durable boxes, or even sturdier packaging than cardboard boxes, but both options were expensive and unwieldy. These approaches also accepted that the bikes would be mistreated in transit, which was disappointing, and guaranteed a significant level of breakage even with packaging upgrades. The bikes would clearly need to be shipped in cardboard boxes—but how could Carlier ensure those boxes would be treated with care?

Carlier asked himself a simple question: *Are* cardboard boxes sometimes treated with care by shipping companies? With a little research, he realized that his breakage rates far exceeded those of, say, TV companies, though TVs were both fragile and shipped in boxes that were similar in shape to VanMoof's. Few TVs arrived broken and damaged because their boxes practically shout *Fragile!* The idea of hearing a TV shatter through mishandling must surely encourage delivery workers to treat them with care. So Carlier did what seemed cheapest and easiest: he asked his box manufacturers to print a picture of a TV on VanMoof's boxes. There was no lie—the boxes still included a picture of a bicycle and explained that they contained a bicycle—but those boxes were dominated by a large picture of a TV.

"That small tweak had an outsized impact," VanMoof's blog explained. "Overnight our shipping damages dropped by 70–80%. We sell 80% of our bicycles online, [and] we still print TVs on our boxes. More than 60,000 of them have now been shipped directly to our riders worldwide." Soon, much to Carlier's displeasure, other companies began using the same approach. "We tried to [maintain the deception] for as long as we could," Carlier explained in an interview, "until a journalist in our store in New York tweeted about it and revealed it to the world. . . . The more companies do this, the less effective it will be." Carlier's box redesign was the perfect expression of Snead's firm-but-flexible approach. Carlier was firm in maintaining that Van-

Moof's bicycles needed to be shipped in cardboard boxes, but flexible in recognizing that the box could be redesigned to gently nudge shipping companies to treat the bicycles more gently.

———

One feature that unites Bob Dylan, David Brown, William Wrigley, and Ties Carlier is that they moved away from expertise to embrace beginnerhood. Dylan knew the electric guitar, but tried his hand at acoustic folk. Brown had spent a decade learning heart drug chemistry, but pivoted to study erectile dysfunction. Wrigley was an expert in soap before selling baking powder, then chewing gum. And Carlier, who knew plenty about bicycles but little about packaging, devised a packaging method that avoided four of every five shipping losses.

All four were novices in their pursuits, but novices have one surprising advantage over experts: they aren't bound by the shackles of knowledge. It's impossible to *un*know what you know already, and this existing knowledge tends to constrain your creativity. Normally this isn't a problem—most of the time what worked in the past will continue to work in the future—but when you're hunting for a breakthrough, and seeking a new and creative path, expertise might prevent you from thinking as broadly as you should.

Expertise endows you with what cognitive scientist Herb Simon called a "hierarchical information structure," or a sense of how different ideas fit together. In 1962, Simon described how expert watchmakers rely on hierarchical information when assembling a watch. Complex watches contain hundreds of tiny parts that form an intricate puzzle. They have names like *lug*, *crown*, *pusher*, and *oscillating weight*, and to an expert these parts form tiny subcomponents that combine to form the watch. The tachymeter, which measures speed, might contain a dozen parts; the mechanism that drives the second hand might contain another two dozen parts; and so on. If the expert watchmaker is interrupted by a phone call while assembling a specific subcomponent of the watch, she can pick up where she left off, losing perhaps only a few minutes of work. The completed subcomponents she assembled earlier remain intact.

In contrast, a novice watchmaker doesn't have the same hierarchical information to organize her knowledge. To her the puzzle might seem impossibly complicated, and she might need to rely on instructions to assemble the watch one step at a time, seeing each part as completely separate from the others. If she was interrupted by a phone call, Simon suggested, she might have to start reassembling the entire watch from scratch.

Assembling a watch demands the opposite of creativity. You can't just decide to *creatively* rearrange some of the watch's parts and expect the watch to work. Watchmaking rewards precision and dexterity, and punishes creativity. Other tasks are open-ended, though, rewarding you for inventiveness instead of precision. In those cases, adopting a hierarchical information structure can be counterproductive, as happened in one study in which researchers asked two groups of students to spend an hour building an alien from hundreds of LEGO bricks. Half of those students represented novices. For them, the LEGO pieces were mixed together haphazardly, mimicking Herb Simon's flat information structure. In contrast, for the "expert" group, the bricks were sorted into forty-eight subgroups, each containing bricks of the same shape and color. These forty-eight subgroups were similar to the watch subcomponents that Herb Simon described sixty years earlier. For the novices, the bricks were disorganized, but for the experts they were neatly partitioned into groups.

You might imagine that the task was therefore easier for the experts. The work of shuffling through the pieces was already done; all they had to do was build the alien. But it was precisely the lack of structure that helped the novices invent wacky aliens. An independent group of raters judged the novices' aliens to be more creative, and less similar to existing creatures on Earth. This seemed to be because the novices spent more time working on the task, and because they thought about it more deeply, exploring more options than did the experts. Knowing *less* and struggling *more* made them more creative.

This is true beyond the lab as well. In 1994, pop artist Seal released the song "Kiss from a Rose," which earned the artist three Grammy Awards, spent weeks at the top of various global charts, and sold millions of copies around the world. The song, written by Seal alone in the late 1980s, was unlike anything else on the pop charts. In 2021, Rick Beato, a music producer and YouTube personality, released a thirty-two-minute video exploring the song. Beato did a beautiful job of deconstructing the song's appeal, but unless you're a music expert yourself, much of his commentary is difficult to follow. It's clear, though, that the song is complex. "The song is a great example of modal interchange," Beato explains. "I always like to talk about the theory of these songs, because these are the things that make them great." He goes on to discuss "tonic chords," "flat sixes and sevens," and "inversions," among other musicological arcana.

The heart of Beato's video, though, is a conversation with Seal himself. "The melody is so complex," Beato began in admiration. "Those odd interval jumps—how do you think of things like that?" Seal responds:

> The best explanation I can come up with is that I didn't know that you couldn't really do those things or those things were really unusual. It just felt like the right thing to do when I wrote that song. . . . The whole thing happened really quickly—it was really an afternoon's work of about two or three hours, and really I wasn't really thinking about the melody.

Even if Seal was being modest, the contrast between his naïveté and Beato's sophistication is striking. Beato seems to have spent more time parsing the song than Seal spent writing it. Seal's approach, untethered to theory and expertise, was clearly what allowed him to create a song that hits the ear perfectly, while sounding different from everything else the pop industry has produced over the past several decades.

This is a theme for Beato. A couple of months after interviewing Seal, Beato interviewed Sting—another pop giant whose style is inimitable. Again, Beato began by exploring the complexities of Sting's approach.

A song like "Fortress Around Your Heart" is incredibly melodic, yet it changes keys three times. [The progression is] very weird, though it sounds completely normal to the ear. And then you go into the chorus, which is in G, E minor, D over F sharp, G, then C, A minor, C, D. . . . How would you even come up with an idea like that song?

Sting's response sounds a lot like Seal's:

It starts with three chords, and then I just go on an adventure. I find it and it writes itself, you know, and you just have to be in a state of grace where the music will tell you where it goes next. . . . I'm not a trained musician; I just have this trust that the harmony will lead me in the right direction. I envy people [who were trained musicians because] it forces you to exercise a different kind of muscle. I know amazing musicians who can play just about anything, but they don't write [at all].

To Sting, melody is all art, whereas to Beato music is art with a serious dose of science. This is the *ology* part of musicology, which is Beato's bread and butter. Sting resisted this. To him, as to Seal, his best melodies are not the product of expertise, but rather the result of naïveté and exploration. I mean no disrespect to Beato, who wears his analytical hat lightly and is himself creative. Expertise isn't always a weakness—but Sting and Seal show that knowing less isn't always the liability it appears to be.

There's a martial arts quality to how the musicians, entrepreneurs, and scientists in this chapter got unstuck or avoided getting stuck in the first place. Instead of thrashing about wildly when faced with friction, they adopted a lighter touch. Some of them, like Bob Dylan and Arlene Harris, embraced an incremental definition of originality that recognizes that new ideas almost always stand on the shoulders of existing ideas. Arch-originality, by this definition, is a myth, and believing that radical novelty is the only path forward is paralyzing. A lighter touch is also valuable when considering a shift in strategy or approach, as David Brown and William Wrigley showed. A lack of expertise is often not such a bad thing, which is incredibly liberating given that most of us are experts in few areas of life and novices in many. It pays not to be completely ignorant, but deep expertise is often a recipe for the kind of rigidity that might entrench rather than unstick. One way to avoid these problems is to distribute expertise across a team of people—to work in diverse groups, and to rely on others to fill in your gaps as you strive together to get unstuck. Behind many of the individual successes described in this chapter are teams of supporters who were essential. The next chapter explores how crowdsourcing drives breakthroughs.

DIVERSITY AND CROWDSOURCING

The human brain is among the world's most resourceful machines. With it, humans have cured diseases, led nations, and invented rockets that carry people to space and back again. Brains are greedy, though. To use yours, you must feed it hundreds of calories a day, and you must be willing to devote your time, attention, and energy to whatever task you're asking your brain to complete. Humans manage these demands by developing patterns and habits that aren't quite perfect, but that most of the time do a satisfactory job. When you buy a soda from a wall of options, for example, you don't examine every label every time you buy. Instead, you reach for one of a couple of options that you've enjoyed in the past. Walking and driving a car are mostly automatic for most people most of the time. That's why your mind wanders while you're walking and driving. You have surplus brain resources to devote to other tasks.

The one downside of living on autopilot is that we sometimes find ourselves in deep ruts. The strategies and habits that simplify the business of everyday life become so entrenched that they're difficult to escape even when we need to try something new.

The good news is that your strategies and habits are probably quite different from mine. We've lived different lives under different conditions and have different personalities, talents, attitudes, and values. My habits might guide me toward a rut, but your habits might set me free. That's exactly what has happened over the past sixty years among the creatives who have worked on the TV show *Doctor Who*.

—

Doctor Who is the world's longest-running TV show. Its first episode aired on BBC TV on November 23, 1963, at 5:16 p.m.—eighty seconds later than planned because the BBC was covering the previous day's assassination of John F. Kennedy. The show revolves around an extra-terrestrial character, known as the Doctor, who travels through time in a blue phone booth. The Doctor is fascinated with planet Earth. He takes on human form and travels with human companions as he saves innocent people from harm. He has been alive for centuries, which is possible because his soul migrates into a new human body whenever he is mortally wounded. The show owes much of its longevity to this conceit, which allows its producers to cast a new actor in the role of the Doctor whenever the previous actor decides to move on. Over the show's six decades, thirteen actors have played the role of the Doctor, some for a single feature film, and others for over six years.

Doctor Who's thirty-nine regular seasons and eighteen specials have been broadcast in more than one hundred countries. The show has inspired museum exhibitions, spin-offs and fan fiction, books and mer-chandise, and has been featured on *The Simpsons*, *South Park*, *Family Guy*, *Futurama*, and *Star Trek: The Next Generation*. At its peak, in the 1970s, the show attracted an average of 11 million viewers per episode, and though its audience is about half as large today, it still scores up to ninety out of one hundred on the British Audience Appreciation Index, a measure of audience sentiment toward British TV shows.

As with its stable of actors, the show's creative team is in constant flux. Each episode is driven by creative artists who occupy one of three "core" roles: producers, directors, and writers. In total there are be-tween two and five creatives across the three roles per episode. These creatives, as with any artists, have their own style. They compose each episode through the lens of personal experience, training, and idio-syncratic preferences. For example, Graeme Harper, who directed fif-teen episodes of *Doctor Who*, had a background in Dickensian theater, whereas Phil Collinson, who directed forty-seven episodes, had a background in sitcoms and comedy. John Nathan-Turner, who produced fifty episodes, was more open to violent story lines and felt strongly that the show should appeal to the lucrative US market.

Despite, or perhaps because of, its longevity, *Doctor Who* has endured many sticking points. Its audience fell by almost 70 percent in the late 1980s, and the BBC placed the show on an indefinite hiatus that lasted sixteen years. *Doctor Who* reemerged in 2005 to great fanfare, but there are fresh rumors of its demise whenever the show's viewership declines.

The show's highs and lows have attracted interest from researchers who specialize in team dynamics. Does *Doctor Who* fare best when its creative team is cohesive and like-minded, or is diversity a virtue? You might imagine that creative teams benefit from consistency. Directors might learn how to coax good ideas from familiar writers, and producers might discover the personalities of the writers and directors who tend to craft the best story lines. In moments of difficulty, perhaps familiarity is the best "unsticker." This is the question one research team asked when they combed through fifty years of *Doctor Who* episodes: Are the creatives on a long-running show more or less likely to get stuck—or to flourish—when they work with familiar, or closed, networks?

The researchers began by gathering all sorts of data on each episode. Who was on its creative team? To what extent had they worked together on other episodes of the show—or indeed on other shows beyond *Doctor Who*? How did viewers feel about the episode? How creative was the episode according to *Doctor Who* experts? (The research team included a small group of devoted *Doctor Who* scholars.) Were the ideas in that particular episode unusual in the context of *Doctor Who*'s past, or did they explore similar (and therefore less creative) themes? With the data in place, the researchers were primed to measure the value of a concept known as network nonredundancy. Put simply, over the show's life span, did creative teams benefit from an injection of new blood, or were they more likely to thrive when their networks were closed?

The answer was clear and unambiguous. Though most creatives prefer working with familiar teams, familiarity breeds friction. The best episodes emerge with new blood. "The more closed the network around an artist," the researchers wrote, "the less creative their work." Creatives benefit from working with new teammates, particularly when those teammates have worked in very different circles in the past. Nonredundancy—or novelty—produced breakthroughs and sometimes moved the show from periods of stagnation to periods of creative rejuvenation.

Working with new people inspires creative unsticking for at least two reasons. The first is that new people bring fresh ideas. The *content* of their creative thoughts is different, and novel ideas shuttled back and forth between two or more people unlock other new ideas. The second reason is that simply shaking things up has value. If part of getting stuck is about stubbornly sticking to old habits, introducing new people forces you to adopt a new style of thinking. As the researchers explained, this isn't just about new content; it's also about reorganizing old content. New blood "stimulates the adoption of new perspectives and ways of seeing, thus [allowing creatives to] successfully apply old notions in different ways."

When you look beyond *Doctor Who*, you'll see the value of nonredundancy over and over. In 2000, Pixar Animation Studios was riding high. Between 1995 and 1999, Pixar released *Toy Story*, *A Bug's Life*, and *Toy Story 2*—three films that changed how the motion picture industry perceived animation. Traditionally, animated films were for kids. They explored simple ideas with two-dimensional drawn characters that appealed to younger audiences. But 1995's *Toy Story* was a feature-length animated film that appealed to kids and adults alike by exploring themes that spoke to both audiences. Its visuals weren't quite realistic, but they were three-dimensional and textured to an extent that hadn't been possible before the mid-1990s. In 1972, the Academy Awards introduced a Special Achievement Oscar for contributions to film. The Special Achievement Oscar was awarded every few years to recognize films that transcended the established boundaries of the motion picture medium. In 1977, *Star Wars* won for its "alien, creature, and robot voices," and in 1990 *Total Recall* won for its "visual effects." *Toy Story* won the fifteenth such award in 1995 as the "first feature-length computer-animated film."

With three successes under its belt, Pixar might have been content to keep doing what it was already doing so well: writing great stories that were realized with beautifully rendered animations. Instead, Pixar's founders sought nonredundancy. They were worried the studio might grow lazy or complacent, so they introduced new blood in the form of Brad Bird, an outsider who did things very differently. Bird recalled when he was approached by Pixar's Steve Jobs, Ed Catmull, and John Lasseter: "[They said], in effect, 'The only thing we're afraid of is complacency—feeling like we have it all figured out. We want you to come shake things up. We will give you a good argument if we think what you're doing doesn't make sense, but if you can convince us, we'll do things a different way.'"

Pixar's artists were understandably invested in the integrity of every image they created for every film. They were purists because the company's signature was its incredible animation. This was what the Academy Awards recognized when it awarded Pixar the Special Achievement Oscar in 1995, so the animators would frequently hold up a film if a particular image wasn't perfectly rendered. Bird saw things differently:

> I had to shake the purist out of them—essentially frighten them into realizing I was ready to use quick and dirty "cheats" to get something on screen if they took too long to achieve it in the computer. I'd say, "Look, I don't have to do the water through a computer-simulation program. If we can't get a program to work, I'm perfectly content to film a splash in a swimming pool

and just composite the water in." This absolutely horrified them. I never did film the pool splash . . . but talking this way helped everyone understand that we didn't have to make something that would work from every angle. Not all shots are created equal. Certain shots need to be perfect, others need to be very good, and there are some that only need to be good enough to not break the spell.

Bird has mastered the process of making animated films, and he recognized that sometimes the only way to create excellent products on time was to fast-track their animation. He was also a big believer in the value of nonredundancy and so brought in a host of new animators and, in his words, "black sheep," to shake things up. "A lot of them were malcontents," Bird remembered. They had big, new ideas, but the established way worked fine, so they rarely had the chance to put their ideas into practice. "We gave the black sheep a chance to prove their theories, and we changed the way a number of things are done here. . . . All this because the heads of Pixar gave us leave to try crazy ideas."

The first two features Bird worked on for Pixar were *The Incredibles* and *Ratatouille*. Both won Oscars for Best Animated Feature, *The Incredibles* in 2004, and *Ratatouille* in 2007. *Ratatouille*, in particular, was a half-made failure when Bird began working on the film, and many of the changes he introduced—including the requirement that all the rats apart from Remy, the central character in the film, walk on four legs instead of two—were critical to the film's success. But perhaps his biggest move, and what made Bird famous in the industry, was his desire to work with black sheep animators—the outsiders with different perspectives whom other directors overlooked.

Bird believed that black sheep were valuable if only because they were different. Their difference, whether or not they were the most talented creatives in the business, forced the rest of the creative team to see things from a new perspective. This, he recognized, made them excellent unsticking agents when his teams hit creative roadblocks.

Black sheep are, by definition, less likely to be mainstream successes. They fall at the fringes of existing networks, and so they tend to be more loosely connected to prevailing norms. A black sheep's primary role is to offer a new perspective that researchers call a positive shock. In the words of the *Doctor Who* researchers, "The addition of new ties to an existing network represents a positive shock that pushes individuals in the network to reconsider the way they work together and coordinate."

But here's the critical point about black sheep—and why you should always consult outsiders for advice when you're stuck: experiments show that even *incompetent* outsiders move a team forward. They don't need to be oracles or geniuses. They just need to be different. According to one study, for example, we believe top performers give better advice than mediocre performers, but in fact their advice is equally good. In the case of word-unscrambling puzzles (for example, reordering the letters MYRDEA to form DREAMY), you might expect an expert unscrambler to give better advice than a mediocre unscrambler. But completing the task, and explaining how it's done, draw on different abilities. The only difference between the best and the mediocre is that top performers give more—but not better—advice than average performers, which we mistake for *better* advice.

In another study, strangers worked together to solve an online puzzle. The strangers couldn't interact, but each could see the moves made by the others. The puzzle could only be solved if the group worked together. The task was difficult, and sometimes the groups failed. Often they needed many attempts to find a solution. In one version of the experiment, the players in the network were humans working toward a solution. In other versions, though, some of the players were actually "noisy bots," or artificially intelligent agents that sometimes made poor decisions. These noisy bots were modestly incompetent black sheep. Their only role was to behave randomly from time to time, which frustrated the other players and forced them to explore new strategies to solve the puzzle.

The bots may have been "noisy," but they also helped the human players find solutions more reliably and quickly, "not only by making the task of humans to whom they are connected easier," as the researchers wrote, "but also by affecting the game play of the humans themselves when they interact with still other humans in the group, thus creating cascades of benefit." Shaking things up is valuable even when the person (or bot) doing the shaking isn't herself (or itself) helpful or competent. It didn't matter that the bots weren't good at their jobs; what mattered is that they were *different*.

If you're stuck, the prescription is obvious: share your situation with someone new and different. It can't hurt to speak to a wise expert, but speaking to someone new even if that someone is neither especially enlightened nor educated is valuable. We tend to be blind to our own habits and patterns, and it's often those habits and patterns that steered us toward a rut in the first place. Nonredundant outsiders bring latent, hidden ideas to the fore by pushing us to look beyond our instinctive defaults.

———

Another, perhaps more familiar, term for nonredundancy is *diversity*. The more you consult with nonredundant outsiders, the more diverse your inputs, and the more likely you are to move beyond stubborn personal defaults. Though humans have been getting stuck and unstuck for millennia, for most of that time they have tackled obstacles in small, like-minded, homogeneous groups. These groups lacked diversity because their members often knew each other quite well, often lived close together, and were sometimes related or close friends.

Even as we began to favor the scientific method over trial and error, research teams remained homogeneous. Most were made up of older, rich, conventionally educated white men. As more women entered the medical profession in the 1980s and 1990s, attention shifted to diseases and health issues that affected women, including osteoporosis, menopause, and breast cancer. Part of this shift arose because the women on these medical research teams nudged them in new directions that had largely escaped male researchers. Even medical trials that were designed to examine human behavior tended to focus on men. The 1958 Baltimore Longitudinal Study of Aging was designed to explore "normal human aging," but for its first twenty years enrolled only men. Likewise, the researchers behind the Physicians' Health Study recommended that low doses of aspirin taken daily might reduce heart disease, but their conclusions were based on data from twenty-two thousand male participants, and *zero* women. The 1982 Multiple Risk Factor Intervention Trial (fittingly abbreviated as MRFIT) explored the role of diet and exercise in heart disease, but enrolled thirteen thousand men and zero women.

One research team wasn't satisfied with scattered anecdotes, so they combed nearly 7 million publications to explore the relationship between gender diversity on medical research teams and innovativeness. Those papers were written by a total of 7 million different medical scientists across fifteen thousand different journals, between 2000 and 2019. Over time, academic fields tend to become echo chambers. The same small groups of researchers cite one another as they make increasingly incremental progress by asking ever narrower questions. One big intellectual leap might spawn hundreds or thousands of related papers that ultimately drive the field toward an intellectual roadblock. In contrast, a field that isn't stuck draws in new researchers from allied fields, attracts citations from nonredundant researchers, and avoids becoming an echo chamber. The research group investigating diversity found that teams that included male and female researchers were more likely to do novel research that drew in novel researchers from novel fields. The diverse teams were also more likely to make a big impact, with large teams of mixed-gender researchers publishing "hit" papers 16 percent more often than large teams with single-gender researchers.

The same is true of the business world. One study examined the performance of more than one thousand firms across thirty-five countries, and twenty-four different industries, and found that gender diversity was associated with superior firm performance in countries that generally supported gender diversity in the workplace. A second team of researchers was careful to establish that diversity drove innovation by randomly assigning start-up entrepreneurs to work on teams that were either gender diverse or gender uniform. Over the course of a year, teams with a roughly even gender split outperformed those with unbalanced gender representation. A third team of scientists randomly assigned research participants in a lab experiment to work in teams that were or were not gender diverse, and they, too, found that diversity drove innovation. Diversity evades the quicksand that keeps groups, teams, firms, and even entire fields from making progress.

One of the great case studies in diversity as an unsticking agent is former NBA basketball player Shane Battier. Battier, who played between 2001 and 2014, was unusual in many respects. Measured against traditional basketball metrics, he was mediocre. Michael Lewis, who profiled Battier for the *New York Times Magazine*, wrote, "He doesn't score many points, snag many rebounds, block many shots, steal many balls, or dish out many assists." When Battier played for the Houston Rockets, the team's general manager said, "He's, at best, a marginal NBA athlete."

But in other respects Battier was different from other NBA players. Though most NBA players are bright, Battier was a *scholar*. He graduated from Detroit Country Day School with a 3.96 GPA and won the headmaster's cup for the best all-around student. Before each game, his coach handed him a packet of information on the opposing team—where each player was most and least likely to score, their strongest and weakest shots, and so on. "He's the only player we give it to," Battier's coach said. "We can give him this fire hose of data and let him sift. Most players are like golfers. You don't want them swinging while they're thinking."

As Battier combed through his nightly dossier, he learned how to use his opponents' idiosyncrasies against them. He might recognize that a particular team relied on one or two players and so spent his night defensively neutralizing those players. Or he might learn that a particular player shot better from the left than the right and so forced the player right. He was eccentric and different—and gave his own teammates more room to play—because he didn't play with a one-size-fits-all approach. He took each opponent as a separate and distinct challenge with his own exploitable weaknesses. This attention to detail dovetailed with Battier's unusual selflessness. Most professional athletes are self-focused, but he always seemed to put his team first. He'd choose a strategy that might dampen his own stats if it would, on average, bring his team an extra handful of points each night. It was hard to measure the effects of his selflessness, because "being unselfish" isn't captured by traditional statistics. To capture his magic, a different stat had to be invented—a metric known as the plus-minus.

The plus-minus measures what happens to a team's score when a particular player is on the court. A plus-minus of five, say, means that a player's team tends to score five more points than the opposition does when he's on the court. By definition, the average across all players in the league at any time must be zero. Across a single season, a solid starting player might score plus-two; an all-star might score plus-four; and an all-NBA player might score plus-six—which was Battier's average across his career. During strong years his plus-minus exceeded ten, which matched the scores of Michael Jordan and LeBron James at their peaks. Battier's plus-minus score was astronomical, particularly relative to his other middling stats. "I call him LEGO," his coach at the Rockets said. "When he's on the court, all the pieces start to fit together." Statistically speaking, having a plus-six player on the court is the difference between winning forty-one games in a season and winning sixty. This is the effect of introducing a player who is eccentric in two important ways: he knows more about how to frustrate his opponents defensively than every other player in the league and he's supremely unselfish.

Here's how we know Battier had a great unsticking effect. When he was drafted by the Memphis Grizzlies, they were winning just 28 percent of their games. By his third year with the team, they were winning 61 percent of the time. Then he moved to the Rockets, who had a win percentage of 41 percent. During Battier's first season with the team, that percentage rose to 63 percent, and the next season it rose to 67 percent. That season included a twenty-two-game winning streak, a mark exceeded by just three other teams in the league's seventy-five-year history. Battier's teams won more often when he played, and even solid opponents with all-star players whose stats dwarfed Battier's seemed to struggle. Much of this was because of his eccentricity as a player—and much of it happened because he disrupted the status quo, unsticking his teammates and allowing them to play their own natural games more effectively.

Battier was an undeniable gift to his teams, but one potential cost of eccentricity is that it might compromise cohesiveness. Just imagine five Battier-like players on the basketball court, each playing a completely different game from the others. Battier shook things up and made way for his more conventional teammates to do what they did best, but five Battiers do not a great team make.

—

There's a mountain of research about exactly when diverse ideas are most useful. The bottom line, these studies agree, is that diversity is particularly helpful when the task is complex rather than brief and simple; when it's novel enough to resist habits and entrenched strategies; and when it requires problem-solving, innovation, or creativity. These criteria describe almost every task that rests on breakthroughs. Sticking points are frustratingly resistant to tried-and-true approaches that worked in the past, and overcoming them requires creativity and innovation.

Take, for example, someone who has an undiagnosed medical ailment. After spending $100,000 on dozens of medical visits, she's no closer to a diagnosis. This is the story entrepreneur Jared Heyman tells about his sister, who spent three years bedridden with a rare genetic disorder. She was fortunate to draw the attention of a large, interdisciplinary group of specialists, who ultimately cracked her case, which inspired Heyman to found CrowdMed in 2012.

CrowdMed was designed to replicate her experience at scale, turning diagnosis into a crowdsourcing operation the same way Wikipedia turned encyclopedia-building into a collective pursuit. In exchange for a monthly fee, patients who signed up for the service shared their medical histories and waited as some of CrowdMed's ten thousand "detectives" tried to diagnose the problem. What makes CrowdMed unusual is that, according to CrowdMed's website, one in four of these detectives don't "work in or study medicine." This nonredundant, eccentric minority is the platform's secret sauce. "That's actually very intentional," says the company's CEO, Danyell Jones. Though that "sounds counterintuitive," she says, there's value in diversity, because "if there's an error in [mainstream medical professionals] being able to catch something, that's an error that's going to be duplicated." This minority of detectives is drawn from a long list of tangential professions, including "acupuncturist," "audiologist," "dentist," "educational psychologist," "podiatric medical doctor," "professional clinical counsellor," and "speech language pathologist."

Detectives are carefully vetted, and they're paid bonuses for valuable suggestions. They receive cash rewards and boosted ratings on the site when they solve mysteries, and CrowdMed minimizes the chances of outlandish suggestions by appointing a carefully vetted moderator for each case. A subset of CrowdMed's users bet on which suggested diagnoses are most likely, and this patented, proprietary betting process tends to yield excellent results. The platform's site claims, "Over seventy-five percent of medically-diagnosed patients tell us that their CrowdMed diagnosis was eventually confirmed to be correct by their physician, which is the most stringent definition of success." An independent academic assessment of the site between May 2013 and April

2015 found similar results. Almost four hundred people stumbled on diagnoses through the site, most of them after visiting five or more physicians, and incurring more than $10,000 in medical expenses. Hundreds of case solvers participated, and almost all reported that the crowdsourcing gave insights that led them closer to the correct diagnoses.

You wouldn't turn to CrowdMed before exhausting the obvious channels, but as the data suggest, CrowdMed is for people who are stuck. These patients have suffered for years—some for much of their lives—so they're desperate for a solution. Obvious paths don't make much sense because, if the answer were obvious, another doctor would already have found it.

Crowdsourcing as an unsticking agent isn't new. In 1714, the British government offered a cash prize to any citizen who could offer a simple method for tracking the position of ships at sea. The reward was £10,000 (around £1.5 million today) for modest accuracy, and £20,000 if the proposed method was accurate to within thirty-five miles. This crowdsourcing was possible because it was run by the government, one of the few institutions that could reach a crowd in the eighteenth century.

Crowdsourcing has never been more feasible for the average person than it is today, because almost anyone can source a crowd online. Sites like MetaFilter, Ask.com, Amazon Mechanical Turk, and Reddit draw billions of eyeballs to millions of questions, many of which boil down to pleas from the stuck and frustrated. Even people who aren't seeking a solution sometimes find their frustration met with crowdsourced advice, as happened to Jimmy Choi. Choi is an elite athlete with early-onset Parkinson's disease. He has more than two hundred thousand followers on TikTok, where he shares videos that document a combination of his impressive bodybuilding and athletic feats and his daily experience with Parkinson's. On December 27, 2020, Choi posted a brief video focusing on his hand as he attempted to fish a small pill from a plastic container. The post's caption read:

Pharma executives: "Hey! Let's make a pill for Parkinson's patients as small as F#€KIN& possible!"

Hey Pharma companies . . . get a clue! Raising #parkinsons #awareness sorry, I get a little angry when I am struggling to move sometimes.

Choi's post caught the attention of dozens of designers and engineers who believed they could design a better pill bottle for Parkinson's patients. One of those was Brian Alldridge, a videographer with plenty of experience as a graphic designer, but none as a product designer. Still, Alldridge tinkered and ultimately devised a 3D-printable pill bottle that seemed to do the trick. The process was pretty simple: the pill fell into a small well at the base of the bottle, and a vertical tube could be rotated to sit above the well so the patient could take the pill like vodka from a shot glass. Alldridge had little experience with 3D printers, so his original attempts to produce the bottle failed. That's where the magic of crowdsourcing came in. TikTok's 3D-printing aficionados took over, including a man named Antony Sanderson, who spent hours working on the project one night before printing a prototype that did the job. Others then fine-tuned the design, introducing an extra quarter turn to the bottle that prevented the pills from spilling out.

Choi was delighted with the final product. With the bottle "the anxiety level goes away," he said. "The time it takes, and your risk of spilling these pills out on the floor in public, it's almost zero." The bottle is now available for $5 on Etsy, and that entire sum is donated to the Michael J. Fox Foundation for Parkinson's Research. Alldridge is pursuing a patent, which he plans to release into the public domain.

———

Jimmy Choi was lucky to attract the attention of the perfect crowd, but sometimes the right crowd is hard to reach. For one reason or another, unsticking is sometimes a solo affair. But even when you're alone, there's a way to simulate the diverse inputs that remedied Choi's pill bottle conundrum. Enter the wisdom of the "internal crowd."

Much of this chapter draws on the idea that crowds are often wiser than individuals, particularly when those crowds are diverse. As the CEO of CrowdMed suggested, a collection of uniform voices is likely to make the same errors over and over, compounding rather than solving a sticky problem. Since each of us is just one person, we are, by definition, as far from "diverse" as possible. We view every problem through a single lens crafted by our life experiences, personalities, talents, and shortcomings. We can't develop new expertise overnight or shed our biases and attitudes just because they're hindering us today. What we can do, though, is refocus that lens by interrogating the biases and attitudes that may be keeping us mired.

One version of self-auditing is to become your own therapist. In 2019, a team of psychologists created a virtual reality environment in which users could switch between inhabiting an avatar of their own bodies (which looked uncannily like they did) and an avatar of Sigmund Freud. The Freud avatar, with his signature white beard and mustache, sat across from the research participant in a gray suit and skinny black tie. Before the session, participants shared a sticking point that they hoped to address. The most common sticking points focused on social anxiety, family issues, and work issues. For example:

"When I talk in public, I feel nervous, overwhelmed, I think that it will not go well, I start to play with my fingers, and my hands sweat, and I would like to control my emotions."

"When I consider looking for a job, I feel insecure. I think I am not prepared to face a job that I do not know."

Half the participants in the study inhabited their own bodies while the Freud avatar delivered generic instructions to consider the issue more carefully. The avatar welcomed them, asked them to expand on the issue, and asked them to think about the problem from a new perspective.

The other half—the participants who switched between playing Freud and playing themselves—effectively communicated with themselves, as though two separate people were in the room. (The platform altered their voices when they played Freud to deepen the sense they were speaking to someone else.)

Participants in the switching condition were moved by the experience. One week later they returned to the lab to discuss how the conversation affected them. Compared to those who spoke to a generic representation of Freud, those who inhabited his avatar were three times more likely to report behaving differently following the session, four times as likely to report feeling their problems were at least partially solved, and twice as likely to say they were more focused on solving the issue.

You don't need a virtual reality headset to replicate this experience. All you need is a conversation with yourself where the second party to the conversation plays devil's advocate to the first. If you think someone else is to blame for your situation, your devil's advocate self might ask you to reconsider your role in the situation. If you're anxious or fearful, your devil's advocate self might ask, "What's the worst that can happen?" Part of what makes this experience so useful is that becoming a second person allows you to shed a lot of the emotional baggage that anchors you to the sticking point. You can be more reasonable and detached as a fictional therapist than you can be as yourself.

The Freud experiment was difficult and expensive to run, so the researchers recruited fewer than sixty participants. Larger-scale studies have found similar results, though. In 2008, two cognitive psychologists proposed the "wisdom of inner crowds" hypothesis when they asked people to make the same estimates twice and found that the average of those estimates was more accurate than either estimate alone. They asked questions like "What percentage of the world's airports are in the United States?" and "What percentage of the world's adult population can read and write?" Half the participants in that study made the second estimate immediately after the first, and the other half made the second estimate three weeks later. The delay was valuable because forgetting the first estimate made the second more independent—almost as though it came from a different person altogether. The average of the two answers delivered one after the other made them 6 percent more accurate than either answer alone, but the average was 16 percent more accurate than either answer alone when the second estimate was made three weeks later. A follow-up experiment published in 2022 showed similar results. Six thousand adults who made two estimates were more accurate on average when they imagined their first estimate was made by someone with whom they disagreed. This disagreement mindset inspired them to consider how they might initially have been wrong and pushed them to overcome some of their initial biases and misconceptions.

The wisdom of inner crowds is a useful last resort, but consulting one or more other people is far more effective. The researchers calculated that asking yourself the same question twice yields an answer about one-tenth as accurate as combining your answer with a random other person's answer, and about one-third as accurate if you deliver your second answer three weeks later. The problem is that the reconsidered answer still overlaps with the first answer, even after a delay. You're the same person three weeks later, so your biases and foibles remain.

Other researchers who built on this work wondered how we might best consult our inner crowds. What should we ask when we're trying to split ourselves in two? Here's a script that worked particularly well:

First, assume that your first estimate is off the mark.

Second, think about a few reasons why that could be. Which assumptions and considerations could have been wrong?

Third, what do these new considerations imply? Was the first estimate too high or too low?

Fourth, based on this new perspective, make a second, alternative estimate.

This approach also works for questions that aren't grounded in numbers. In other studies, researchers have asked participants to "consider the opposite" of their original view, or "if you imagine you're wrong, for a minute, how exactly are you wrong?" Consulting your internal crowd is flexible—you just have to adapt the script to the sticking point you're battling to overcome. It's also often worth reconsidering because follow-up responses are sometimes more valuable than first attempts. In one experiment, people were asked to invent four new pieces of fitness equipment. They tended to believe their first idea was best, but a separate panel of consumers routinely rated their second idea as superior to their first. The second was more abstract, more unusual, and in many ways more surprising because it required that the inventors go beyond their entrenched ideas about the nature of fitness equipment.

———

It's no accident that humans have thrived for millennia in groups. Whether in tribes or megacities, we do better together because we compensate for our neighbors' weaknesses—and vice versa. The more complicated and sticky the problem, and the more diverse the inputs, the more valuable the crowd. Even when a real crowd isn't available, asking yourself the same question twice is better than relying on your first instinct alone.

As easy as it is to ask yourself the same question twice, few of us naturally question our instincts. We need to be guided in the moment or taught to reconsider. There are, however, natural experimenters among us who treat every sticking point as an opportunity to test alternatives before settling on a path forward. The next three chapters examine what makes these people different from the rest of us, why they tend to be stuck relatively rarely and briefly, and what the rest of us can learn from their approach to breaking free. The first of those is an athlete named Dave Berkoff, who experimented his way onto the 1988 US Olympic team.

PART IV

HABIT

EXPERIMENTATION

Elite male swimmers are generally tall, broad shouldered, and dedicated. Those who set world records weigh an average of two hundred pounds and stand a shade over six feet, three inches tall. They swim up to twelve miles per training session, up to ten sessions per week, often beginning the first of their two daily workouts at four in the morning. When they aren't swimming, they're working out; when they aren't working out, they're eating; and when they aren't eating, they're sleeping.

This combination of natural size and dedication presented a problem for Dave Berkoff, an ambitious collegiate backstroke swimmer in the mid-1980s. Berkoff was several inches shorter and forty pounds skinnier than most elite swimmers, and he despised swimming practice. When Australian swimming coach Laurie Lawrence met Berkoff in 1988, Lawrence was struck by how much smaller Berkoff was than the giants who loped around the pool. "This kid was quite small," Lawrence said. "He had a build that wouldn't attract even a second glance from the ladies. 'This bloke shouldn't be here,' I thought."

Talent scouts from the top swimming colleges ignored Berkoff, so he attended Harvard on the back of strong grades rather than swimming prowess. "I wasn't a top recruit," Berkoff told me. "My high school swimming career was good, but not great, and I didn't get a ton of attention." Everybody knows Harvard for its academic program, but Harvard wasn't the natural place for elite swimmers. "Harvard was a nonscholarship school," Berkoff said. "You showed up because you wanted to be part of a team, and not because you were being paid to show up." Despite these challenges, Berkoff dreamed of a spot on the 1988 US Olympic backstroke squad.

Berkoff's sticking points were emotional, mental, and physical. He wasn't hungry enough, he was frustrated and despondent, he wasn't big enough, and he wasn't sure what to do to improve. "Swimming was boring," he told me. "I had a problem getting to practice. Coaches always wanted me to work harder." For a while Berkoff was ranked fifth or sixth among backstroke swimmers in the United States—solid, but not strong enough to qualify for the Olympic team—which further eroded his will to practice. If a solution existed, it had to motivate Berkoff to train, while enabling him to transcend his physical stature.

Despite his various shortcomings, Berkoff was endowed with an insatiable curiosity. He was uncommonly bright and open to experimenting. Other swimmers defaulted to the dominant techniques of the day, but Berkoff tended to question everything. Why swim the same technique better than everyone else when you could find a better technique? This taste for experimentation suited Joe Bernal, Berkoff's innovative coach at Harvard. Bernal learned that Berkoff loved sampling new techniques but hated to practice, so Bernal coaxed Berkoff to train by teaching him new methods at the end of long practice sessions. Together they refined Berkoff's technique with a series of small and moderate tweaks.

"Joe was the kind of coach who was willing to take the time to experiment with new techniques," Berkoff recalled. "He told us, 'Try and do something to get an advantage.'" First, they broke the process down into its components, beginning with the start of the race. Backstrokers begin by spending a short time underwater, and Berkoff calculated that swimmers are 82 percent faster when their bodies are completely immersed than when they swim on the surface of the water. In a sport decided by milliseconds, an 82 percent difference is enormous. To break through, Berkoff decided, he needed to spend as much time as possible underwater.

Spending time underwater sounds easy, but Berkoff almost abandoned the technique because his body rebelled each time he immersed himself for longer than a few seconds. The human body rushes to resurface as soon as it's submerged, fearing that it might asphyxiate without a fresh pull of oxygen. That's why, until Berkoff pushed the envelope, humans had swum above the surface for millennia. Launching into a race is exhausting, so a swimmer's body cries out for oxygen almost immediately. The only way to suck in that oxygen is to rise to the surface. Berkoff trained his body to resist this urge while dolphin-kicking underwater for as long as he could. At first the exertion forced him to rise after fifteen meters, but over several months he trained his body to remain underwater for forty meters, or 80 percent of the first lap of an Olympic pool.

Berkoff's breakout race came at the 1987 NCAA Nationals in Austin, Texas, where he broke the NCAA record in the 100-yard backstroke. The following year, at the Olympic trials in preparation for the 1988 Olympic Games, he broke the 100-meter world record twice. Though he won Olympic gold in the team 4 × 100-meter medley relay, he was edged to the wall in the 100-meter Olympic final by Japan's Daichi Suzuki—another swimmer who spent much of the first lap underwater after learning Berkoff's technique from grainy video footage.

Commentators dubbed Berkoff's method the Berkoff Blastoff, and it revolutionized the sport. During that same 100-meter Olympic backstroke final, one commentator remarked, "Look at this! Ten—twenty meters into the race and only three competitors on the surface, five underwater." Another says, "[Berkoff] has turned this into a thirty-five-meter start and a sixty-five-meter swim!" The podium featured Suzuki, Berkoff, and Igor Polyansky, all three of whom spent the first third of the race underwater.

The Blastoff was so effective that it rocked the sport. After the 1988 Olympics, swimming's governing body, FINA, added a fifth rule to its four existing rules governing backstroke:

Some part of the swimmer must break the surface of the water throughout the race. It is permissible for the swimmer to be completely submerged during the turn, and for a distance of not more than 10 metres [later increased to 15 meters] after the start and each turn. By that point the head must have broken the surface.

The *New York Times* published an article titled "Fastest Backstroker Loses a Revolution," noting that FINA had ruled the technique too dangerous for young swimmers and claimed that "it simply wasn't backstroke." Berkoff wasn't pleased with the change. It offended his sense that innovation and experimentation were legitimate paths to success. "I'm very upset by what FINA did," he said. "It's completely ludicrous. It doesn't really affect me because I decided a year ago that I would retire after this meet. But for future swimmers, the kids who started doing this, it's a shame."

For Berkoff, success had two elements: swimming fast and swimming smart. "FINA's always been conservative," Berkoff told me. "They've never celebrated ingenuity." He believed speed and smarts were both legitimate, and FINA had diminished the sport by putting tradition before innovation. It had also elevated the natural talent of a perfectly built swimmer above the earned talent of a swimmer like Berkoff. There's a democracy to earned talent—the sense that anyone, with the right combination of skill and enterprise, can succeed—and that element disappears when you privilege the natural endowment of having a one-in-a-million physiology.

In contrast to organized sports, few firm rules govern how you can approach art, music, business, writing, parenting, and relationships. Much of the time, there's a better way, and there's nothing wrong with making that shift. The best unstickers are hungry to experiment. They're open to trying new techniques and strategies, and they're quicker to stumble on breakthroughs because experimenting exposes them to more solutions than are available to those who cling to the status quo.

—

Colonel John Boyd was a fighter pilot who, like Berkoff, refused to accept the status quo. Boyd finished first in his class at the Fighter Weapons School and went on to be a fighter-pilot instructor. In contrast to Berkoff, Boyd was endowed with many natural gifts. He reacted and maneuvered more quickly than other pilots and as an instructor offered $40 to any young pilot who could evade him in simulated air-to-air combat for longer than forty seconds. He defeated the vast majority of his students within twenty seconds and never lost a battle. Those who came closest would gather in the nearest bar to relive each move with their friends.

Despite his gifts, Boyd wasn't satisfied. Like Berkoff he was itching to experiment—to try new approaches, and to record and share the strategies that served him best. He completed an engineering degree, and in 1959 began to write what became the first tactical manual for the US Air Force. He spent a month creating an outline, during which he slept just two or three hours a night, and then began to dictate his ideas into a tape recorder. The result was a 150-page manual titled *Aerial Attack Study*, by Capt. John Boyd. Almost overnight, the manual became the gold standard among air force pilots. Boyd printed six hundred copies in his first run, and within a day they were snapped up by eager students and instructors.

Boyd's approach reflected his passion for experiments and his training as an engineer. Over time, he honed his approach to air-to-air combat, developing a four-step loop that he repeated rapidly, over and over, until the battle had ended. This loop, committed to paper, was designed to teach fighter pilots how to joust, but could also be used "in competitive business practices, in sports, or in personal relationships." The key to victory, Boyd suggested, was completing the loop more quickly and efficiently than your opponents, whether in the skies, in business, or elsewhere.

The loop's four stages went by the acronym OODA: *observe, orient, decide*, and *act*. Together they describe an excellent recipe for unstick-ing. The first step, *observe*, asks combatants to interpret the situation as accurately as possible. For Dave Berkoff, this meant recognizing two sticking points: that he disliked and therefore avoided traditional training, and that he was neither tall enough nor endowed with a long enough torso to compete on natural talent alone. If you aren't sure why you're stuck, it's impossible to break free.

Boyd believed the second step, *orient*, was probably the most im-portant. Once you've appraised the situation, you need to develop an effective action plan. Your orientation depends on all sorts of factors that arose years earlier: your cultural beliefs, attitudes, personality, ed-ucational experience, genetic heritage, and so on. Berkoff was both un-usually intelligent and unusually curious, he was well educated, and he wasn't especially genetically gifted. His profile therefore made him the perfect candidate for experimentation—for treating the training he so disliked as a testing ground for novel swimming techniques. This ori-entation prepared Berkoff to overcome his two primary sticking points because he enjoyed experimenting, and he used it to identify technical advantages that might compensate for his anatomical limitations.

Next comes the decision-making phase, *decide*. Having examined his options, Berkoff recognized that swimming beneath the water made him faster, so the natural decision was to exploit this piece of information that may have eluded his competitors. Having decided to hone his underwater swimming skills, Berkoff embarked on the *act* phase: making a concrete plan to enact his decision. This meant draw-ing up an underwater-training plan with advice from his coach, Joe Bernal, and sticking to that plan as his tolerance for swimming under-water grew.

Boyd described OODA as a loop because, in air-to-air combat as in life, situations change. If the clouds clear, and suddenly you're flying blindly toward the sun, your original plan might need to shift. You'll return to the first stage of the model, observing the situation afresh with a new set of facts. Berkoff experienced something similar when

FINA outlawed his Blastoff technique. Instead of abandoning the sport, Berkoff experimented with a new technique and found a new coach who he believed was better suited to his new training regime. "After the 1988 Games, when FINA banned my technique," Berkoff said, "I came out of retirement in 1990 and decided I wanted to win an Olympic medal in 1992, to show FINA and the skeptics that I could swim backstroke [their] way."

A different athlete might have quit for good, but Berkoff wasn't just smart and curious; he was also stubborn and proud. "I went back to my old coach, Dick Shoulberg, and I basically relearned how to swim conventional backstroke," Berkoff said. He spent a year swimming much farther than his target distance of one hundred meters—an approach known as overdistance training, which mirrors the hardship inoculation concept I mentioned earlier—and capitalized on some of his other natural gifts. Berkoff was unusually flexible, and relatively small, which allowed him to turn more tightly and rapidly at the wall, buying him precious fractions of a second midway through each race. This second run at the OODA loop paid off. Berkoff won a gold medal in the 4 × 100-meter medley relay, and a bronze in the 100-meter individual backstroke event, at the 1992 Barcelona Olympics.

Experimentation is at the heart of the first two phases of the OODA loop. Observing is about identifying the problem and collecting data for potential solutions, and orienting is about analyzing the data and deciding how your particular background, abilities, and experiences might guide your next steps. Boyd's training as an engineer convinced him that data gathering and experimenting was the best way to make progress in any situation. How could you evolve if you didn't understand the options and which ones were likely to produce the outcomes you were seeking?

———

Experimentalism is the belief that carefully comparing two or more alternatives illuminates the best path forward. How can you know which path to follow if you haven't tested them first? In practice, there are two reasons to collect data: to determine the best among a set of approaches, and, where you feel you have the answer already, to convince others that your approach is superior.

This philosophy drove an English wine merchant named Steven Spurrier to stage a now-famous wine-tasting event in 1976. Spurrier owned a wine shop and a wine school in Paris, a city overrun with Old World wines from traditional wine-making countries like France, Italy, and Spain. It was difficult to develop a competitive edge selling these wines because so many merchants were selling the same bottles for similar prices.

Spurrier had a couple of options. He could drum up publicity for his shop and his school, or he could convince the Parisian public to buy the New World Californian wines that he believed were just as good as Paris' beloved Old World labels. Spurrier tried to do both by hosting a blind tasting featuring ten white wines and ten red wines. Six of the reds and whites were from California and the remaining four of each were French. He invited nine of France's most distinguished wine experts to sip and rate each wine, and to note whether it seemed French or American. The event went better than he imagined, and a journalist from *Time* captured what became known as the Judgment of Paris.

In the mid-1970s, anyone who knew anything about wine believed that French wines were superior to Californian wines. Spurrier's judges were no different, and from the first glass every judge clearly used a simple "good = French" rule. But while this dogma may have been accurate once upon a time, over the years Californian winegrowers and their wines had become more sophisticated. "Ah, back to France," one judge pronounced after sipping a Napa Valley chardonnay. Another, sniffing a Bâtard-Montrachet, said, "This is definitely California. It has no nose." The two unanimous winners that day were a 1973 chardonnay from Chateau Montelena, and a 1973 cabernet sauvignon from Stag's Leap Wine Cellars. Both were produced in the Napa Valley.

With his simple experiment, Spurrier began to dismantle centuries of resistance to New World wine producers. Even die-hard Old World fans were forced to concede that the New World had something to offer. Lovers of French wine certainly didn't switch to Californian wines overnight, but the wheels began to turn. "It rocketed us to fame," said Bo Barrett, whose father was the proprietor of Chateau Montelena. In 1983, Warren Winiarski, the founder of Stag's Leap Wine Cellars, said, "The phone started to ring pretty quickly. The wines really took off."

Spurrier's experiment achieved two things: it showed that New World wines could compete with Old World staples, and it convinced the wine world that New World labels merited a second look. This second consequence was a legitimate breakthrough—a force that changed how wine aficionados appraised New World wines. This was the unsticking power of a blind experimental taste test: strip away the bottle's label and you're left with the unassailable truth.

As with Spurrier's wine-tasting demonstration, experimentation is an excellent tool for questioning entrenched assumptions about the order of the world. For example, much of the developed world is stuck on the idea that the full-time workweek encompasses five days of eight hours each. In truth, there's no good reason why we do or should work according to that structure. In the 1700s, most Americans worked six twelve-hour days a week, for a total of seventy-two hours, pausing only to attend church on Sundays. With industrialization, workweeks shrank to sixty-eight hours by 1860, sixty-five hours by 1900, and fifty hours by 1930. During the Great Depression, the workweek shrank to forty hours, on average, where it remains almost a century later. Work parameters have changed dramatically since the 1930s, so why have we worked the same schedule for almost a hundred years?

Why don't we work, say, for four days each week instead of five? In February 2018, an estate-planning firm in New Zealand called Perpetual Guardian trialed this four-day structure for six weeks. The company's founder, Andrew Barnes, asked each of the company's 240 staff to nominate a day off each week, while promising to pay them the same salaries they earned before the trial. Barnes wasn't just committing an act of charity—he believed that the four-day week made business sense. "The four-day week is not just having a day off a week," Barnes says on the company's website, "it's about delivering productivity, and meeting customer service standards, meeting personal and team business goals and objectives." The word *productivity* punctuates the company's "four-day work week" explainer page: "At Perpetual Guardian we set out to test our assumptions about productivity through a company-wide trial. . . . We seek to generate useful data and insights to share with organizations that wish to develop their own productivity and flexibility policies."

Perpetual Guardian ran the experiment between March and April 2018, and the company worked with two universities in New Zealand to monitor its effects on productivity and staff satisfaction. The results were unambiguous: staff reported more time for their "families, hobbies, completing their to-do lists, and doing home maintenance." Barnes trained a careful eye on staff output and discovered that his workers were more efficient, more engaged with customers, less stressed, and reported enjoying a superior work-life balance. The company's revenue remained stable, but its costs shrank because its power bill fell dramatically. Barnes made the policy permanent and founded a nonprofit community titled 4 Day Week Global. The benefits persisted through 2019 and deepened further during the COVID-19 pandemic, when work-life balance became a particularly pressing corporate concern. "Sixty-three percent of businesses following the four-day work week found it easier to attract and retain talent," the nonprofit's site explains. "Seventy-eight percent of employees are happier and less stressed working a four-day work week."

There are certainly open questions here. This four-day structure might not work in every workplace, across every industry, in every country. Some of its benefits might be attributed to the so-called Hawthorne effect, which suggests that merely changing conditions at a company tells workers that their welfare matters, and that they're being monitored, which might inspire an artificial rise in productivity and self-reported welfare. But that seems unlikely to explain the entire effect here. Perpetual Guardian has benefited from this policy for several years now, and dozens of other organizations across other countries have reported similar benefits across long stretches of time. One percent of Iceland's workforce worked shorter workweeks between 2015 and 2019 and reported similar effects on well-being, productivity, and efficiency. The same was true among workers at Microsoft Japan in 2019, civil service workers in the Gambia between 2013 and 2017, and at a raft of companies in the United Kingdom between 2018 and 2019.

What matters here is not whether the four-day structure is optimal, but that experiments forced policymakers to reconsider a practice that had gone unquestioned for decades. A theoretical white paper written by several academics has nothing on the persuasive power of real-world field experiments. To move the needle—or to convince people to ask whether the needle might need moving in the first place—few tools are as compelling as experiments. Andrew Barnes at Perpetual Guardian knew this, and forty years earlier Steven Spurrier knew that elitist attitudes toward New World wines were unlikely to change without a gentle nudge from blind-tasting experiments.

———

There are two ways to experiment. The first, practiced by Berkoff, Spurrier, and Barnes, is to tackle a specific problem by comparing potential solutions. The second is to be globally curious—to treat life as one long experiment. The benefit of this approach is that you're less likely to become stuck in the first place, and more likely to stumble on serendipitous breakthroughs.

Globally curious adults are rare, but children are almost universally curious nearly all of the time. By one estimate, five-year-olds ask between two hundred and three hundred questions a day, whereas adults ask an average of just twenty or thirty. Our species sheds 90 percent of its natural curiosity by adulthood, which is a shame, because curiosity is one of the greatest drivers of creativity, and consequently one of our best unsticking tools.

Every now and then you'll meet someone who's unusually curious, who refuses to accept defaults and conventions just because they've hardened into norms. That was the case when I spoke to Max Deutsch early during the COVID-19 pandemic. It was May 2020, and Deutsch was stuck in his San Francisco apartment. He had become famous in certain circles in November 2016 when he decided to spend a year experimenting with twelve new skills. He called this his Month to Master (or M2M) project. That first month he taught himself to memorize the order of a deck of cards in under two minutes. On his blog he recounted a daily mix of progress and setbacks. On day five his confidence was "unwavering at 90%," but by day seven he was only 65 percent sure he'd complete the challenge by November 30. On November 24 he'd overcome those early jitters, recalling the order of a deck of cards perfectly in one minute and forty-seven seconds.

I asked Max how many hours he'd spent honing his memorization skills that November. I expected the answer to be hundreds, but Max told me he was too busy to devote more than an hour each day. "Some days I spent only forty-five minutes training," he said. "I couldn't blow up my entire life." He was so busy that most of his training took place during the Caltrain commute between his home and work. He'd sit wearing a pair of bizarre "memory glasses," reciting lists of cards under his breath as puzzled commuters pretended not to notice.

In December, Max decided to teach himself to draw realistic self-portraits. Despite describing his "strong artistic tendencies," he observed that his first self-portrait attempt on December 1 "sadly doesn't look very much like me." He spent most of the month following a studio drawing course, while drawing an impressive portrait of the British illusionist Derren Brown. During the second half of the month, Max spent eight hours drawing a realistic self-portrait that finally came together on Christmas Day.

Max spent most of the following year experimenting with ten diverse challenges. Some were physical (landing a backflip in March and completing forty consecutive pull-ups in August); some were artsy (playing a blues guitar solo in March and freestyle rapping in September); and others still were intellectual (learning in June to complete a challenging Saturday *New York Times* crossword puzzle and in April holding a thirty-minute Hebrew conversation on the future of tech).

Max nailed the first eleven challenges, but his pièce de résistance seemed impossible:

Month 12: Defeat world-champion Magnus Carlsen at a game of chess.

If you know anything about chess, you know all about Carlsen. The Norwegian world champion, who was twenty-six at the time, became a grand master—the highest ranking in chess—at age thirteen, assumed the world's top ranking in three different variants of the game between 2010 and 2012, and has held all three rankings ever since. Only one player in the history of the game has spent longer atop the world charts.

On his blog Max explained that he obviously wouldn't play Carlsen face-to-face, but would instead challenge a computer program infused with Carlsen's prowess and playing style. Max's blog had attracted a significant following by this twelfth challenge. "The project resonated with a lot of people," Max said. "So, on day one, ten people were following along, and by the end over six million people were [tuned in]." Given his blog's popularity, a writer at the *Wall Street Journal* offered to introduce Max to Carlsen's manager. Carlsen, known for being "a bit of a showman," agreed, and so the two chess players with vastly different backgrounds met in a hotel room in Hamburg, Germany, in mid-November 2017.

Max wasn't a great chess player, but, as with his other challenges, he experimented, using a crash course that taught him to recognize classic patterns and board positions. For a while Max held his own. Carlsen had defeated Bill Gates in nine moves, and on Max's ninth move he made a small but fatal mistake. The game wrapped after each player had made thirty-nine moves—an impressive showing from a challenger who was colossally outmatched. Carlsen was so impressed he agreed to a rematch once Max had more time to devote to the game.

The first thing to know about Max is that his M2M project wasn't just a stunt. "This was the culmination of something I'd been doing my entire life," Max told me. "I just thought it would be cool to capture a more structured effort in this format."

Max was describing ingrained experimentalism: an innate drive to experiment with new hobbies, pursuits, and skills, that began when he was a child. "I grew up just an extremely curious kid. Most of my childhood was pursuing these interesting kinds of things. When I was seven or eight, I got this cheap camcorder for my birthday, and I ran around for the next ten years making films and learning about visual effects. Then I got into music and learned all sorts of instruments. And art. And writing. And Rubik's Cubes. And sleight-of-hand magic . . ." Max continued to list skills as varied as his M2M domains had been.

Experimentalism opened doors to Max that were closed to other people. Meeting and playing against Carlsen were perks, but the deeper benefits of his approach extended far beyond bragging rights and moment-to-moment fun. Each experiment allowed Max to try on a new identity as you might try on clothes in a fitting room. His overarching conclusion, across these twelve M2M tasks, was that he loved being an entrepreneur who could marry the intrinsic rewards of learning with the external rewards of earning a living. The experiment continued when Max founded Monthly, an online business that pairs you with an expert who teaches you a new, creative skill in one month, from music production and painting to singing and filmmaking. Monthly is venture-backed and profitable. It's Max's full-time job at the moment, and if you look for its origins, you'll find a seven-year-old boy with a camcorder on the brink of twenty years of experimentation.

You don't have to turn your life upside down to become more like Max. What Max does particularly well is that he pushes back and delves deeper the way a child might, asking "Why?" and "Why not?" where other adults might accept the world at face value. There are several ways to cultivate a practice of curiosity. The first is to ask questions relentlessly about concepts you've historically taken for granted. One of my friends pushes back on every convention that the rest of us take for granted. He refuses to meet for lunch on the hour, for example, suggesting that we meet at, say, 12:48, when no one else will be arriving for a meal. He came upon this nugget by asking, "Why do people always meet on the hour? Is there value in following that convention?" He realized quickly that following the herd in this case was counterproductive, and so he breaks convention when he makes lunch and dinner plans.

A second step toward becoming globally curious is to browse rather than to search. To search, you need to know enough about the topic you're exploring to have a rough goal in mind. With searching, you specialize, which is valuable, but you're unlikely to engage with novel ideas. Technology, for better and worse, funnels us toward searching. The analog world, in contrast, rests on browsing. When you walk through a physical library or a bookstore, for example, you're likely to find books on topics that interest you already, but you're also likely to stumble on entirely new topics. Browsing fosters curiosity by sketching the contours of a world beyond your existing interests. In practice, that means using search bars less often and drop-down menus and buttons more often, and reading books and articles on topics you've never before considered, rather than diving ever deeper into the small set of topics that occupy your mind today.

Finally, a third approach toward becoming globally curious is to keep an ongoing list of facts, ideas, and experiences that puzzle you. What we don't know dwarfs what we do know, but most of us allow these moments to pass us by without pausing to examine them more deeply. Throughout my childhood, my dad placed a list of countries and capitals and "obscure words" on our fridge. Each time we came upon a new word or heard about a country in the newspaper or on TV, we'd add it to the list. The immediate effect of these lists was to broaden my vocabulary and deepen my understanding of world geography—but the longer-term effect was to make me generally curious, to encourage me to explore rather than to take my sense of the world for granted.

—

Curiosity is an effective unsticker because it inspires idea linking. Idea linking is the tendency to bounce from one concept to the next. Each jump takes you further from where you began and culminates in a dense map of connected ideas. The Wright brothers imagined humans flying on winged bicycles, for example, perhaps because they owned a bicycle store. As soon as they built a prototype, they realized that flying bicycles were almost impossible to balance. On the ground they tended to veer left or right, and in the air—even for a fraction of a second—their wings were irresistibly drawn sideways and downward. The brothers compared their failures to the successes of birds, who were perfectly balanced in the air, and realized immediately that their metaphor had been all wrong. Birds' wings move quickly—and not just up and down. They twist and turn in three dimensions, with one part of the wing facing one direction while another part faces a completely different direction. From there, the brothers built a winged glider with flexible wings, which took them far closer to sustainable flight—and carried them a long way from their original winged-bicycle concept. Their map of ideas had been thickened and enriched by the links they had drawn between bicycles, birds, and balance.

There isn't just one way to make a heavier-than-air vehicle fly, but often there's a *right* answer to a problem. With curiosity you're more likely to find that answer. Take the high-stakes arena of professional basketball. Roughly half of all games are decided by a margin of eight points or fewer, and a third of all games by five points or fewer. Since scoring shots count for between one and three points, a five-to-eight-point margin amounts to just three or four critical scoring shots per game. Any team that can improve its scoring efficiency even modestly stands to win a significant number of games that it might have lost by a handful of points.

Until several years ago, few teams showed much interest in scoring efficiency. Each player seemed to have one or more "sweet spots" from where he preferred to shoot, and those sweet spots varied widely. Some players preferred to shoot from right beneath the basket; others shot to the left or right of the basket; and others still preferred long-range three-point perimeter shots. If you mapped the most common shot locations for each team during the early 2000s, you'd see a random mess of dots in every case.

Eventually, though, the game was swept up in an efficiency craze. Instead of suggesting players shoot from wherever they liked, mathematicians began to figure out the most effective shot-taking locations on the court. Shooting from directly beneath the bucket yields the highest return: more than 1.20 points per shot taken. This isn't surprising—you're likely to score a high percentage of shots from close range—but getting to that part of the court is difficult when you're facing a determined defensive outfit. The other profitable region is the region beyond the three-point line, near the corners of the court. Here, the average yield is roughly 1.10 to 1.20 points per shot taken. In a conspicuous no-man's-land the yield drops to fewer than 0.85 points per shot taken, and that covers most of the two-point scoring zone beyond the region directly below the bucket. So, looking at the most popular shot-taking regions during a typical early 2000s season, some were very efficient, some were highly inefficient, and some fell in between.

The difference between these regions is monumental. Take one hundred shots from the efficient regions and you stand to score between forty and fifty more points than if you'd taken them from the inefficient regions. And often we're talking about a matter of steps to the left or right.

Not a single team in the NBA was optimizing for efficiency until suddenly *every* team got wind of these efficiency stats. Updated shooting maps show that since the 2017–2018 season, almost every player has taken his shots from the most efficient regions of the court.

———

This approach isn't available only to NBA strategists. Like the Wright brothers, you just need to be curious enough to question the status quo. Is the way things are right now optimal—or, adopting a lower standard, acceptable? And if you're stuck, the search for a new approach is even more urgent. With a mix of curiosity, and the right experiments that yield the right data, you're far more likely to find a path through the weeds. The experiments themselves don't need to be costly or intensive. They can be as simple as varying the time of day you tackle a particular responsibility, the order in which you complete a series of tasks, the mindset you adopt when you interact with another person, or whether and how you prepare mentally for a job that requires creativity. There's an experiment for every context, and if nothing else you'll confirm empirically that your existing approach is the most effective among a palette of options.

Experimentation is valuable, but eventually you need to buckle down and pursue whichever outcome triumphs over the rest. Max Deutsch tackled twelve different pursuits during his M2M year, but ultimately decided they pointed him toward a career in digital entrepreneurship. Dave Berkoff experimented with different swimming techniques, but only long enough to discover the benefits of swimming underwater for as long as possible. Experimentation is known as a divergent process. Done well, it exposes you to a menu of novel, diverse ideas and solutions. If you want to avoid getting stuck, though, the trick is working out when to switch from experimentation to implementation—to buckling down for the hard work of making your chosen option stick. Berkoff could never have won Olympic medals and broken world records had he not trained his body to tolerate the discomfort of remaining underwater even as his reptilian brain urged him to return to the surface. Breakthroughs may be one part experimentation, but they'll elude you forever unless you also add one part implementation.

EXPLORING AND EXPLOITING

In 2018, a team of researchers examined the career paths of thousands of artists, film directors, and scientists. The researchers discovered that most workers experienced one hot streak during their careers. That golden period occupied about 20 percent of their working lives, whereas they spent the remaining 80 percent of their careers churning out lower-quality products. Some of them spent much of that time stuck, producing little quality work at all. These creatives didn't produce *more* work during hot streaks, but the work they produced was more inventive and influential, and it went on to become their best-known work.

One detail puzzled the authors, though. Hot streaks seemed to arise randomly. They were common, occurring at least once in 90 percent of the careers the authors examined, but their timing was unpredictable. Some careers began with a hot streak, others ended with a hot streak, and others featured hot streaks partway through. It was hard to see why the arrival of these fruitful periods varied so greatly.

A new team including many of the original researchers began to investigate that question more deeply. If they measured the right inputs, they might discover signature behaviors that herald hot streaks ahead of time. With this information, they could coach budding artists, film directors, and scientists to manufacture hot streaks, rather than waiting for them to arrive.

The answer came three years later, in a second piece of research. The authors identified two behaviors that, executed in the right order, seemed to produce hot streaks. The first behavior was a period of "exploration," and the second was a period of "exploitation." The causal chain seemed to suggest that first you explore, then you exploit; then begins your hot streak. "Despite the differences in the three types of careers we studied," the researchers wrote, "the observed associations between exploration, exploitation, and hot streaks appear universal across all three domains."

Exploration and exploitation are opposites. "Exploration," the authors wrote, "engages individuals in experimentation and search beyond their existing or prior areas of competency." It's risky because sometimes you don't find what you need, but it's also the only way to upgrade an approach that isn't working for you. Dave Berkoff's period of exploration introduced him to the underwater technique that became the Berkoff Blastoff. It isn't enough to explore endlessly, though. Once Berkoff discovered the magic of swimming underwater, he had to train and train and train. This was his period of exploitation. The research team wrote, "Exploitation allows individuals to build knowledge in a particular area and to refine their capabilities in that area over time." To exploit you need to work hard, training for hours at a time, refining and fine-tuning. You can't make breakthroughs without a period of exploration, but you'll never succeed if you don't follow a period of exploration with precise, targeted exploitation.

Film director Peter Jackson explored and exploited his way to great success. His hot streak came in the early 2000s, when he won a string of awards for his *Lord of the Rings* trilogy. When Jackson accepted the Academy Award for Best Director, for the third of those films, he noted that his earliest films had been "wisely overlooked by the Academy at the time." Those early films were part of an exploratory period that ranged far and wide, encompassing, among other genres, comedic horror, a self-referential mockumentary about a filmmaker, and a somber true-crime biography. These films were diverse, but through them Jackson developed a taste for creating richly drawn worlds, which he applied to a string of films in the mid- to late 1990s. This was the beginning of his exploitation phase—a period when he cofounded a special effects studio and created films that perfected many of the techniques and approaches that made his *Lord of the Rings* trilogy such a success. The hot streak researchers found Jackson's case fascinating because his career mimicked their pattern perfectly. He explored during much of the 1990s and exploited—and hit his hot streak—during much of the 2000s.

Like Peter Jackson, Jackson Pollock explored before he exploited. Between 1942 and 1946, Pollock experimented with a range of new techniques. Buoyed by a contract to paint at Peggy Guggenheim's gallery in New York City, Pollock was liberated to paint works that ranged from small to large, figurative to abstract, down-to-earth to surrealist. He began painting large murals, but also produced smaller, intricate works. He also explored different venues, painting in Manhattan studios, but also painting at a home he shared with his wife, fellow artist Lee Krasner, in East Hampton. No single approach stuck for long, until late 1946, when Pollock discovered the poured "drip" technique that defined his five-year hot streak. This new technique marked Pollock's transition from exploration to a half decade of exploitation. His works during this period were exclusively large and conceptual, and though the drip technique produced a stunning variety of visual effects, each mural relied on pouring paint directly onto the canvas. As with Peter Jackson, Pollock's drip technique combined many of the elements he'd discovered during his period of exploration, and he wisely cast aside other techniques that were less successful.

Beyond both Jacksons, the researchers showed that many other creatives hit hot streaks after that same pattern of exploratory-then-exploitative behavior. Both ingredients in just that order were essential. "When exploitation occurs by itself, not preceded by exploration," the researchers wrote, "the chance that such episodes coincide with hot streaks is significantly lower than expected, not higher." Exploit before you know whether a particular patch of terrain is fertile, and you're unlikely to succeed. The same goes for exploring in the absence of exploitation: "When the episode of exploration is not followed by exploitation," the researchers explained, "the chance for such exploration to coincide with a hot streak again reduces dramatically."

It's important to understand where hot streaks come from because they represent the hopes and dreams of breakthrough hunters everywhere. If sticking points are periods of stagnation, hot streaks are periods of change, development, and growth. The explore-exploit combo the researchers identified in 2021 is powerful because it provides a recipe for turning periods of stasis into periods of change, and a tool for diagnosing where your actions might be leading you astray. Some people explore constantly, roaming new pastures one after another, never seeming to settle before they move on to the next field. You probably know some of these people. And you probably also know their opposites: people who work incredibly hard, incredibly diligently, nose to the grindstone at all times, rarely floating above the metaphorical workbench to ask whether their efforts might be more fruitfully expended somewhere else. Both kinds of people are onto something, but they need to trade places in precisely the right order to unlock the hot streak they both desire.

Before deciding whether you're spending too much time pursuing one strategy over the other, you need to learn to distinguish exploration from exploitation. One litmus test is to ask how often you answer yes or no to opportunities and requests. Saying yes as a rule is a sign that you're exploring. You're open to uncertainty and novelty. Saying yes forces you to take up an activity that may waste your time, but some yeses expose you to new opportunities that are worth mining. Once you find those opportunities, you can kick into exploit mode, in which you say no most of the time. Saying no protects your time and energy. It allows you to devote yourself to the pasture you've already found—presumably after having said yes many times in the past. That shift from yes to no is a sure sign that you've shifted from exploration to exploitation. The many rules about when to say yes and when to say no all revolve around this basic explore-exploit distinction. For example, when starting college, a new career, or moving to a new city, there's great value in exploring broadly—and in adopting yes as your default response to opportunities to encounter new people and new experiences. When you're happy with your existing career, your circle of friends, and the city in which you live, or if you're struggling to make time for the people and interests that are already important to you, there's more value in exploiting—and adopting a no default.

Once you know whether you're exploring or exploiting, you'll need to decide when to switch from one strategy to the other. Whether you're switching at the right time is hard to know, but bad timing is easy to fix because you aren't locked into either strategy. Researchers have found that you can jump back and forth between the two, returning to a period of exploration as soon as you realize your exploitative phase isn't bearing fruit. This switching strategy is known as ambidexterity, and the only thing stopping most people and organizations from switching readily is fear and uncertainty. In one study, people who were forced to switch—to begin anew with an exploratory phase, or to jump from exploration to exploitation—were more successful than those left to their own devices. We find comfort in inertia, so we stick for far too long with what seems to be working just well enough. The answer, the researchers discovered, is that jumping from exploration to exploitation, and back again, is almost always productive. Since switching back is always an option, the only unproductive strategy is to switch too seldom.

I didn't realize it at the time, but I had an explore-exploit moment as a young college student a quarter century ago. In the United States, most undergrads spend a couple of years exploring before they're forced to choose—or "exploit"—a major. In Australia, you apply to both a college *and* to a specific degree at that college. A law degree might require a higher entrance score than, say, a commerce degree, which in turn requires a higher entrance score than an arts degree. I was awarded a full-ride scholarship to study actuarial science, which was an incredible honor—but it forced me to exploit before I'd begun exploring.

Those first three months of college were among the unhappiest of my life. My college math professor and the material he was teaching were impossible to understand. We covered everything I'd learned in high school during the first week of college, a crash course that the professor described as "getting the easy stuff out of the way." I'd been a motivated student in high school, but dreaded college so much that I started to dislike the smell of campus.

For several reasons I felt stuck. The scholarship not only paid my tuition but included a small biweekly stipend. Turning my back on free money seemed ungrateful. My family wasn't wealthy, and we'd been forced to leave behind the majority of our modest assets when we moved from South Africa to Australia in the 1980s. More important, though, I had no backup plan. Having never explored the menu of degrees, I was blind to the alternatives.

As the semester drew to a close, the scholarship administrator told us we had one week to decide whether we wanted to stay in the program. If we decided to stay past that date, we had two choices: complete the degree or leave before the end of the four-year program and pay back in its entirety the stipend we'd been given. Faced with those options, I left the program later that day.

I had several months to choose a new degree program before the next academic year began, and above all I wanted to avoid making another terrible decision. During my first few months on campus, I'd heard friends describe their classes in art, English, philosophy, sociology, law, psychology, medicine, finance, computer science, business, engineering, and dozens of other disciplines. I had no idea what a degree (never mind an entire career) in any of those disciplines involved, so I decided to explore them with the help of a friend who was also ditching actuarial science.

For three months we attended lectures across as many departments as we could. We took in dribs of Chaucer and drabs of Plato; a week of computer programming and a week of stagflation; a month on World War I and a month on the advertising industry. When I liked a lecture, I'd attend a second and then a third—small bursts of exploitation following exploration—and when I didn't, I'd move on to another course. By the end of that semester, I knew that I wanted to study psychology and law. So I spent five years exploiting for those degrees and went on to complete a doctorate in psychology at Princeton University.

———

To understand why exploration and exploitation are excellent partners, it's helpful to understand the lucrative truffle business. I moved from Sydney, Australia, to Princeton, New Jersey, in the summer of 2004 and spent my first afternoon in the United States shopping at a local supermarket. A table near its entrance had a stack of small jars and a sign that caught my eye:

Was $1,999; Now Just $999

I'd never seen jars of food with three- or four-figure prices. A label on the jar said WHITE ITALIAN TRUFFLES, which turn out to retail for thousands of dollars per pound.

White truffles are absurdly expensive because they're as desirable as they are elusive. They taste like a unique combination of what experts variously describe as earth, garlic, nuts, minerals, roots, and shallots, and they're among the rarest foods on the planet. Truffles grow underground, at the base of certain trees, which makes them almost impossible to find. Humans have tried to farm them for centuries, but they're difficult to cultivate or control, so most continue to grow wild in tiny pockets of the world. For centuries, truffle hunters relied on female pigs—sows—to sniff out hidden truffles, but the truffle scent was so similar to the scent of testosterone emitted by male pigs that crazed sows often ate the truffles before they could be retrieved. Today, specific breeds of dog lead white truffle hunts, particularly in parts of Italy and Croatia. One retriever breed, the Lagotto Romagnolo, has specifically been bred for several centuries to hunt truffles.

The distribution of white truffles is, to use a technical term, lumpy. On the overwhelming majority of our planet you won't find a truffle even with the best truffle-hunting dogs. Even in the Piedmont region of Italy, where you're most likely to find white truffles, you need to find a patch of land with just the right climate and soil conditions. And even in the best patch of land, you won't find white truffles at the base of every beech, poplar, oak, or hazelnut tree. You need to explore—to rule out the 99.9999 percent of the land that isn't fertile before striking a particularly rich vein worth exploiting. Exploitation is then critical because once you find a fertile patch, chances are decent you'll find truffles worth hundreds or even many thousands of dollars.

The lumpiness of white truffle distribution makes exploration then exploitation your only chance of success. Exploit in the wrong spot, and you won't find a single truffle; explore far and wide without exploiting a rich patch of land, and you're almost guaranteed to leave a specimen or two behind. Getting unstuck is often just as lumpy as the distribution of white truffles. In many domains, you'll spend a lot of time throwing darts at a dartboard with a tiny bull's-eye surrounded by blank space. Every now and then, you'll hit the bull's-eye, which will compensate for dozens of earlier failed shots.

This bull's-eye analogy is a specific case of the eighty-twenty rule (also known as the Pareto principle). The eighty-twenty rule suggests that, say, for many businesses 80 percent of all sales come from 20 percent of all customers. In the case of white truffles, the ratio is even more extreme, as the vast majority of all truffles grow on a vanishingly small proportion of the planet's land. The numbers vary—for example 1 percent of movies earn 80 percent of box office revenue (an eighty-one rule)—but the basic idea is that outcomes are lumpy. In the business world, some customers spend lots of money, and most don't spend much at all. If you're a savvy entrepreneur, you're supposed to find and cultivate relationships with the 20 percent who will really move the needle. When Richard Koch coined the term, in 1997, he suggested this lumpiness rule held in dozens of domains. "Seven hundred words, or fewer than one percent of all words, are used eighty percent of the time," he said. "Eighty percent of a computer's time is spent executing about twenty percent of the operating code. Eighty percent of the market will tend to be supplied by twenty percent or fewer of the suppliers."

The eighty-twenty rule suggests two things. First, as Koch argued, you should spend your time, energy, and effort cultivating the 20 percent that brings 80 percent of your benefits. Second, the flip side of this rule is that you'll probably spend a lot of time, energy, and effort on the 80 percent that brings only 20 percent of your benefits. That's a natural consequence of the lumpiness of outcomes—and why, say, even the best creatives and scientists tend to have one or maybe two relatively brief hot streaks during their long careers, or why investors tend to earn the vast majority of their profits from a small proportion of their investments. The same is true of large tech companies, which tend to run thousands of small and large experiments to improve their products. One team of researchers examining the extent to which these experiments improved Microsoft's Bing search engine between 2013 and 2016 found that 75 percent of the gains Microsoft experienced came from just 2 percent of all tweaks—a seventy-five–two rule. Lumpiness is everywhere, which underscores the danger of exploiting prematurely, before you've explored for early signs of promise.

Lumpiness is a bit disheartening because it makes the world seem random and difficult to control. But it's also empowering because it suggests that a gold mine, whether filled with white truffles or great ideas, could be around the next corner. What determines whether you'll succeed, and whether you'll manage to unstick yourself if you're stuck, is your decision to keep going. The more you try, the more times you aim darts at the dartboard, the more likely you are to hit your mark.

This "just keep going" mentality was central to the insights of

Robert Merton, an American sociologist who studied the origins of scientific breakthroughs. In the 1930s, Merton was a graduate student at Harvard. Strolling through town one day, he saw the thirteen-volume edition of *The Oxford English Dictionary* in the window of his favorite bookstore. It was love at first sight. "I came upon the resplendent volumes of the *OED*," he recalled six decades later, "that very expensive reference work, which I obviously had no intention, expectation, or hope of acquiring." Merton couldn't afford the *OED* outright, but the bookseller agreed to sell the books on credit. "It was truly a huge investment," Merton later remembered. "I devoted almost a third of my cash resources to the serendipitous purchase of the *OED*."

Merton's purchase was serendipitous because it introduced him to the concept of *serendipity*. "While in search of the history of a word beginning with the letters *se*," he remembered, "my eye happened upon the strange-looking and melodious-sounding word *serendipity*." Merton spent the next sixty years studying serendipity, and its role in unsticking those who were stuck.

Serendipity, as Merton saw it, is "the natural gift for making useful discoveries by accident." It's different from ordinary, unearned luck because serendipitous luck requires skill. Merton believed that people could manufacture luck under the right conditions, and the right conditions were largely a matter of behavior. It wasn't simply an accident that, say, Isaac Newton stumbled on gravity when he saw an apple fall from a tree. Millions of people had watched objects fall, but it took 2 million years, between the dawn of our species and the year 1666, for one particular human to ask, "Why, if an apple could fall from a tree, shouldn't the moon similarly fall toward Earth?" Newton had what Merton called a "prepared mind." A chance discovery, he said, involves "both the phenomenon to be observed and the appropriate, intelligent observer."

A prepared mind ensures that, even when you find yourself stuck, you'll rarely be stuck for long. To be prepared, your mind must be poised to do two things: to seek similarities and to seek differences.

For Newton, this meant asking, "What else in the world is similar to an apple as it falls to the ground? And how is this falling apple unique and different from other phenomena I've witnessed?" The answer, for Newton, was that the moon is similar to a gigantic apple falling toward Earth, so they must be experiencing the same universal force. In contrast to the apple, though, the moon doesn't actually reach Earth. Instead it orbits Earth at a consistent distance, following a curved path that suggests the force pulling the moon toward Earth is strong enough to prevent the moon from escaping Earth completely, but not strong enough to bring them together as an apple hitting the ground.

Newton is one of thousands of scientists to benefit from serendipity. In 2002, a British chemist named Walter Gratzer published a book cataloging the role of serendipity in science. "Because science in general proceeds slowly, and is short on day-to-day drama," he wrote, "it is the moments of sudden startling illumination, and especially of those rarest of all gifts from nature, chance revelations, that live in the memory."

Many of the zero-calorie commercial sweeteners on the market, from NutraSweet and Equal to Sweet'N Low and Splenda, were discovered when scientists accidentally tasted pinches of white powder that were designed for other purposes. In one case, a badly behaved research assistant was working to fine-tune a fever-reducing drug when he lit up an illicit cigarette in the lab. A small puff of the drug, in fine powder form, had coated the cigarette, and the assistant noticed immediately that the tip of his cigarette tasted cloyingly sweet. The drug failed as a fever reducer, but succeeded as a new commercial sweetener called cyclamate. James Schlatter, a chemist working on ulcer treatments in 1965, similarly noticed a sweet taste when he licked his finger to turn a book's page. "I traced the powder on my hands back to the container into which I had placed [crystallized aspartame]," Schlatter remembered. "I felt it was unlikely to be toxic and I therefore tasted a little of it and found that it was the substance which I had previously tasted on my finger." Schlatter had discovered a substance that was both easy to synthesize and two hundred times sweeter than regular sugar. These serendipities in aggregate spawned an artificial-sweetener industry worth billions of dollars.

Gratzer identified dozens of other serendipitous discoveries. The common thread running through each was consistency: researchers who consistently asked the right questions and inquired further when they were surprised by an experience tended to create their own luck. Even if they'd been stuck for years, serendipity as a combination of luck and skill seemed to unstick them. This was true for, among other discoveries, the causes of color blindness, the role of refrigeration in preserving meat, the function of the pituitary gland, the power of vaccination, the dangers of rising to the surface too quickly after an ocean dive, the importance of vitamins in animal health, the contraceptive pill, the Antabuse alcoholism treatment, and treatments for dozens of ailments, from high blood pressure to heart disease. The scientists who made these discoveries were deeply educated, but in many cases their major discoveries relied on doggedness and curiosity rather than book smarts and intellect. For many, the search began with a serendipitous Aha! moment—the combination of some unexpected event, and the insight to recognize why that event was important.

Even if you aren't a scientist seeking breakthroughs, there are lessons here for serendipity in everyday life. The most important of those is that in productive questioning you behave more like a child than an adult—asking questions about everything, and refusing to stop until the answers are completely satisfying. This is a high bar, and most adults give up long before they reach this level of comprehension. (If you have small kids, as I do, you'll know that kids ask follow-up questions till they're completely satisfied. In other words, they never stop asking questions, which explains in part why they learn so much more rapidly than adults do.) If something goes wrong, ask why—and don't stop delving until you understand why it went wrong with such precision that you can reliably avoid the same outcome in the future. If something goes well, ask why to the point where you're able to bottle it and reproduce the same magic later. That's true of ideas that work well and poorly, relationships that thrive and fail, personal interactions that produce desirable and unwanted results, and days studded with wins and losses. Serendipity is about stumbling on luck, but long-term success is about understanding so deeply what made you lucky that you're able to concoct the same conditions at will.

———

As Merton's examination of serendipity suggests, Aha! moments are elusive. Sometimes the best way to find them is to ignore them altogether. In 2019, three psychologists asked hundreds of physicists and professional writers to record their best ideas each day for a week or two. The researchers chose physicists and writers because they lead very different creative lives. If writers and physicists come by Aha! moments similarly, the same principles might apply more broadly to people who are stuck in other domains. Each day, the research participants recorded their best idea of the day, what they were doing when it arrived, and whether it resolved a sticking point or contributed to an ongoing project that was progressing smoothly.

There are, broadly speaking, two ways to conjure good ideas. One is to work hard to find inspiration—to toil deeply and consistently until you find a promising path forward. This is the orthodox route we're taught to pursue at school, in college, and at work. The other approach is to hope inspiration strikes while your mind wanders. Mind wandering has a bad rap because it seems like a form of weakness. It takes discipline and grit to keep going, and mind wandering is unfocused and undemanding. This bad reputation makes sense if mind wandering short-circuits a period of progress and slows you down. That's probably why the researchers found that only 10 percent of good ideas on a task that was progressing smoothly came during mind wandering. The other 90 percent emerged during active task engagement.

But the same wasn't true when the physicists and writers were stuck. If you're stuck, it's because whatever you've been doing isn't working. If it were working, you'd be making progress. When the participants were stuck, 25 percent of their good ideas came during mind wandering. "These findings provide the first direct evidence that a significant proportion of creative individuals' ideas occur while engaged in [mind wandering]," the researchers wrote. Several months later, the researchers returned to the same physicists and writers to ask them to revisit their ideas. They wondered whether the ideas sourced by a wandering mind might be weaker or compromised because they were products of unfocused thought. In fact, the study's participants believed those ideas were just as creative and important as the ideas that emerged when they were absorbed in the problem.

Dozens of studies have shown that mind wandering unsticks because it inspires creativity. In one small study, nine jazz musicians improvised over twelve different chord progressions while a researcher periodically measured whether their minds were wandering. Though their minds wandered just 10 percent of the time, those brief periods of disengagement produced much of their most creative work. In other studies, people were more likely to produce creative uses for everyday items, like bricks and paper clips, when their minds had been left to wander during the task. Mind wandering is valuable because it allows people to disengage from their bad ideas—the ideas that entrenched them in the first place—freeing them to consider new, possibly subtler ideas. There's also some evidence that it liberates people to form new associations between disparate ideas already in their heads, inspiring novel solutions that rest on the connections between distantly related concepts. It's also restorative, allowing tired minds to rest between bouts of concerted effort.

Despite these benefits, the solution isn't to let your mind wander all day, every day. More good ideas come when you're focused than when you're unfocused. But you can't always be focused, and when you're at an impasse, stepping away from the roadblock yields measurable returns. Over two weeks, you can expect three or four strong unsticking ideas to arise during mind wandering—and over a year, you may make dozens or more breakthroughs when your mind is unfocused. Mind wandering is a lot like the exploratory process that precedes exploitation. A wandering mind explores, but when you're making good progress, and it's time to exploit again, you'll do better actively focusing on the task at hand.

One practical approach is to adopt two different strategies that map onto broad and narrow thinking. Broad thinking requires a long view, so you might set aside a couple of hours every three to six months to ask the broadest questions about each important area of your life. Are you broadly satisfied with your life at home, at work, and in other domains that matter to you? Do you have a sense of how your life might progress within each domain over the coming year, three years, five years, and ten years? If you're tacking in the wrong direction, you can begin to consider how you might reorient yourself. Are there global steps you might take? Do you need to consider seeking a new job, relationship, or living arrangement?

In tandem, you need to think narrowly as well, because narrow thinking is responsible for concrete change. You might begin by making a list of the specific sticking points in each domain, then revisiting that list once every month or two to track your progress. If you're just as stuck as you were the previous month, consider a set of specific, concrete steps you might take over the following month. The key to making breakthroughs is to keep moving in the right direction, even if slowly, rather than allowing yourself to become fixed in place. This approach to progress is incremental, but effective, and it often explains the difference between succeeding modestly and succeeding wildly. Whether you're stuck at work, at home, in love, friendship, or entrepreneurship, it's critical to alternate between thinking broadly and narrowly.

———

Strategies, like alternating between broad and narrow thinking, are most valuable if you assume that all of us, regardless of ability, can improve. If you believe talent and outcome are fixed quantities determined by genes and fortune, even the strongest strategy brings little benefit. This worldview is largely outdated now, but in the 1930s it drove a Russian physicist named Lev Landau to rank his fellow physicists on a scale of achievement. This scale was designed to capture not only their contribution to the field, but their innate talent. To Landau, the greatest physicists were fundamentally different from the remaining 99.9 percent of the field. Landau's scale ranged from 0 to 5, where Isaac Newton alone scored a 0, and "mundane physicists," who made up the majority of the field, scored a 5. Albert Einstein scored 0.5 on Landau's scale, and the founding fathers of quantum mechanics, including Niels Bohr, Werner Heisenberg, and Erwin Schrödinger, as well as Richard Feynman, Paul Dirac, and "a few others," scored 1. Landau assigned himself a score of 2.5, which he revised in his favor to 2 after he won the Nobel Prize in 1962. Landau's scale was logarithmic, which meant that a physicist with a score of 1 contributed ten times more to the field than did a physicist with a score of 2, and so on. In Landau's estimation, it would take one hundred Landaus and one hundred thousand mundane physicists to approach Newton's contribution to the field. Landau believed that the dozen or so brightest stars in his field were light-years ahead of the remaining thousands. He considered those dozen to be part of a "super league" and believed that they weren't just brighter than their colleagues, but were of a completely different species.

As interesting as Landau's scale is—and as much as it continues to inspire conversation among physicists—it magnifies the relative contributions of different physicists. In truth, the careers of lesser lights aren't so different from the careers of Nobel Prize winners. In one analysis, published in 2019, a team of researchers compared the careers of Nobelists in physics, chemistry, and physiology or medicine to those who might have scored a 5 on Landau's scale. "Apart from the prizewinning work, which may be subject to peculiarities of the Nobel," they wrote, "there is no known major difference that distinguishes patterns governing the careers of scientific elites from those with Landau's rank of five." Strip away the work that won these scientists the Nobel, and their careers look similar to the careers of thousands of other researchers whom Landau might have disparaged. The researchers concluded on an upbeat note, "These results offer reasons to remain hopeful: perhaps the ranks of scientists are not fixed, and barriers to leapfrog out of rank five may be less insurmountable than imagined."

The same idea is just as hopeful when applied more broadly. What seems like a gulf between top performers and the rest of us isn't as cavernous as it appears. Because outcomes are generally so lumpy, that difference is often razor-thin. If an average performer rounds the right bend, she might just discover the gold that separated her from her higher-achieving peers. And before those high achievers stumbled on their own gold nuggets, they were stuck, too.

This insight—that striking gold and continuing to fail aren't so far apart—drove a team of researchers to ask why some people turn failure into success, where others keep failing. The research team examined performance in a number of domains, including the performance of start-ups and the ability of scientists to attract grant funding. Some of their findings were quite surprising. Instead of failing less often, those who eventually succeeded were *more* likely to fail. "Failures are characterized by longer-than-expected streaks before the onset of success," the researchers explained, suggesting that winning becomes likelier the longer you've been losing. If you keep losing, but remain in the game, your chances of succeeding rise. This isn't just because winning is almost guaranteed with enough attempts, but rather because it takes time to learn from failures. For that reason, failures in a string become progressively smaller misses, so that the failure that comes immediately before success is usually a near miss. "The penultimate attempt shows systematically better performance than the initial attempt," the researchers found. "We find significant improvement for the successful group, which is absent for the unsuccessful group." Businesses and scientists who ultimately win do a better job of recognizing what it means to be close, whereas those who continue to miss the mark struggle to tell by how far. "Edison once said," the authors noted, "'Many of life's failures are people who did not realize how close they were to success when they gave up.'"

Some near misses are hard to detect, but others are obvious by design. When scientists apply for government grants, they receive a single score that tells them whether and by how much they've missed out on funding. It hurts to receive a very low score, but in some cases it hurts more to receive a "borderline score," which falls just a few percentage points below the funding threshold. (Some researchers even score above the threshold, but fail to secure funding perhaps because one reviewer was particularly negative.) A borderline score suggests you're close, but it might be demoralizing.

In 2019, a team of researchers examined whether near misses early in a scientist's career are more helpful or harmful than early narrow wins in the long run. The answer is both, depending on the researcher. "On the one hand," they wrote, "near misses significantly increase attrition, predicting more than a ten-percent chance of disappearing from the system. Yet, despite an early setback, individuals with near misses systematically outperform those with narrow wins in the longer run." Researchers who withstand the pain of having to dig deeper tend to do better than those whose early grants were approved by hairline margins. "Overall these findings are consistent with the concept that, 'what doesn't kill me makes me stronger,'" the researchers wrote. The near losers who continued to apply for grants after missing out ultimately won by a significant margin, producing hit papers 21 percent more often than did narrow winners.

Near misses are easy to see when feedback falls along a numerical scale, but you can also discern the size of a miss without objective feedback. Even if you can't be precise, in most cases it's easy to tell if you're getting nearer or farther from your goal across repeated attempts. That information comes from three sources: feedback from the context (for example, visual feedback if the goal is physical); your internal sense of whether you're improving or deteriorating; and feedback from other people. In concert, those three sources of information are usually sufficient to describe the size of a miss, and whether you're approaching or receding from your goal across time.

Near misses mean different things to different people. Some see them as a signal to keep exploiting—as valuable signposts that they're on the right track. To those people, a near miss says something like "You're almost there; with one or two small tweaks, success is yours." Those who are demoralized by near misses overlook or choose to ignore those signs. Instead of exploiting, they begin exploring anew, losing focus on just how close they are to success, and beginning to scratch elsewhere instead. This is where Edison's adage comes in— where missing how close you are to success when you give up becomes a tragic cause of failure. Never go back to exploring when success should follow another burst or two of exploitation. At its heart, this exploitation phase is about acting with purpose—about just plain *doing* after you've spent much of your energy developing a strategy for getting unstuck. The final ingredient that stands between good ideas and genuine breakthroughs is the action that takes them from theory to reality.

ACTION ABOVE ALL

In the early 1970s, Paul Simon was riding high. He'd released a string of wildly successful albums with Art Garfunkel in the 1960s, and Simon's solo career was booming. Several times during that period, TV personality Dick Cavett invited Simon on his talk show to discuss music and creativity. You can find those interviews online, and they all begin the same way: Simon, sitting awkwardly opposite Cavett, is unsure where to focus his eyes. He looks at the camera, at Cavett, at the studio audience, and then repeats that script.

Simon's answers to Cavett's first few questions are whispered, self-conscious, and brief. During one interview, Simon looks up to discover a boom mic sitting just above his head and asks, "Am I speaking too softly? Is that why the mic just went up?" There's a gulf between Paul Simon's towering musical prowess and his discomfort as a talk-show guest.

But then during each interview something shifts. And it shifts the same way each time. Cavett asks a well-timed question about some aspect of Simon's music, and Simon picks up his guitar. A question about how he wrote "Mrs. Robinson," the song tied forever to Mike Nichols' film *The Graduate*. Or a question about how Simon wrote "Bridge over Troubled Water," which won five Grammys and became a spiritual hymn for a generation of atheists.

As soon as Simon plays his guitar and starts *doing* rather than thinking or speaking, he becomes a different guest. He's charming and fluid. His answers are longer and easier to follow, and he's luminous. Many of the people watching these videos of Simon have noticed the same thing. "The second he picks up the guitar, he blooms," says a commenter named Davi. Nearly five hundred people agree. In reply to another clip, jontgreene says, "He is so much more comfortable speaking after he sings. That's great." Four hundred people agree. Rhys, a third commenter, says, "The moment the guitar was in his hand, he softened. He felt in his natural habitat again. I appreciate that." Nicole Marie replied, "Yeah, Paul seems shy until that guitar is in his hands."

What unsticks Simon is action. As soon as he holds and then plays his guitar, he relaxes. His words flow again. Perhaps the most fascinating aspect of watching Simon bloom is that he's aware of the change. He knows that action is his unsticker. Walking Cavett and his audience through a series of phrases from "Bridge over Troubled Water," Simon explains how he connected each element to the next. The video's viewers comment on this ethereal moment, on how lucky they are to have a genius walk them through his process. Simons admits that the song was easy to write, until it wasn't. He plays and hums to a fifteen-second melody, then stops abruptly. "I was stuck there. That was all I had of that melody." Cavett asks, "What made you stuck?" Simon replies, Zen-like, "Well, everywhere I went, I didn't wanna be." The audience laughs, and Cavett calls that "the best definition of stuck I've heard in my life."

Cavett asks, "When you get a block like that, how do you break through?" Simon explains that he listened to a fast-paced gospel song over and over, which inspired him to sit down with his guitar. The rest is history. It's not a flippant answer, but it doesn't demystify the process much. All Simon can point to is a kernel of inspiration paired with action. The action is key. He sits with his guitar, noodles a bit, loosens up, and the creative impasse relents.

If getting unstuck is a combination of feelings, thoughts, and actions, the driving force among this trio is actions. Feelings and thoughts, as important as they are, exist largely in the service of actions. Paul Simon's creative process, and his loosening up in front of the camera as soon as he picks up his guitar, are strong illustrations of the primacy of action. Without guitar in hand, Simon is shy and reserved; as soon as he starts to act, he produces a hymn for the ages.

This isn't just true of Paul Simon, or of musical geniuses in general. Psychologists have been interested in the relationships between feelings, thoughts, and actions for a long time, and one of their key insights is that actions are paramount. You may have heard the idea, for example, that smiling makes you feel happier and think happy thoughts. The mere act of smiling matters so much that wearing a fake smile can fool you into feeling happy. The same basic idea applies to making breakthroughs more broadly. If you're trying to write a song on the guitar, you can get nowhere by humming melodies in your head, over and over, or you can pick up the instrument and begin strumming. Paul Simon found inspiration in a gospel tune, and he listened to that tune hundreds of times. But not until he picked up his guitar did the tune turn into more than idle inspiration. It was the marriage of inspiration and action that produced magic.

As important as actions are for unsticking in the moment, they're critical for building habits that make getting stuck less likely in the long run. Thinking or feeling the same thing every day is useful, but *doing* the same thing every day is much more likely to endure. In one study, an economist tracked the handwashing behavior of thirteen thousand health-care workers during more than 2 million shifts across five years. Hospitals struggle with this sort of compliance, many considering it a major sticking point. They introduce mantra-driven policies with names like "Gel-in, gel-out," which require workers to sanitize their hands every time they enter and exit a patient's room, but the results are modest. In this study, for example, compliance rates hovered around 50 or 60 percent for most workers. Some complied more than others, but across more than 100 million opportunities to sanitize, the health-care workers failed to wash their hands 52 *million* times. Each failure to sanitize is a potential disaster for patients with weakened immune systems, particularly as hospitals grapple with superbugs that respond poorly to antibiotics. Four percent of patients suffer a health-care-associated infection, and one hundred thousand die in US hospitals each year alone. Every 1 percent rise in hand sanitizing reduces these infections by 2 percent, so the stakes are significant.

The best way to predict whether health-care workers will wash their hands in the future is to consider how they've acted in the past. Compliance rates rise the more opportunities workers have to wash their hands in a particular room—to develop action habits that become automatic. By the tenth visit to a particular room, compliance rates rise 1.5 percent over their initial levels. By thirty visits, they rise by 2 percent, and by fifty visits by almost 3 percent. The more workers sanitize their hands, the less susceptible they become to fatigue. Those who develop action-based habits continue to sanitize their hands even as their shifts stretch beyond eight, nine, or ten hours—but those who haven't developed the same habit tend to sanitize much less often as the day wears on. Habitual sanitizers also continue sanitizing even after they've taken a weeklong break from work, whereas those who haven't formed those habits become noncompliant relatively quickly. Education and catchy policy names aren't enough to encourage compliance; what matters most is the act of washing over and over.

Action also matters because it changes how we see ourselves, which in turns unsticks us. If you run occasionally, you might tell someone, "I run," but if you run habitually, say four times a week, you might instead say, "I'm a runner." The difference is subtle but critical. "I run" focuses on the action that you do from time to time; but "I'm a runner" focuses on your essence. The label attaches itself to you, and you become a runner whether or not you're running at any particular moment. Running is central to your identity, so running regularly changes how you think and feel about yourself. Seeing yourself as a runner, rather than as someone who runs sometimes, is a great force for unsticking. A person who's struggling to exercise regularly after an extended illness has far less to overcome if she sees herself as a runner who has not been running recently, rather than as someone who hasn't run in a long time. A break in running doesn't compromise her status as a runner.

Psychologists have shown that doing an action repeatedly—moving from verb (run) to noun (runner)—prevents friction and encourages action across many contexts. People who say "I'm a voter" are more likely to vote than those who say "I vote." People who say "I'm a water saver" are more likely to conserve water than those who say "I save water." Kids aged three to six years are more likely to help an adult when they think of themselves as "being a helper" rather than merely "helping."

"Action" takes on different meanings in different contexts. Sometimes the appropriate unsticking act is obvious, as it was to Paul Simon sitting across from Dick Cavett.

Sometimes it's not as easy to act—or to find the right action. To act you need to be motivated, or to overcome the absence of motivation, and you need to be clear about which kind of action might work best. If you aren't a great songwriter picking up your guitar, the right next step isn't always clear. But when you're saddled with uncertainty, often the right next step is any step at all.

———

The value of action doesn't speak against taking one of Tara Brach's "sacred pauses." If you're anxious and uncertain how to proceed, pausing is valuable. But if you have a general sense of the direction in which you'd like to move, acting is the best way to get there. That's because of the bright line between being stuck and moving forward. As soon as you act, even modestly, you're no longer stuck. That's true no matter the context, and a kernel of action should be within reach no matter the situation.

Consider writing. Writing is hard. Some people write more fluidly than others, but almost everyone who writes gets stuck from time to time. To writers, the relevant kernel of action is a single word or a single sentence or, say, sixty seconds tapping at the keyboard. Sometimes, when I'm really stuck, I make one of these kernels my target. I might set the timer on my watch for, say, sixty seconds, and I'll write till the timer rings. I don't expect to write much, but writing briefly is an unsticking agent. I go from *not writing* to *writing*. If that sixty-second period passes easily—as often happens—I ignore the timer and continue writing. If I need more structure, I might reset the timer and write for two minutes, or ten minutes, and repeat the process after that period has passed. What's important isn't the quantity of action, but that action takes place at all.

Using a timer to govern behavior seems rigid, which might seem like exactly the wrong approach when you're stuck. What could be more constraining than rigidity? But structure turns out to be freeing when you're stuck. The more structure you have, the fewer decisions you need to make, and so the more cognitive capacity you have for the task at hand. If you know you're, say, writing for sixty seconds, all that remains is to allow your brain to empty its ideas onto the page. You've allowed your brain to do that because it isn't preoccupied with other questions like "What else could I be doing with this sixty-second period?" or "How long should I spend on this task before I give up completely?" When you're stuck, you can connect kernels of activity together. Write for several periods of a few minutes each, and then read for several periods of a few minutes each. Connecting these kernels is known as microscheduling.

Microscheduling requires breaking a longer time into briefer periods—chunks of ten, fifteen, or twenty minutes each, for example. Before that longer period begins, you decide how you'll use each chunk. You might plan to spend fifteen minutes writing; then fifteen minutes reading; then fifteen minutes taking a break; then fifteen minutes taking a walk; and so on. You can connect two chunks together if one particular task requires more time.

What matters when you microschedule is that you give yourself up to the schedule. You allow the schedule to dictate what you'll do, when, and for how long so you can concentrate on the act itself. So much of what paralyzes us when we're stuck isn't the act we're supposed to be doing, but rather the questions that hover above the act like a curious vulture. "Why is this so hard?" "Why am I not making more progress?" "Should I be doing something else instead?" "How much longer do I need to spend on this?" Most of those questions dissolve instantly when you microschedule because you're committed to spending a certain amount of time on the act no matter how difficult it is. By forcing yourself to spend that time on the task—by removing the option to disengage—you liberate yourself to focus on the task completely. By choosing a short burst of action, rather than a block of many hours, you're unlikely to feel overwhelmed. You silence the questioning voices in your head by defining your goal as simply and narrowly as possible—as the ability to simply spend a predetermined period on a certain action, regardless of your output.

Microscheduling isn't the way to live your life in general. Scheduling leisure time, for example, is the best way to strip it of pleasure, and the more precisely we structure our lives, the less time we feel we have. But when you're absolutely mired, with no apparent way through, rigidity is freeing. This is the same mental unloading that drove Steve Jobs to wear his black turtlenecks day after day, to adopt a "uniform" in an industry famous for lionizing creativity and difference, while working at a company that implored its consumers to "think different." Jobs himself was able to "think different," he claimed, because he was assiduous about delegating or shaving off any mental intrusion that might soak up the cognitive resources he needed to devote to creative unsticking.

Once you've microscheduled bite-size actions, the next question to ask is whether some actions more reliably unstick you than others. At least one class of candidate actions seems to unstick quite reliably. Several years ago two architects were poring over a data set that captured the locations of thousands of US firms. The data set included dozens of pieces of information about each location—or census tract, as the neighborhoods were known—and the level of innovation associated with the firms in each census tract. One result stood out to the researchers: firms that were located in highly walkable census tracts filed for many more patents—and so were more innovative—than those in census tracts that require cars or public transportation. This result wasn't definitive, but it suggested that walking, or moving more generally, might promote creative unsticking.

Other studies found similar results. One geographer found that early-stage start-ups tend to be in highly walkable census tracts, whereas more established firms tend to cluster in less walkable areas. "The mean walk score of science/tech start-ups was significantly higher than for any other group of firms," he noted, "and twenty points higher than for established tech firms." Early-stage start-ups, he argued, rely on creative unsticking far more than do established firms, which have usually moved beyond the stubborn "early ideas" phase of business.

These studies weren't definitive because dozens of factors might have explained the relationship between walkability and innovation. For example, innovative firms might prefer to be near one another so they can share ideas, which suggests that walking, per se, might not be what drives creativity. To test the idea more carefully, other researchers asked a small group of students to spend forty minutes reading a book while either sitting still or walking on a treadmill. The researchers administered a memory test later while the participants were hooked up to sensors that measured their brain activity as they completed the task. Those who'd walked on the treadmill for forty minutes recalled 35 percent more information, were more focused on the task, and showed increased activity in areas of the brain associated with memory and attention.

Dozens of studies have now shown that moving your body is a reliable path to mental unsticking. Both during and for some time after moving, your decisions are more incisive, you're more likely to generate creative solutions to problems that are designed to make you feel stuck, and you're more likely to work well with teams and groups that are trying to solve creativity problems in the workplace.

Walking unsticks you for many reasons. Walking and movement broadly are beneficial because they introduce change and variance. If you're sitting for hours a day, walking breaks the pattern, which, both metaphorically and more concretely, seems to break the pattern of being stuck. Among other techniques, author Hilary Mantel said getting away from her desk was the best remedy for writer's block. "Take a walk," she said, "exercise; whatever you do, don't just stick there scowling at the problem."

Fluid movement is particularly important when you're trying to get unstuck. Studies have shown, for example, that free-flowing dance, rhythmic walking, and even tracing smooth rather than jagged, disjointed shapes inspire creativity and insight. Other studies have shown that movement doesn't benefit every kind of thinking. Rather, it helps with stubborn problems that require innovation, novelty, and creativity, but less so with problems that simply require focused attention. You may not solve dozens of simple math puzzles more accurately, but you're more likely to generate creative and unusual uses for a brick or a paper clip or a bucket of paint. These creativity tasks measure so-called divergent thinking, which requires you to think broadly, rather than narrowly and precisely, about a subject. Divergent thinking is critical for unsticking, because thinking convergently—focusing more and more narrowly on the task at hand—is probably what got you stuck in the first place. Divergence solves the problem by taking you beyond your instincts and intuitions to ideas and approaches that are relatively well hidden.

———

Strategically lowering your standards is another excellent way to move forward when you're stuck. That's the position of Jeff Tweedy, the singer and guitarist in the bands Wilco and Uncle Tupelo, who has also written one of the best how-to guides for frustrated creatives. Tweedy writes about his ongoing struggle with addiction and mental health issues, so it's natural to assume his music is the product of suffering. This is one popular model of creativity: that sublime art, music, and writing are almost always the silver lining encompassing a cloud of suffering. Not so, says Tweedy. In an interview with Ezra Klein of the *New York Times*, Tweedy dispelled the idea that suffering fuels his creativity. Instead, he suggested that art was a medication for suffering. People misunderstand the relationship between art and suffering: it's not that suffering produces great art, but that people who suffer tend to medicate themselves by turning to creative pursuits. "I think it's a horrible cop-out," Tweedy says, "and it's a pervasive myth. . . . If that was all it took, there'd be so much more great art."

Suffering isn't Tweedy's key to creativity. Instead, he overcomes creative roadblocks by "disappearing"—by ignoring his presence in creativity by jettisoning all self-consciousness, and allowing whatever occupies his mind to pour forth. That means lowering the filters that might normally critique new ideas as "not quite good enough." Tweedy told Klein that he's least likely to succeed when he's self-critical: "I think if I'm putting really high demands on what I want to come out of myself, or when I'm just coming at it wanting to get something out of it, thinking I'm going to get a song out of this—I feel like I'm aiming at the wrong thing."

Tweedy's approach is to act consistently but without self-criticism or self-reflection. In his case that means writing prose, or composing music, for ten or fifteen minutes a day either before he leaves his bed in the morning or before he fires up his smartphone to read the news and check his emails:

> Like all types of writers—poets, authors, songwriters—I do rely upon a certain amount of freewriting, and emptying yourself with regularity, as a daily practice. So I would start there for anybody wanting to do this. Just exercise the muscle that pushes the ego out of the way. And that, to me, is just getting better

and better at writing without judgment, without direction, without trying to steer your mind to the specific things that make you feel good about yourself, or make you think you're smart, or make you think you're writing well.

This is acting without the baggage of emotion and thought, and for Tweedy it has produced decades of creative output—hundreds of songs, several books, and plenty of good ideas. All of this *despite*, not because of, his complicated history of mental health and addiction struggles.

Tweedy takes this idea further than simply being nonjudgmental, though. He recommends not only giving yourself a pass when you're stuck, but actively "emptying" your mind of baggage every day. Klein struggles at being bad at things, he tells Tweedy—to be a bad drawer or poet. Tweedy takes a different tack, overtly trying to produce bad work. As he explains, "To avoid writer's block, I write songs I don't like. I get an idea for a song, and I just go ahead and do it, even though I don't think I'm going to like it. And that frees me up to go to the next song."

This "emptying" is a kind of unsticking magic because it achieves two things that are difficult when you're stuck: it frees you to act with little emotional or mental baggage, and it puts no demands on the output that flows from your actions.

Obviously writing the worst poem or song or generally performing poorly isn't the desired end. But it moves you from inert to active. Instead of being stuck, you're moving. Once you're moving—and once you've emptied your mind of its worst ideas—you're primed to start making real progress. There's support for this idea, too. Entertaining bad ideas is likely to produce good ideas in time by showing you what doesn't work. In some experiments, for example, people who hold strong beliefs about a topic are asked to think about the strongest arguments against, or the weakest arguments in favor of, those beliefs as a means to shoring up their intellectual positions. You improve by learning the difference between what works and what doesn't, and you can fast-track that learning by forcing yourself to produce what doesn't work before you strive to succeed. This is inoculation by opposition: the idea that you can protect yourself from failure and "doing a bad job" by exhausting yourself of bad ideas before you make a concerted effort to succeed.

Another reason to privilege the number of actions you take, rather than their quality, is that quality follows from quantity. People who generate more creative ideas tend to have better ideas, all else equal. The same is true of actions. The more you act, the more likely one of those actions is to move you forward, and the higher the average quality of those actions is likely to be. Quantity and quality may be related because both rely to a large extent on your ability to lower your filters and inhibitions. Filters and inhibitions stifle the production of new ideas and tend to produce ideas that hew to accepted norms and standards, rather than the creative or unusual ideas that might unstick you. Jeff Tweedy's approach to creativity is grounded in a similar kind of disinhibition: the importance of switching off the judgmental voice in your head that forces you to question the quality of your ideas even as you're generating them. Bad ideas are the essential foundations, Tweedy suggests, on which good ideas are built. The simple rule is that you should allow yourself to think and act "badly," "wrongly," and "poorly," particularly if lowering the bar gives you permission to think and act more fluently and reliably than you otherwise might. There's nothing wrong with being wrong if wrongness reliably predicts the arrival of rightness.

———

One hallmark of learning is "wrongness that reliably precedes rightness," and broadly speaking there are two ways to learn new things. You can learn by accumulating information, or you can learn by doing. Most schools convey information using the first approach, but in the real world, learning by doing tends to be the great unsticker. Of the world's many experiential learners, Hamilton Naki must rank among the most successful.

Naki was born in 1926 in a small village in South Africa's Eastern Cape Province. His formal education was limited by apartheid and opportunity. Naki's six years of schooling came to a close when he was fourteen, and he eventually moved seven hundred miles west to work as a gardener in Cape Town.

As a Black man in apartheid South Africa, Naki was forbidden from pursuing a range of elite professions. It would have been difficult for him to study, let alone to practice, law or medicine, for example, but from a young age Naki had an eye on the medical profession. As he was forced to observe from a distance, the closest he got to a medical career in those early days was to tend the grounds of the University of Cape Town. One day, when Naki was in his late twenties, a surgeon approached the gardening foreman asking for help with a range of basic lab duties. Naki was working that day, and soon he was feeding, cleaning, and anesthetizing animals in the university's research lab.

Naki split his time between gardening and lab work, but the medical lab captured his imagination. Over time, he spent more and more time in the lab, attempting and then mastering increasingly technical procedures that were generally reserved for advanced students or even medical graduates. Naki was unusually dexterous, a skill he so honed that eminent surgeons sought him out as an anesthesia assistant. Eventually, he became the lab's principal surgical aide.

In the mid-1960s, Naki began working with heart surgeon Christiaan Barnard. Barnard was a star transplant surgeon, and the head of the university's department of experimental surgery. In 1967, Barnard would perform the world's first human-to-human heart transplant on a fifty-five-year-old man with incurable heart disease. (Naki didn't attend the transplant procedure, though at his death in 2005 a number of reports and obituaries claimed in error that he acted as Barnard's surgical partner.) Barnard's opinion carried tremendous weight, and he praised Naki publicly and often. "Hamilton Naki had better technical skills than I did," Barnard said some years later. "He was a better craftsman than me, especially when it came to stitching, and had very good hands in the theater." During another interview, Barnard described Naki as "one of the great researchers of all time in the field of heart transplants. . . . If Hamilton had had the chance to study, he probably would have become a brilliant surgeon."

Though Naki never operated directly on humans, he pioneered a number of surgical techniques and taught thousands of medical students. Eventually, he left Barnard's lab to specialize in liver transplantation. Naki eventually taught Del Khan, who became the head of the university hospital's organ-transplant department. "A liver transplant on a pig in the US would involve a team of two or three medically qualified surgeons," Khan said during an interview. "Hamilton can do this all on his own." Ralph Kirsch, the head of the hospital's liver-research unit, described Naki as "one of those remarkable men who really come around once in a long time. As a man without any education, he mastered surgical techniques at the highest level and passed them on to young doctors." Naki's career was therefore a triumph of *action* over passive learning—of doing over simply consuming information. In an era when the color of his skin was a major sticking point, what unstuck Naki was a combination of opportunity and experience.

Naki's story is both personal and sociological. He overcame individual barriers, but also challenged the juggernaut of apartheid as one of the first Black men to approach the peak of the medical research field in South Africa. It's almost impossible to shatter systemic barriers with thoughts and feelings alone, and what made Naki's story irresistible to journalists and medical journals was the improbability of his ascent, and the concrete actions that carried him from the gardens at the University of Cape Town to its lecture halls and research labs.

As Naki demonstrated, sometimes nothing short of action can convince people that a barrier is surmountable. In this sense, action unsticks at the level of populations just as it unsticks individuals. This was true of runner Roger Bannister, and mountaineer Edmund Hillary, two pioneers who changed how the world viewed their respective sports during a twelve-month period in the mid-1950s. Bannister ran a mile in three minutes and fifty-nine seconds in May 1954, breaking the four-minute barrier for the first time. The mile record had fallen dozens of times since the 1850s, but a race time that began with the digit 3 seemed impossible. The record barely budged for a decade, hovering around the four-minute-one-second mark between 1944 and 1954. But as soon as Bannister showed there was nothing magical about the four-minute mark, the record plunged. Just one month after his three fifty-nine, Australian John Landy ran the mile in three fifty-eight. By 1964, ten years after Bannister's historic race, the record time had fallen five times, to three fifty-four.

The same was true after Hillary reached the peak of Mount Everest with Sherpa Tenzing Norgay, in 1953. When the two men ascended the mountain, they licensed others to break the same barrier. Soon a trickle and then a flood of climbers attempted the feat, and today more than five thousand mountaineers have summited Everest. A successful act—particularly an audacious act that surmounts conspicuous boundaries—unsticks others who may be game to try themselves, but prefer to be second or third movers rather than pioneers. Only a particular and rare personality tackles the kinds of boundaries that Naki, Bannister, Hillary, and Norgay overcame in the 1950s and 1960s, but the obliteration of those barriers even once licenses others to try, too. Firsts are hard; seconds and thirds are slightly less daunting because the task is obviously possible; and the attempts that follow become progressively less threatening because they're both anonymous and enjoy the confidence that comes from seeing others succeed.

Acting is the king of unstickers because it is propulsive by definition. You can't act and be inert, and as Jeff Tweedy observed, even writing deliberately bad poetry or courting failure more broadly brings delayed progress. Empty yourself of bad ideas and unskilled actions and you'll learn to recognize their productive counterparts—and learn to be less judgmental as you progress from sticking point to breakthrough. But perhaps the strongest argument for acting is that it's the best way to learn, and learning is the greatest unsticker. By learning to recognize the difference between what works and what doesn't, we become better thinkers, partners, parents, friends, entrepreneurs, artists, writers, and musicians.

CONCLUSION

100 WAYS TO GET UNSTUCK

I've given hundreds of academic lectures. One of the rules I was taught early is "After the punch line, wrap up as quickly as possible." People don't want to wade through dozens of concluding slides, glancing at the clock as they wonder how long you'll stand between them and lunch.

In that spirit, I'm not going to leave you with a traditional epilogue. Instead, consider this a cheat sheet: a summarized collection of one hundred unsticking techniques and principles I covered in *Anatomy of a Breakthrough*.

I hope you find yourself stuck only rarely and that when you do, breakthroughs aren't too far behind.

Introduction: The First Rule Is That You Will Get Stuck

1. The first step to getting unstuck is accepting that barriers are universal.
2. When you see other people succeeding, remember you're getting the "after" shot; the "before" shot included one or two or a hundred barriers that were hidden from you.
3. You'll be stuck for reasons within your control, and reasons beyond your control. Learn to distinguish them, and focus your energy on addressing the reasons within your control.

Chapter 1: Why Getting Stuck Is Inevitable

4. When you're tackling an extended goal, expect lulls in the middle. This almost always happens, and it's known as the goal gradient. You'll gather speed early, and again late, but in the middle you'll probably find yourself stuck.

5. The best way to avoid lulls in the middle is to shorten the middle. Break bigger goals into subgoals or smaller chunks that eliminate or shrink the midpoint. This is called narrow bracketing.

6. More broadly, plateaus are inevitable. Many will happen near the middle, but some may happen early and others late in the process. There's no one size fits all when it comes to sticking points.

7. The best way to avoid plateaus is by varying your approach; by adopting new and different methods and strategies over time.

8. To avoid plateaus, make the majority of your decisions for the long term. Occasionally you can prioritize the short term, but across time you'll get stuck less often, and move more smoothly, if you aren't greedy about short-term gains.

9. Natural end points—like the end of a decade of your life span (age twenty-nine, thirty-nine, etc.)—are overwhelming, and they tend to drive short-term, myopic decisions. Learn to recognize when your decisions may be driven by these irrelevant, extraneous forces.

10. The flip side: these natural end points can be motivating. If you lack motivation, end points are springboards for action.

11. You'll probably experience modest life changes every year or two—and large "lifequakes" that are major sticking points every decade or so. No one escapes at least a few of these across the life span.

12. There's no one way to respond to a lifequake, but it's useful to anticipate them, because accepting and recognizing them is the first step toward moving beyond them.

13. Beyond the midpoint lull, people often get stuck immediately before a goal. This happens particularly when they apportion their resources *almost perfectly*—but fall slightly short. If you've ever seen long-distance runners collapse just short of the finish line, you'll recognize the idea. This ability to apportion energy is known as teleoanticipation, and while humans do it well, even a modest error creates sticking points.

14. Some goals don't have obvious end points—and you're far more likely to get stuck in the face of these boundless goals. You can overcome this issue by creating artificial waypoints that break the goal into chunks.

Chapter 2: Keep Going

15. Before you quit, keep going for longer than you believe you should. Most successes take longer than people anticipate.

16. People mistakenly tend to believe their best ideas, and their best work more broadly, will come early in a process. That's not true. This is known as the creative cliff. Often your best ideas come later.

17. People tend to associate challenges with failure. But challenges—and the sense that you're struggling—are a signal that you're moving beyond the obvious. The obvious rarely produces great results, so struggling past the obvious is an early signal that you're on the path to success.

18. At the same time, learn to quit when the costs of continuing massively dwarf the benefits of continuing.

19. Time is your friend. The longer you spend on any task—and the older you are in general—the more experience you gain, and the more likely you are to overcome sticking points.

20. Slow down. Being a first mover is almost always a recipe for long-term failure. Being second or third or twentieth is often more rewarding.

21. Duration = success. Last longer in almost any domain and you're more likely to succeed.

22. Success is lumpy and difficult to predict—and the role of luck varies by career and domain. If you're dealing with a luck-laden domain, longevity is even more important.

23. A lot of sticking points arise through mismatches in timing. It's not good to have a good idea too late—but it's also easy to get stuck when your good ideas come too early. Learn to identify when you're stuck because a good idea is timed poorly by considering the prevailing technological, political, cultural, and economic context.

Chapter 3: Traps and Lures

24. Many stubborn traps don't look like traps at all—which is a large part of what makes them so stubborn. We respond to them too slowly or not at all.

25. It's difficult to be truly novel in any domain. It's smarter to strive for modest differences and advances. This is known as optimal distinctiveness.

26. You're rarely as well understood as you think you are—particularly when you aren't communicating face-to-face and can't see how people are reacting to you. Assume people are significantly less savvy—and that you're significantly less savvy a communicator—and you'll generally avoid miscommunication sticking points.

27. Small communication gaps are often bigger problems than large communication gaps. Two people speaking slightly different dialects are more likely to get stuck in a miscommunication loop than are two people who speak completely different languages. This is known as the pseudo-intelligibility trap.

28. We ignore small problems longer than larger problems—and that makes smaller problems more difficult to overcome. They

also often turn into larger problems when ignored. Deal with small problems soon—or at least make a plan for dealing with them later.

29. Preventive maintenance is better than treating issues as they arise. Form a plan for anticipating and sanding away future friction points before they become barriers.

30. Learn to find a sweet spot between smooth, slow, continuous progress and bursts of rapid progress punctuated by sticking points.

31. Think ahead. When you make any decision, ask yourself how it will affect you in a year, five years, ten years, and twenty years.

32. Much of the time we're stuck because we're focusing too myopically—on the short term—when we should be focusing on the medium and long term. Learn to vividly paint a mental picture of the future whenever you're making decisions and choices that will have implications beyond the immediate present.

Chapter 4: Exhale

33. Mental traps are often more dangerous than physical traps. Humans deal quickly with physical traps, but slowly, if at all, with mental traps.

34. Removing pressure from yourself and others is the first (easy) step to improving creativity and general performance.

35. Our culture celebrates boldness, but—as with moving first—it's often a trap. Being slightly less bold, and slightly more careful, is almost always a better approach.

36. When you're paralyzed by a decision or a task, imagine the worst-case outcome that might follow your next step. If it's either revocable (you can undo it) or bearable (you can deal with it), move ahead. A mindset of *radical acceptance* in the face of anxiety eliminates or shrinks most anxiety-driven sticking points.

37. Learn when to maximize and when to satisfice (find an option that's just good enough). Occasionally, in limited situations, you should maximize. The vast majority of the time, though, satisficing is sufficient, and less likely to fix you in place.

38. Strive for excellence rather than perfection. Striving for perfection is one of the surest guarantees you'll find yourself stuck.

39. Make large tasks granular. Focus on one aspect of the larger task at a time. Rarely if ever focus on more than one at a time.

40. When stuck, your instinct will be to thrash about mentally. The quicker you override that urge, the more briefly you'll find yourself stuck.

41. Many of us adopt the stubborn, unhelpful mantra to set high standards. Setting standards that are too high, rather than progressively raising them across time, is a sure road to friction. In general, lower your standards by default unless there's an excellent reason why good enough isn't good enough.

Chapter 5: Pause Before You Play

42. We're driven to make progress, which we measure by action. Appraising for an extra minute, day, or year is often a cure to getting stuck in the longer term. Engage less and prepare more.

43. Anxiety levels vary, but even the best performers in any domain experience anxiety. Giving yourself a pass for being anxious in the midst of sticking points is one of the best routes to getting unstuck.

44. In moments of anxiety and tension we tend to focus on ourselves. It's far more productive to focus outward—on others, and on the situation at large—particularly when anxiety fixes us in place.

45. Embrace silence—also called the sacred pause. Resist the urge to make noise (whether spoken or otherwise) just to end a silence.

46. When anxious, adopt the RAIN approach: *recognize* what is arising; *allow* it to be there; *investigate* your emotions and thoughts (e.g., "What is happening in my body now?"); *note* what is happening from moment to moment.

47. Exposing yourself to modest discomfort makes you more resilient in the long run and reveals hidden weaknesses.

48. When timing isn't governed by someone or something else, wait till you're ready. Pausing till you're in that ready state makes it far less likely you'll get stuck later.

Chapter 6: Failing Well

49. The more driven you are, the more likely you are to be hard on yourself. Many of the greatest success stories are from people who were surprisingly lenient on themselves when they made mistakes.

50. Make room for failure. Don't just accept it when it happens; invite it to happen.

51. Build failure into any extended forecast. Assume it'll happen significantly more often than you first imagine.

52. The optimal failure rate to stay motivated—and not to get stuck—is roughly one in five or one in six, in most situations. If you're failing more than every fifth or sixth attempt, you'll get stuck in the short term. If you're failing less than every fifth or sixth attempt, you'll get stuck in the long term.

53. People react to winning quite uniformly. They react to losing with a huge variety of responses that range from very useful to completely self-defeating. You can learn to move yourself toward the useful end of the spectrum.

54. Put yourself through stress tests. If you expect you'll need to deal with a particular challenge, prepare by putting yourself through a challenge 20 or 50 or 200 percent greater.

55. The flip side of stress tests: If you're overwhelmed by a

challenge, desensitize yourself by tackling scaled-down versions of the challenge at first. Over time, increase the dosage till you approach the full dosage.

56. It's a mistake to ration praise. You can never give too much *deserved* praise to yourself or other people.

57. If you don't deal with your lower-order needs first—food, shelter, emotional safety, and so on—you'll never be able to tackle loftier sticking points.

Chapter 7: Friction Audits and the Art of Simplification

58. Actively seek out patterns across challenges and experiences. Patterns help you understand and simplify what at first seems novel, which makes those barriers less imposing.

59. Complete *friction audits* often. Look for friction points; sand them down; assess whether you've successfully eliminated them. Repeat.

60. Look for rules and algorithms, which will guide you most of the way most of the time. Don't be afraid to stand on the shoulders of giants, or to hitch a piggyback when it's made available.

61. One of the greatest unsticking skills isn't recognizing what's most important, but recognizing what *isn't* important. Strip any problem down to its bare essentials, and it becomes far easier to overcome.

62. When tackling a problem, we usually begin by making the situation more complex. Often, the best solution is to subtract. Begin by looking to simplify, then consider adding complexity.

63. Rules and algorithms are valuable—but they're almost all optional. Before you blindly apply a rule, ask if it's essential, consider alternatives, and then only implement it if it seems the best way forward.

64. From time to time, impose artificial constraints on yourself. They'll improve your performance once they're removed, and

they'll force you to look for new, subtly different approaches to the problems you've been tackling the same way for months or years.

Chapter 8: Recombination and Pivoting

65. Instead of keeping an eye out for big leaps forward, look for small steps that ask relatively little of you. Take those first, unless they compromise your ability to take larger steps later.

66. Nothing is truly original. Don't strive for radical originality, which will only paralyze you.

67. Strive for original combinations of two or more existing ideas. This is the recipe that drives the vast majority of what we consider new and innovative.

68. Hold your ideas lightly. Look for opportunities to pivot and adjust.

69. Embrace beginnerhood. Being an expert is narrowing, and once you're an expert, it's almost impossible to return to the mind-expanding experience of being a novice. Don't race toward narrowness and depth (but get there eventually, because that's how you differentiate yourself).

Chapter 9: Diversity and Crowdsourcing

70. Seek other people's opinions. Seek many more than you think you need. Seek them before, during, and after you tackle any task, experience, or problem.

71. Seek, particularly, the opinions of novices and outsiders—smart people who aren't domain experts.

72. Seek nonredundancy. Assemble a motley band of people to critique, comment on, and verify every idea or path forward. Friends can offer moral support, but they're less likely to bring intellectual benefits because they're often too similar to you and everyone else you know.

73. A good black sheep, brought into the fold, is often better than an excellent in-house expert. That's particularly likely to be true after excellent in-house experts have failed once or twice already.

74. Even incompetent or barely competent outsiders provide some value through their diversity.

75. The value of diversity and nonredundancy goes up the more complex the task. Simple tasks work best with teams of people who think and approach issues the same way; complex tasks benefit from difference.

76. Crowdsource particularly complex problems. Ask people you've never met, possibly by the thousand or more, for advice and input.

77. Learn to be your own therapist. Question your own decisions the way a smart outsider might. Ask yourself complex questions more than once, answering with a different lens each time. This takes advantage of the so-called wisdom of the inner crowd.

78. The four steps when tapping into the inner crowd: First, assume that your initial estimate is off the mark; second, think about a few reasons why that could be. Which assumptions and considerations could have been wrong? Third, what do these new considerations imply? Was the first estimate too high or too low? Fourth, based on this new perspective, make a second, alternative estimate.

Chapter 10: Experimentation

79. Conduct experiments. Knowledge evolves constantly, and we're almost always wrong to assume that the way any one thing is now done is optimal. All ideas are updated over time—and much of that updating comes from smart experiments.

80. When stuck, cycle rapidly through the OODA loop: *observe, orient, decide,* and *act.*

81. Experiments are also useful if you're trying to unstick other people's minds—they're the most convincing demonstrations that a new approach or idea might outperform an existing approach or idea.

82. Learn to be curious the way children are curious. Adults become less naturally curious over time, which helpfully allows us to focus, but sabotages us when we're stuck.

83. Collect data whenever you can about whatever you can. About yourself, about your actions, about your ideas.

Chapter 11: Exploring and Exploiting

84. Explore first. Roam widely, but shallowly.

85. Next, exploit. Once you've identified fruitful pastures, go narrow, and develop expertise.

86. If you're not sure whether you're exploring or exploiting, do a "yes/no audit." If you say yes to most requests and new opportunities, you're in explore mode. If you say no more often, you're either exploiting or you're disengaged.

87. The Pareto principle suggests gains are lumpy. Some decisions and actions bring huge gains, but the vast majority bring no gains at all. If you can identify which is which, spend time on the actions that bring huge gains. If you can't identify which is which, don't worry about spending a lot of time and energy making only modest progress. That's the inevitable downside of lumpiness, but it's the necessary cost to enjoying the rarer nuggets of rapid progress.

88. You can prepare for serendipity—a blend of luck and skill. Some people seem luckier than others, but much of that luck is invited by skill.

89. Allow your mind to wander. A lot of excellent ideas come from what seems like idle mind wandering.

90. The difference between excellent and merely good performance

often comes down to capitalizing on near misses. It's critical to recognize and harness near misses.

Chapter 12: Action above All

91. When you're stuck, act. Those actions should feel comfortable—and ideally they should be actions at which you excel.

92. Acting is the best way to build helpful habits that prevent long-term friction.

93. To drive yourself forward when you're stuck, describe yourself using nouns rather than verbs. "I'm a runner" drives people to run on days when they feel lazy. "I run" doesn't. The former describes who you are at your essence; the latter merely describes what you do.

94. Do very, very small things when large or even moderate things are overwhelming. Small things take you from stuck to unstuck, even if you're making only modest progress initially. That binary leap is the first step in making meaningful progress.

95. Rigidity—doing the same thing over and over, or sticking to a strict regime—is paradoxically freeing when you're stuck. Being rigid about some things allows you to be more flexible about others. Selectively embrace rigidity.

96. Moving your body is one of the best ways to unstick yourself mentally. That's particularly true if you've been sitting—or sedentary—for long periods. It's especially true of movements that feel fluent.

97. If you're striving for a quality product and you're stuck, begin by pouring out your worst. Do the exact opposite of what you're striving to do, which "empties out" the bad, liberates the good.

98. When you're striving for creativity or novelty, quality and quantity overlap. The more ideas you have, the higher their quality will be (both the best idea and the average of those

ideas). Don't interrogate those ideas too closely at first. Allow them to emerge, then question them later.

99. Learning and education are key, but *doing* the thing you're learning is essential. (This rule borrows from the medical school guideline for mastering new procedures: see one; do one; teach one. The quicker you progress from consuming information to acting, the quicker you'll learn.)

100. Artificial barriers function as sticking points—think of the four-minute mile, for example. These are largely illusory (as evidenced by the number of people who broke the four-minute barrier soon after it was broken for the first time). Don't allow artificial barriers to mire you.

ACKNOWLEDGMENTS

Writing is a balance of being stuck and breaking through. I'm fortunate that *Anatomy of a Breakthrough* was more breakthrough than roadblock thanks to a cast of family, friends, colleagues, and contributors.

A huge thank-you to the teams at Simon & Schuster and InkWell Management: at Simon & Schuster, in particular to my generous and incisive editor, Eamon Dolan, who pointed me in the right direction when I was stuck, and nudged me to refine my wooliest ideas. Also at Simon & Schuster, thanks to Jonathan Karp, Tzipora Baitch, Rebecca Rozenberg, Alyssa diPierro, Sara Kitchen, Jackie Seow, Irene Kheradi, Amanda Mulholland, and Max Smith. At InkWell, thanks to my wise, generous agent, Richard Pine, who continues to be as much a friend, cheerleader, and teacher of Yiddishisms as he is a font of excellent advice and unwavering good taste. At InkWell, thanks also to Alexis Hurley, Eliza Rothstein, Laura Hill, Hannah Lehmkuhl, Tizom Pope, and Jessie Thorsted.

For reading earlier drafts of *Anatomy of a Breakthrough*, sharing their ideas, and patiently answering my questions, thanks to Nicole Airey, Dean Alter, Jenny Alter, Ian Alter, Sara Alter, David Berkoff, Andrea Bonezzi, Ben Caunt, Shai Davidai, Max Deutsch, David Epstein, Bruce Feiler, John Finger, Scott Galloway, Malcolm Gladwell, Hal Hershfield, Brian Lucas, Steve Magness, Tom Meyvis, Cal Newport, Mike Olesker, Suzy Olesker, Eesha Sharma, and Charles Yao. Thanks also to my many friends and colleagues at New York University, particularly in the marketing department at the Stern School of Business, who inspired many of the ideas in this book.

And thanks, always, to the great unstickers who make every breakthrough possible: my wife, Sara; my son, Sam, and daughter, Izzy; my parents, Ian and Jenny; and Suzy and Mike and my brother, Dean.

NOTES

Introduction: The First Rule Is That You Will Get Stuck

xi *Brianne Desaulniers was born in Sacramento, California, in 1989*: For more on Brie Larson's childhood and acting background, see A. Radloff, "Meet Brie Larson, the Rising Star You Need to Know About in 2014," *Glamour*, January 14, 2014, https://www.glamour.com/story/the-rising-star-you-need-to-kn; L. Sandell, "Brie Larson's 20-Year Climb to Overnight Stardom: 'I'm Totally out of My Comfort Zone,'" *Hollywood Reporter*, January 20, 2016, https://www.hollywoodreporter.com/features/brie-larsons-20-year-climb-857011; T. Lewis, "Brie Larson Interview: 'I Just Wanted to Do Weird Stuff,'" *Guardian*, October 19, 2013, https://www.theguardian.com/film/2013/oct/20/brie-larson-short-term-12-interview.

xii *On August 13, 2020, she uploaded a fourteen-minute*: B. Larson, "Audition Storytime! (pt. 1)," YouTube, August 13, 2020, https://www.youtube.com/watch?v=zE3togjm2tw.

xii *In the second part of "Audition Storytime"*: B. Larson, "Audition Storytime! (pt. 2)," YouTube, September 3, 2020, https://www.youtube.com/watch?v=t9CcjI0SOcU.

xiii *The first lies in the headwinds/tailwinds asymmetry*: See, for example, S. Davidai and T. Gilovich, "The Headwinds/Tailwinds Asymmetry: An Availability Bias in Assessments of Barriers and Blessings," *Journal of Personality and Social Psychology* 111 (2016): 835–51; K. Hansson et al., "Losing Sense of Fairness: How Information about a Level Playing Field Reduces Selfish Behavior," *Journal of Economic Behavior & Organization* 190 (2021): 66–75; C. Sanchez and T. Gilovich, "The Perceived Impact of Tax and Regulatory Changes," *Journal of Applied Social Psychology* 50 (2020): 104–14.

xv *"At the time, I had one thousand dollars"*: C. McCann, "Scaling Airbnb with Brian Chesky," Medium, November 20, 2015, https://medium.com/cs183c-blitzscaling-class-collection/scaling-airbnb-with-brian-chesky-class-18-notes-of-stanford-university-s-cs183c-3fcf75778358.

xvi *In the summer of 2015 he shared screenshots*: B. Chesky, "Seven Rejections," Medium, July 12, 2015, https://medium.com/@bchesky/7-rejections-7d894cbaa084.

xvii *"Amazon launched in July 1995, and every Xmas"*: Tweet thread begins at @DanRose999, Twitter, September 12, 2020, https://twitter.com/DanRose999/status/1304896586086928384?s=20&t=jnuKEFcoCdIZ4s2QnX9-Iw.

xviii *In an interview Wilke gave*: "Keynote: Fireside with Jeff Wilke," Amazon Seller University, YouTube, September 30, 2020, https://www.youtube.com/watch?v=bLMWu90O45U.

xviii *The company had gone public in May 1997*: For a summary of Amazon's early critical press, see M. Novak, "Here's What People Thought of Amazon When It First Launched in the 1990s," Gizmodo, July 3, 2019, https://paleofuture.gizmodo.com/heres-what-people-thought-of-amazon-when-it-first-launc-1836008229.

xix *A young Fred Astaire complained of being stuck*: See, for example, A. Tate, "Celebs Who Went from Failures to Success Stories," CBS News, July 12, 2019, https://www.cbsnews.com/pictures/celebs-who-went-from-failures-to-success-stories/2/; "33 Famous People Who Failed Before They Succeeded," *Business Insider India*, October 27, 2016, https://www.businessinsider.in/careers/33-famous-people-who-failed-before-they-succeeded/slidelist/55102204.cms.

xix *Close famously claimed*: A. Henry, "Chuck Close's Advice on Inspiration and Getting Things Done," Lifehacker, August 2, 2016, https://lifehacker.com/chuck-closes-advice-on-inspiration-and-getting-things-d-1784527805.

xix *Harper Lee flirted with a similar fate*: S. Marche, "Harper Lee's Last Year Was the Most Interesting of Her Career," *Esquire*, February 19, 2016, https://www.esquire.com/entertainment/books/news/a42282/harper-lee-death-marche/.

xx *Martin has been candid about his struggles*: J. Hibberd, "George RR Martin Gets Candid about New Book," *Entertainment Weekly*, November 19, 2018, https://ew.com/author-interviews/2018/11/19/george-rr-martin-interview/; J. Pantozzi, "George RR Martin Is Just Like All of Us," Mary Sue, July 25, 2013, https://www.themarysue.com/grrm-writing-troubles/.

xxi *The same "block" affects other creatives, too*: See, for example, J. Acocella, "Blocked: Why Do Writers Stop Writing?," *New Yorker*, June 14, 2004, https://www.newyorker.com/magazine/2004/06/14/blocked; M. Castillo, "Writer's Block," *American Journal of Neuroradiology* 35 (2014): 1043–44; R. Winston, "How Great Artists Have Fought Creative Block," BBC News, July 27, 2010, https://www.bbc.com/news/magazine-10766308; M. Kantor, *Understanding Writer's Block: A Therapist's Guide to Diagnosis and Treatment* (Westport, CT: Praeger, 1995); R. Sharp, "How Pollock, Picasso, and Seven Other Iconic Artists Overcame Creative Block," Artsy, June 30, 2015, https://www.artsy.net/article/artsy-editorial-how-pollock-picasso-and-6-other-iconic-artists.

xxi *hundreds of English art lovers voted his Water Lilies series*: H. Furness, "The Nation's Favorite Paintings Revealed," *Telegraph*, February 22, 2015, https://www.telegraph.co.uk/news/newstopics/howaboutthat/11427972/The-nations-favourite-paintings-revealed.html.

xxii *Psychologists call this a classic case of pluralistic ignorance*: D. A. Prentice and D. T. Miller, "Pluralistic Ignorance and Alcohol Use on Campus: Some Consequences of Misperceiving the Social Norm," *Journal of Personality and Social Psychology* 64 (1993): 243–56.

Chapter 1: Why Getting Stuck Is Inevitable

3 *Hull spent three decades as a professor at Yale*: On Hull's research, see, for example, C. L. Hull, "The Goal-Gradient Hypothesis Applied to Some 'Field-Force' Problems in the Behavior of Young Children," *Psychological Review* 45 (1938): 271–99; C. L. Hull, "The Conflicting Psychologies of Learning: A Way Out," *Psychological Review* 42 (1935): 491–516; C. L. Hull, "The Concept of the Habit-Family Hierarchy and Maze Learning: Part II," *Psychological Review* 41 (1934): 134–52. On Hull's early life and development, see C. L. Hull, "Clark L. Hull: A History of Psychology in Autobiography," *Psychological Review* 57 (1950): 173–80; C. I. Hovland, "Clark Leonard Hull, 1884–1952," *Psychological Review* 59 (1952): 347–50.

4 *In one experiment from a paper published in 2006*: R. Kivetz, O. Urminsky, and Y. Zheng, "The Goal-Gradient Hypothesis Resurrected: Purchase Acceleration, Illusionary Goal Progress, and Customer Retention," *Journal of Marketing Research* 43, no. 1 (2006): 39–58.

4 *In one experiment designed by my NYU colleague Andrea Bonezzi*: A. Bonezzi, C. M. Brendl, and M. De Angelis, "Stuck in the Middle: The Psychophysics of Goal Pursuit," *Psychological Science* 22 (2011): 607–12.

5 *As researchers continued to monitor goal progress in other domains*: See, for example, C. E. Cryder, G. Loewenstein, and S. Seltman, "Goal Gradient in Helping Behavior," *Journal of Experimental Social Psychology* 49 (2013): 1078–83; J. D. Jensen, A. J. King, and N. Carcioppolo, "Driving toward a Goal and the Goal-Gradient Hypothesis: The Impact of Goal Proximity on Compliance Rate, Donation Size, and Fatigue," *Journal of Applied Social Psychology* 43 (2013): 1881–95; M. R. vanDellen, J. Rajbhandari-Thapa, and J. Sevilla, "Does Serving Vegetables in Partitioned Portions Promote Vegetable Consumption?," *Food Quality and Preference* 78 (2019): 103750; A. Emanuel, "Perceived Impact as the Underpinning Mechanism of the End-Spurt and U-shape Pacing Patterns," *Frontiers in Psychology* 10 (2019): 1082; Z. Meng, Y. Yang, and C. K. Hsee, "The Mere Urgency Effect," *Journal of Consumer Research* 45 (2018): 673–90; M. Lukas, "The Goal Gradient Effect and Repayments in Consumer Credit," *Economics Letters* 171 (2018): 208–10; A. Anderson and E. A. Green, "Personal Bests as Reference Points," *Proceedings of the National Academy of Sciences of the U.S.A.* 115 (2018): 1772–75; M. Toure-Tillery and A. Fishbach, "Too Far to Help: The Effect of Perceived Distance on the Expected Impact and Likelihood of Charitable Action," *Journal of Personality and Social Psychology* 112 (2017): 860–76; C. Teng, "Strengthening Loyalty of Online Gamers: Goal Gradient Perspective," *International Journal of Electronic Commerce* 21 (2017): 132–51; V. Kuppuswamy and B. L. Bayus, "Does My Contribution to Your Crowdfunding Project Matter?," *Journal of Business Venturing* 32 (2017): 72–89; T. H. Song, S. Y. Kim, and W. L. Ko, "Developing an Effective Loyalty Program Using Goal-Gradient Behavior in Tourism Industry," *Journal of Tourism Marketing* 34 (2017): 70–81; B. Van den Berg et al., "Altering Speeding of Locomotion,"

Journal of Consumer Research 43 (2016): 407–28; E. Shalev and V. G. Morwitz, "Does Time Fly When You're Counting Down? The Effect of Counting Direction on Subjective Time Judgment," *Journal of Consumer Psychology* 23 (2013): 220–27; M. Toure-Tillery and A. Fishbach, "The End Justifies the Means, but Only in the Middle," *Journal of Experimental Psychology: General* 141 (2012): 570–83; D. Gal and B. McShane, "Can Small Victories Help Win the War? Evidence from Consumer Debt Management," *Journal of Marketing Research* 49 (2012): 487–501; H. Mishra, A. Mishra, and B. Shiv, "In Praise of Vagueness: Malleability of Vague Information as a Performance Booster," *Psychological Science* 6 (2011): 733–38; M. Amar et al., "Winning the Battle but Losing the War: The Psychology of Debt Management," *Journal of Marketing Research* 48 (2011): S38–S50.

6 *This is known as narrow bracketing*: For a review on bracketing, see D. Read, G. Loewenstein, and M. Rabin, "Choice Bracketing," *Journal of Risk and Uncertainty* 19 (1999): 171–97.

7 *Ebbinghaus studied learning and forgetfulness*: See H. Ebbinghaus, *Memory: A Contribution to Experimental Psychology*, trans. H. A. Ruger and C. E. Bussenius (New York: Teachers College Press, 1913). For related work, see E. C. Tolman, "Cognitive Maps in Rats and Men," *Psychological Review* 55 (1948): 189–208.

8 *so was born the plateau effect*: For a recent review, see B. Sullivan and H. H. Thompson, *The Plateau Effect: From Stuck to Success* (New York: Penguin, 2013).

8 *a study of fifteen thousand people who followed an "ultra-minimalist" training plan*: A. Hutchinson, "The Data behind a Once-a-Week Stength Routine," *Outside*, February 2, 2021, https://www.outsideonline.com/2420657/ultra-minimalist -strength-workout-research. See also J. Steele et al., "Long-Term Time-Course of Strength Adaptation to Minimal Dose Resistance Training: Retrospective Longitudinal Growth Modelling of a Large Cohort through Training Records," *SportRxiv Preprints*, January 27, 2021, https://doi.org/10.31236/osf.io/eq485.

10 *In 1965, Jaques noticed that dozens of creative geniuses lost their mojo*: E. Jaques, "Death and the Mid-life Crisis," *International Journal of Psychoanalysis* 46 (1965): 502–14.

11 *Several years later, my colleague Hal Hershfield and I discussed*: A. L. Alter and H. E. Hershfield, "People Search for Meaning When They Approach a New Decade in Chronological Age," *Proceedings of the National Academy of Sciences of the U.S.A.* 111 (2014): 17066–70.

13 *Far from being unusual, Feiler's setbacks were mirrored*: B. Feiler, *Life Is in the Transitions* (New York: Penguin Press, 2020).

16 *The footage of Self's legs "giving out" is hard to watch*: C. Self, "Chandler Self's Dallas Marathon," *Dashing Whippets* (blog), December 18, 2017, https://www.dashing whippets.org/2017/12/18/chandler-selfs-dallas-marathon-recap/; "Stranger Carries Woman to Marathon Finish Line" (video of Self stumbling before the finish line, viewed over 4.5 million times), *Inside Edition*, YouTube, December 11, 2017, https:// www.youtube.com/watch?v=-z9NqVYPoXI.

17 *They're guided by teleoanticipation*: H.-V. Ulmer, "Concept of an Extracellular Regulation of Muscular Metabolic Rate during Heavy Exercise in Humans by Psychophysiological Feedback," *Experientia* 52 (1996): 416–20; A. Hutchinson, "COVID-19 Is like Running a Marathon with No Finish Line. What Does Sports Science Say about How We Can Win It?," *Globe and Mail*, November 21, 2020, https://www.theglobeandmail.com/opinion/article-covid-19-is-like-running-a-marathon-with-no-finish-line-what-does/; G. Wingfield, F. Marino, and M. Skein, "The Influence of Knowledge of Performance Endpoint on Pacing Strategies, Perception of Effort, and Neural Activity during 30-km Cycling Time Trials," *Physiological Reports* 6 (2018): e13892; M. Katzir, E. Aviv, and N. Liberman, "Cognitive Performance Is Enhanced If One Knows When the Task Will End," *Cognition* 197 (2020), article 104189.

Chapter 2: Keep Going

21 *Furuholmen's band was the Norwegian synth-pop trio a-ha*: For background on Furuholmen and a-ha, see T. Gulbrandsen, "Morten Harket Threatened to Quit Due to the 'Take On Me' Riff" (translated from the original Norwegian), *Underholdning*, September 26, 2014, https://www.tv2.no/a/6051904; D. Kreps, "The Secret History of a-ha's Smash 'Take on Me,'" *Rolling Stone*, May 14, 2010, https://www.rollingstone.com/music/music-news/the-secret-history-of-a-has-smash-take-on-me-95480/; a-ha, "Take On Me" (1984 version), YouTube, 1984, https://www.youtube.com/watch?v=liq-seNVvrM; M. Millar, "Interview: a-ha Cofounder Magne Furuholmen on Third Solo Album, *White Xmas Lies*," XSNOIZE.com, October 23, 2019, https://www.xsnoize.com/interview-a-ha-co-founder-magne-furuholmen-on-third-solo-album-white-xmas-lies/; Official Community of a-ha, *The Story So Far*, "Chapter 3."

23 *When psychologists Brian Lucas and Loran Nordgren first described*: B. J. Lucas and L. F. Nordgren, "The Creative Cliff Illusion," *Proceedings of the National Academy of Sciences of the U.S.A.* 117 (2020): 19830–36; B. J. Lucas and L. F. Nordgren, "People Underestimate the Value of Persistence for Creative Performance," *Journal of Personality and Social Psychology* 109 (2015): 232–43. For more on creativity across time, see R. E. Beaty and P. J. Silvia, "Why Do Ideas Get More Creative across Time? An Executive Interpretation of the Serial Order Effect in Divergent Thinking Tasks," *Psychology of Aesthetics, Creativity, and the Arts* 6 (2012): 309–19. For more on insight and Aha! moments, see J. Kounios and M. Beeman, "The Aha! Moment: The Cognitive Neuroscience of Insight," *Current Directions in Psychological Science* 18 (2009), 210–16; J. W. Schooler and J. Melcher, "The Ineffability of Insight," in *The Creative Cognition Approach*, ed. S. M. Smith, T. B. Ward, and R. A. Finke (Cambridge, MA: MIT Press,1995), 97–133; T. M. Amabile, *Creativity in Context* (Boulder, CO: Westview Press, 1996); A. Newell, J. C. Shaw, and H. A. Simon, "The Processes of Creative Thinking" (paper presented at sympo-

sium at University of Colorado, 1958), in *Contemporary Approaches to Creative Thinking* (New York: Atherton Press, 1962).

27 *Only, this isn't true. The average age*: Decades of research suggests that older adults outperform younger adults in many domains where precocity and youth have been celebrated. See, for example, M. Gladwell, "Late Bloomers: Why Do We Equate Genius with Precocity?," *New Yorker*, October 20, 2008, https://www.newyorker.com/magazine/2008/10/20/late-bloomers-malcolm-gladwell; J. Hamilton, "Study Makes Case for Late Bloomers," *All Things Considered*, NPR, March 29, 2006, https://www.npr.org/templates/story/story.php?storyId=5310107; K. Evers, "The Art of Blooming Late," *Harvard Business Review*, May–June 2019, https://hbr.org/2019/05/the-art-of-blooming-late; B. Jones, E. J. Reedy, and B. Weinberg, "Age and Scientific Genius," NBER Working Paper Series no. 19866, 2014, http://www.nber.org/papers/w19866; J. M. Berg, "One-Hit Wonders versus Hit Makers: Sustaining Success in Creative Industries," *Administrative Science Quarterly*, 2022; P. Azoulay et al., "Age and High-Growth Entrepreneurship," *American Economic Review: Insights* 2 (2020): 65–82; H. Zhao et al., "Age and Entrepreneurial Career Success: A Review and a Meta-Analysis," *Journal of Business Venturing* 36 (2021): 106007; "Science Says This Is How Many Dates You Have to Go On Before You Find 'the One,'" Her, n.d., https://www.her.ie/life/whats-your-number-study-finds-the-average-number-of-dates-and-relationships-before-we-find-the-one-90330; U. N. Sio and T. C. Ormerod, "Does Incubation Enhance Problem Solving? A Meta-Analytic Review," *Psychological Bulletin* 135 (2009): 94–120; H. C. Lehman, *Age and Achievement* (Princeton, NJ: Princeton University Press, 1953); D. T. Campbell, "Blind Variation and Selective Retentions in Creative Thought as in Other Knowledge Processes," *Psychological Review* 67 (1960): 380–400; D. K. Simonton, "Creative Productivity and Age: A Mathematical Model Based on a Two-Step Cognitive Process," *Development Review* 4 (1984): 77–111; D. K. Simonton, "Age and Outstanding Achievement: What Do We Know after a Century of Research?," *Psychological Bulletin* 104 (1988): 251–67; A. Spitz and E. Horvát, "Measuring Long-Term Impact Based on Network Centrality: Unraveling Cinematic Citations," *PLoS ONE* 9 (2014): e108857; B. Yucesoy et al., "Success in Books: A Big Data Approach to Bestsellers," *EPJ Data Science* 7 (2018): 7; O. E. Williams, L. Lacasa, and V. Latora, "Quantifying and Predicting Success in Show Business," *Nature Communications* 10 (2019): 1–8; R. Sinatra et al., "Quantifying the Evolution of Individual Scientific Impact," *Science* 354 (2016): aaf5239.

30 *In 2020, three European data scientists showed the importance of persevering*: M. Janosov, F. Battison, and R. Sinatra, "Success and Luck in Creative Careers," *EPJ Data Science* 9 (2020): 1–12.

32 *researchers tracked the creative output of a sample of European adults*: D. W. Weinberger, S. Ute, and J. Weggem, "Having a Creative Day: Understanding Entre-

preneurs' Daily Idea Generation through a Recovery Lens," *Journal of Business Venturing* 33 (2018): 1–19.

34 *Harris was an internet pioneer during the golden age*: For a comprehensive biography, see A. Smith, *Totally Wired: The Rise and Fall of Josh Harris and the Great Dotcom Swindle* (New York: Grove Press, 2012). See also the movie about Harris and his company, Pseudo: O. Timoner (director), *We Live in Public*, Interloper Films, 2009.

Chapter 3: Traps and Lures

40 *As it turned out, I did get lost in a sea of Adams*: On how names evolve, and why they mimic one another, see J. Berger et al., "From Karen to Katie: Using Baby Names to Understand Cultural Evolution," *Psychological Science* 23 (2012): 1067–73; J. Berger and G. Le Mens, "How Adoption Speed Affects the Abandonment of Cultural Tastes," *Proceedings of the National Academy of Sciences of the U.S.A.* 106 (2009): 8146–50.

41 *During the twentieth century, a swarm of artists known as color field artists*: See, for example, T. Campbell, "The Monochrome: A History of Simplicity in Painting," *Artland Magazine*, n.d., https://magazine.artland.com/the-monochrome-a-history -of-simplicity-in-painting/.

42 *An Instagram account called @insta_repeat*: https://www.instagram.com/insta_repeat/.

42 *a process known as carcinization*: See S. K. Watson, "Why Everything Eventually Becomes a Crab," *Popular Science*, December 14, 2020, https://www.popsci.com /story/animals/why-everything-becomes-crab-meme-carcinization/; J. Keiler, C. S. Wirkner, and S. Richter, "One Hundred Years of Carcinization: The Evolution of the Crab-Like Habitus in Anomura (Arthropoda: Crustacea)," *Biological Journal of the Linnaean Society* 121 (2017): 200–222.

43 *Christophe Courtois has done for film photography*: See S. Fussell, "Hollywood Keeps Using These Same Thirteen Movie Poster Clichés Over and Over Again," *Business Insider*, May 19, 2016, https://www.businessinsider.com/movie-poster -cliches-2016-5.

46 *This is known as the pseudo-intelligibility trap*: J. Harkins, *Bridging Two Worlds: Aboriginal English and Crosscultural Understanding* (Brisbane: University of Queensland Press, 1994); D. Eades, "Communicative Strategies in Aboriginal English," in *Language in Australia*, ed. S. Romaine (Cambridge, UK: Cambridge University Press, 1991), 84–93; A. L. Alter, "Aborigines and Courtroom Communication: Problems and Solutions," Australian Human Rights Centre Working Paper 2004/2, 2004; *Rahman v. Minister for Immigration and Multicultural Affairs*, unreported, High Court of Australia, McHugh and Callinan JJ, March 10, 2000, S136/1999. Pseudo-intelligibility also plagues email and other written communication, where we tend to believe subtle emotional signals are clearer to readers

than they actually are. See J. Kruger et al., "Egocentrism over Email: Can We Communicate as Well as We Think?," *Journal of Personality and Social Psychology* 89 (2005): 925–36.

47 *Matthew Fray, a relationship coach, has said*: M. Fray, *This Is How Your Marriage Ends* (New York: Harper One, 2022); M. Fray, "The Marriage Lesson I Learned Too Late," *Atlantic*, April 11, 2022, https://www.theatlantic.com/family/archive/2022/04/marriage-problems-fight-dishes/629526/.

49 *Most blisters aren't fatal, so there's a reason*: We tend to allow minor injuries—both psychological and physical—to fester, whereas we pounce on major injuries almost immediately: D. T. Gilbert et al., "The Peculiar Longevity of Things Not So Bad," *Psychological Science* 15 (2004): 14–19.

50 *technique known as preventive maintenance*: See, for example, "The A, C, and D of Aircraft Maintenance," Qantas.com.au, July 18, 2016, https://www.qantasnewsroom.com.au/roo-tales/the-a-c-and-d-of-aircraft-maintenance/; H. Kinnison and T. Siddiqui, *Aviation Maintenance Management*, 2nd ed. (New York: McGraw-Hill, 2011). For more on the basics of preventive maintenance in engineering, see D. Stangier and R. Smith, *Preventive Maintenance Made Simple* (Reliabilityweb.com, 2016).

53 *what would become known several decades later as the Y2K Bug*: On Y2K, Bemer's forecasts, and the role of early intervention in preventing what might otherwise have been a major disaster, see M. Stroh, "Programmer Saw Y2K Bug Coming," *Baltimore Sun*, April 25, 1999, https://www.baltimoresun.com/news/bs-xpm-1999-04-25-9904250201-story.html; F. Uenuma, "Twenty Years Later the Y2K Bug Seems like a Joke—Because Those behind the Scenes Took It Seriously," *Time*, December 30, 2019, https://time.com/5752129/y2k-bug-history/; N. Oren, "If You Think the Millennium Bug Was a Hoax, Here Comes a History Lesson," Conversation, December 30, 2019, https://theconversation.com/if-you-think-the-millennium-bug-was-a-hoax-here-comes-a-history-lesson-129042; Z. Loeb, "The Lessons of Y2K, 20 Years Later: Y2K Became a Punchline, but Twenty Years Ago We Averted Disaster," *Washington Post*, December 30, 2019, https://www.washingtonpost.com/outlook/2019/12/30/lessons-yk-years-later/; P. Sullivan, "Computer Pioneer Bob Bemer; 84," *Washington Post*, June 25, 2004, https://www.washingtonpost.com/archive/local/2004/06/25/computer-pioneer-bob-bemer-84/d7a31166-b00f-48b5-b7cc-d53bf106f194/; "Bob Bemer, 84; Helped Code Computer Language," *Los Angeles Times*, June 27, 2004, https://www.latimes.com/archives/la-xpm-2004-jun-27-me-bemer27-story.html; D. Williamson, "Y2K: Nightmare or Inconvenience?," *Kitsap Sun* (Washington State), June 29, 1999, https://products.kitsapsun.com/archive/1999/06-29/0039_y2k__nightmare_or_inconvenience__.html.

55 *About ten years ago I tested a kind of Bemerization intervention*: "Prudential: Your Brain Is to Blame; Episode One: Your Future Self," video, https://www.dailymotion.com/video/x1121u1. On temporal discounting, or the tendency for people to prioritize their present selves over their future selves, see H. E. Hershfield et al.,

"Increasing Saving Behavior through Age-Progressed Renderings of the Future Self," *Journal of Marketing Research* 48 (2011): S23–S27; K. Keidel et al., "Individual Differences in Intertemporal Choice," *Frontiers in Psychology* 12 (2021): 643670; G. W. Harrison, M. I. Lau, and M. B. Williams, "Estimating Individual Discount Rates in Denmark: A Field Experiment," *American Economic Review* 92 (2002): 1606–17.

Chapter 4: Exhale

61 *When artist Jack Kirby created the Incredible Hulk*: See, for example, J. Hill, "Green with Anger," *Guardian*, July 17, 2003, https://www.theguardian.com/film/2003 /jul/17/comment.features; A. Liptak, "The Incredible Hulk Was Inspired by a Woman Saving Her Baby," Gizmodo, August 30, 2015, https://gizmodo.com/the -incredible-hulk-was-inspired-by-a-woman-saving-her-1727562968.

61 *He could be "volatile," "arrogant," and "aloof"*: J. Pareles, "Miles Davis, Trumpeter, Dies; Jazz Genius, 65, Defined Cool," *New York Times*, September 29, 1991, https://www.nytimes.com/1991/09/29/nyregion/miles-davis-trumpeter-dies-jazz -genius-65-defined-cool.html.

62 *There's an incredible video of Davis and Hancock performing in Milan in 1964*: "Miles Davis Angry at Herbie Hancock," Urban Sense, March 31, 2017, https:// www.youtube.com/watch?v=sUG0P7tcCto&t.

62 *"I got to his house," Hancock remembered*: Hancock describes this experience in a video: "Herbie Hancock Highlights Early Moments Working with Miles Davis," SiriusXM, November 4, 2014, https://www.youtube.com/watch?v=hUYS2av5zdM.

63 *"Forty-eight hours after arriving in New York," he remembered*: L. Applebaum, "Interview with John McLaughlin (Conclusion)," Let's Cool One: Musings about Music, April 12, 2013, https://larryappelbaum.wordpress.com/2013/04/12/inter view-with-john-mclaughlin-conclusion/.

65 *We know this, in part, from the results of an experiment*: L. A. Dugatkin, "Tendency to Inspect Predators Predicts Mortality Risk in the Guppy (*Poecilia reticulata*)," *Behavioral Ecology* 3 (1992): 124–27.

67 *I decided to run a small experiment*: A. L. Alter et al., "Rising to the Threat: Reducing Stereotype Threat by Reframing the Threat as a Challenge," *Journal of Experimental Social Psychology* 46 (2010): 166–71.

70 *Brach describes the fear of failure*: T. Brach, *Radical Acceptance: Embracing Your Life with the Heart of a Buddha* (New York: Random House, 2004).

71 *In 1956, the cognitive scientist and economist Herb Simon*: H. A. Simon, "Rational Choice and the Structure of the Environment," *Psychological Review* 63 (1956): 129–38. See also H. A. Simon, "A Behavioral Model of Rational Choice," *Quarterly Journal of Economics* 59 (1955): 99–118.

71 *Almost fifty years later, psychologist Barry Schwartz and several of his colleagues*: B. Schwartz et al., "Maximizing versus Satisficing: Happiness Is a Matter

of Choice," *Journal of Personality and Social Psychology* 83 (2002): 1178–97; B. Schwartz and A. Ward, "Doing Better but Feeling Worse: The Paradox of Choice," in *Positive Psychology in Practice*, ed. P. A. Linley and S. Joseph (Hoboken, NJ: John Wiley and Sons, 2004), 86–104.

73 *Self-imposed decision and action deadlines have similar benefits*: M. Burgess, M. E. Enzle, and R. Schmalz, "Defeating the Potentially Deleterious Effects of Externally Imposed Deadlines: Practitioners' Rules-of-Thumb," *Personality and Social Psychology Bulletin* 30 (2004): 868–77.

73 *Maximizing overlaps substantially with perfectionism*: On perfectionism, see C. Aschwanden, "Perfectionism Is Killing Us," Vox, December 5, 2019, https://www.vox.com/the-highlight/2019/11/27/20975989/perfect-mental-health-perfectionism; P. L. Hewitt, G. L. Flett, and S. F. Mikail, *Perfectionism: A Relational Approach to Conceptualization, Assessment, and Treatment* (New York: Guilford Press, 2017); K. Limburg et al., "The Relationship between Perfectionism and Psychopathology: A Meta-Analysis," *Journal of Clinical Psychology* 73 (2017): 1301–26; T. Curran and A. P. Hill, "Perfectionism Is Increasing over Time: A Meta-Analysis of Birth Cohort Differences from 1989 to 2016," *Psychological Bulletin* 145 (2019): 410–29.

75 *The value of "letting go," or choosing not to fight*: See, for example, L. Feldman-Barrett, "Buddhists in Love: Lovers Crave Intensity, Buddhists Say Craving Causes Suffering. Is It Possible to Be Deeply in Love Yet Truly Detached?," Aeon, June 4, 2018, https://aeon.co/essays/does-buddhist-detachment-allow-for-a-healthier-togetherness; T. Brach, *Radical Acceptance: Embracing Your Life with the Heart of a Buddha* (New York: Bantam, 2003); T. Brach, "Radical Acceptance Revisited," YouTube, 2015, https://www.youtube.com/watch?v=vFr_zQCUMD4; T. N. Hanh, *How to Relax* (Berkeley, CA: Parallax Press, 2015). For applications to Western psychiatry and psychology, see Georg H. Eifert and John P. Forsyth, *Acceptance & Commitment Therapy for Anxiety Disorders: A Practitioner's Treatment Guide to Using Mindfulness, Acceptance, and Values-Based Behavior Change Strategies* (Oakland, CA: New Harbinger, 2005); R. Whitehead, G. Bates, and B. Elphinstone, "Growing by Letting Go: Nonattachment and Mindfulness as Qualities of Advanced Psychological Development," *Journal of Adult Development* 27 (2020): 12–22. See also A. L. Alter, "Do the Poor Have More Meaningful Lives?," *New Yorker*, January 24, 2014, https://www.newyorker.com/business/currency/do-the-poor-have-more-meaningful-lives.

77 *Jonathan Safran Foer, in the first chapter of* Eating Animals: J. Safran Foer, *Eating Animals* (New York: Hachette, 2009).

Chapter 5: Pause Before You Play

79 *Take the world's best soccer player, an Argentinean named Lionel Messi*: E. Bretland, "Lionel Messi's Habit of Being Sick during Matches Is Down to Nerves, Claims Argentina Coach Alejandro Sabella," *Daily Mail*, June 11, 2014, https://

www.dailymail.co.uk/sport/worldcup2014/article-2655113/Lionel-Messis-habit
-sick-matches-nerves-claims-Argentina-coach-Alejandro-Sabella.html; S. Pisani,
"Messi: Argentina Struggled with Nervousness in First Game Back," Goal, October 9, 2020, https://www.goal.com/en-kw/news/messi-argentina-struggled
-with-nervousness-in-first-game/1p341lyf5uap31nijrhi1azq3d; "Diego Maradona: Lionel Messi Is No Leader, He Goes to Toilet 20 Times before a Game,"
ESPN, October 13, 2018, https://www.espn.com/soccer/argentina/story/3668443
/diego-maradona-lionel-messi-is-no-leader-he-goes-to-toilet-20-times-before-a
-game; C. Pellatt, "Lionel Messi Has Visited a Specialist Doctor to Stop Him
from Vomiting on the Pitch," Complex UK, April 24, 2015, https://www.com
plex.com/sports/2015/04/lionel-messi-vomit; N. Elliott, "Lionel Messi Deliberately Does Nothing for the First Five Minutes of Every Game . . . and It Works,"
Dream Team FC, May 2, 2019, https://www.dreamteamfc.com/c/news-gossip
/446751/lionel-messi-five-minutes-barcelona/; "Why Messi Doesn't Touch the
Ball in the First Five Minutes," Goalside!, August 27, 2019, https://www.youtube
.com/watch?v=HP3r4SUvyFY.

83 *"Boris Becker beat me the first three times we played," Agassi remembered*: "The
Andre Agassi Interview: Beat Boris Becker by Observing His Tongue," Tomorrow
Beckons, April 14, 2017, https://www.youtube.com/watch?v=ja6HeLB3kwY.

84 *Brach doesn't just advocate slowing down*: See, for example, T. Brach, "The Sacred
Pause," *Psychology Today*, December 4, 2014, https://www.psychologytoday.com
/us/blog/finding-true-refuge/201412/the-sacred-pause; T. Brach, *Radical Acceptance: Embracing Your Life with the Heart of a Buddha* (New York: Random House,
2004). For more on the value of silence and deliberation, see J. R. Curhan et al.,
"Silence Is Golden: Extended Silence, Deliberative Mindset, and Value Creation
in Negotiation," *Journal of Applied Psychology* 107 (2022): 78–94.

85 *The anecdote, first described by Tom Wolfe, centers on a group of US test pilots*:
T. Wolfe, *The Right Stuff* (New York: Farrar, Straus and Giroux, 1979).

87 *Paul Simon has said of his music that some lines are difficult*: P. Simon, "Isn't It
Rich?," *New York Times Book Review*, October 31, 2010, https://www.nytimes
.com/2010/10/31/books/review/Simon-t.html. On the value of pausing and slowing down, see F. Partnoy, *Wait: The Art and Science of Delay* (New York: Public
Affairs, 2012).

87 *In 1974's Blazing Saddles*: "Blazing Saddles . . . You Know, Morons," 099tuber1,
July 26, 2009, https://www.youtube.com/watch?v=KHJbSvidohg.

88 *About fifteen years ago, Brewer developed a mindfulness-based treatment*: J. A. Brewer,
*The Craving Mind: From Cigarettes to Smartphones to Love—Why We Get Hooked
and How We Can Break Bad Habits* (New Haven, CT: Yale University Press, 2017);
A. L. Alter, "Review: On Mindfulness as an Alternative to Mindless Modern Consumption," *American Journal of Psychology* 131 (2018): 510–13.

90 *A famous experiment illustrates how strongly*: For a summary of the experiment,
which was widely discussed but never published, see M. Luo, "Excuse Me, May

I Have Your Seat?," *New York Times*, September 14, 2004, https://www.nytimes
.com/2004/09/14/nyregion/excuse-me-may-i-have-your-seat.html.

92 *Honnold has been stuck many times*: G. Raz, "Alex Honnold: How Much Can Preparation Mitigate Risk?," *TED Radio Hour*, NPR, November 8, 2019, https://www
.npr.org/transcripts/774089221. See also J. Chin and E. C. Vasarhelyi, directors,
Free Solo, National Geographic Films, 2018.

Chapter 6: Failing Well

98 *In 1981, Malcolm Forbes asked his editor in chief to compile*: C. Peterson-Withorn,
"Birth of the Forbes 400: The Story behind Forbes' First Rich List," *Forbes*, September 19, 2017, https://www.forbes.com/sites/chasewithorn/2017/09/19/birth-of
-the-forbes-400-the-story-behind-forbes-first-rich-list.

99 *If you want to succeed really, really badly*: On the benefits of failing, see S. Johnson,
"The '85% Rule.' Why a Dose of Failure Optimizes Learning," Big Think, January
8, 2020, https://bigthink.com/personal-growth/learning-failure; M. Housel, "Ca-
sualties of Perfection," Collaborative Fund, June 30, 2021, https://www.collabo
rativefund.com/blog/inefficient/; L. Babauta, "The Number One Habit of Highly
Creative People," *Zen Habits* (blog), n.d., https://zenhabits.net/creative-habit/;
T. Dufu, *Drop the Ball: Achieving More by Doing Less* (New York: Flatiron Books,
2017); M. Cassotti et al., "What Have We Learned about the Processes Involved
in the Iowa Gambling Task from Developmental Studies?," *Frontiers of Psychology* 5 (2014): 915.

100 *According to the researchers, the optimal error rate*: R. C. Wilson et al., "The Eighty-
Five Percent Rule for Optimal Learning," *Nature Communications* 10 (2019): 4646.

101 *Motorola launched a satellite phone provider called Iridium*: J. Gertner, "The Fall and
Rise of Iridium," *Wall Street Journal*, June 3, 2016, https://www.wsj.com/articles
/the-fall-and-rise-of-iridium-1464980784.

102 *In "Failing and Flying," American poet Jack Gilbert suggested*: J. Gilbert, *Refusing
Heaven* (New York: Alfred A. Knopf, 2005).

103 *Most of the time, when we focus our attention on losses, failures, and mistakes*: Hu-
mans tend to train their attention on losses and threats more than on gains.
See, for example, A. Dijksterhuis and H. Aarts, "On Wildebeests and Humans:
The Preferential Detection of Negative Stimuli," *Psychological Science* 14 (2003):
14–18; G. S. Blum, "An Experimental Reunion of Psychoanalytic Theory with
Perceptual Vigilance and Defense," *Journal of Abnormal and Social Psychology* 49
(1954): 94–98; F. Pratto and O. P. John, "Automatic Vigilance: The Attention-
Grabbing Power of Negative Social Information," *Journal of Personality and Social
Psychology* 61 (1991): 380–91; D. Wentura, K. Rothermund, and P. Bak, "Automatic
Vigilance: The Attention-Grabbing Power of Approach- and Avoidance-Related
Social Information," *Journal of Personality and Social Psychology* 78 (2000):
1024–37.

103 *When American golfer Phil Mickelson isn't playing championship golf*: Z. Melton, "This Is the Clever Mental Trick Phil Mickelson Uses to Keep His Mind Sharp," Golf, May 21, 2021, https://golf.com/instruction/clever-mental-trick-phil-mickelson -pga-championship/.

104 *To test this idea, three of my colleagues and I examined*: H. B. Kappes et al., "Difficult Training Improves Team Performance: An Empirical Case Study of US College Basketball," *Behavioural Public Policy* 3 (2019): 1–24.

105 *The best human players in the world routinely lost to the Go AI*: S. Choi et al., "How Does AI Improve Human Decision-Making? Evidence from the AI-Powered Go Program," working paper, April 2022, https://hyokang.com/assets/pdf/CKKK-AI -Go.pdf.

106 *In 2014, Poler overcame a basket of fears*: M. Poler, *Hello, Fears: Crush Your Comfort Zone and Become Who You're Meant to Be* (New York: Sourcebooks, 2020). Poler's list of fears (and videos accompanying each one): http://100dayswithoutfear .com/list.

108 *This technique draws on a psychological phenomenon*: A. L. Alter, D. M. Oppenheimer, and J. C. Zemla, "Missing the Trees for the Forest: A Construal Level Account of the Illusion of Explanatory Depth," *Journal of Personality and Social Psychology* 99 (2010): 436–51; L. Rozenblit and F. Keil, "The Misunderstood Limits of Folk Science: An Illusion of Explanatory Depth," *Cognitive Science* 26 (2002): 521–62.

109 *This exposure therapy gives them progressively larger doses of fear*: K. M. Myers and M. Davis, "Mechanisms of Fear Extinction," *Molecular Psychiatry* 12 (2007): 120–50; I. Marks, "Exposure Therapy for Phobias and Obsessive-Compulsive Disorders," *Hospital Practice* 14 (1979): 101–8; T. D. Parsons and A. A. Rizzo, "Affective Outcomes of Virtual Reality Exposure Therapy for Anxiety and Specific Phobias: A Meta-Analysis," *Journal of Behavior Therapy and Experimental Psychiatry* 39 (2008): 250–61.

111 *As the data trickled in, it became clear*: P. Caldarella et al., "Effects of Teachers' Praise-to-Reprimand Ratios on Elementary Students' On-Task Behaviour," *Educational Psychology* 40 (2020): 1306–22.

111 *One study examined the extent to which abusive NBA coaches*: E. L. Carleton et al., "Scarred for the Rest of My Career? Career-Long Effects of Abusive Leadership on Professional Athlete Aggression and Task Performance," *Journal of Sports and Exercise Psychology* 38 (2016): 409–22. In other domains, see M. A. Yukhymenko-Lescroart, M. E. Brown, and T. S. Paskus, "The Relationship between Ethical and Abusive Coaching Behaviors and Student-Athlete Well-Being," *Sport, Exercise, and Performance Psychology* 4 (2015): 36–49; E. N. Smith, M. D. Young, and A. J. Crum, "Stress, Mindsets, and Success in Navy SEALs Special Warfare Training," *Frontiers in Psychology* 10 (2020): 2962; J. P. Jamieson et al., "Optimizing Stress Responses with Reappraisal and Mindset Interventions: An Integrated Model," *Anxiety, Stress and Coping* 31 (2018): 245–61; A. J. Crum et al., "The Role of Stress Mindset in Shap-

ing Cognitive, Emotional, and Physiological Responses to Challenging and Threatening Stress," *Anxiety, Stress and Coping* 30 (2017): 379–95; A. J. Crum, P. Salovey, and S. Achor, "Rethinking Stress: The Role of Mindsets in Determining the Stress Response," *Journal of Personality and Social Psychology* 104 (2013): 716–33.

112 *UBIs are negative taxes that are paid to every member*: For a good summary on UBI research, see S. Samuel, "Everywhere Basic Income Has Been Tried, in One Map," Vox, October 20, 2020, https://www.vox.com/future-perfect/2020/2/19 /21112570/universal-basic-income-ubi-map; E. Hayden, "J. K. Rowling Chats with Jon Stewart about Welfare and Why America Needs 'a Monarch,'" *Hollywood Reporter*, October 16, 2012, https://www.hollywoodreporter.com/tv/tv-news/jk -rowling-chats-jon-stewart-casual-vacancy-379302/; D. McKenzie, "Identifying and Spurring High-Growth Entrepreneurship: Experimental Evidence from a Business Plan Competition," *American Economic Review* 107 (2017): 2278–307; B. Watson, "A B.C. Research Project Gave Homeless People $7,500 Each—the Results Were 'Beautifully Surprising,'" CBC, October 7, 2020, https://www.cbc .ca/news/canada/british-columbia/new-leaf-project-results-1.5752714; S. Sigal, "Finland Gave People Free Money. It Didn't Help Them Get Jobs—but Does That Matter?," Vox, February 9, 2019, https://www.vox.com/future-perfect /2019/2/9/18217566/finland-basic-income.

Chapter 7: Friction Audits and the Art of Simplification

117 *Hillier devised the mathematical term* intelligibility *to capture*: R. Dalton and N. Dalton, "How to Escape a Maze—According to Science," Conversation, January 26, 2017, https://theconversation.com/how-to-escape-a-maze-according -to-maths-71582; N. Geiling, "The Winding History of the Maze," *Smithsonian Magazine*, July 31, 2014, https://www.smithsonianmag.com/travel/winding-his tory-maze-180951998/.

117 *The human body combines dozens of bones*: R. Eveleth, "There Are 37.2 Trillion Cells in Your Body," *Smithsonian Magazine*, October 24, 2013, https://www.smithsonianmag .com/smart-news/there-are-372-trillion-cells-in-your-body-4941473/.

118 *For the most complex cases, expert diagnosticians*: Discover staff, "The Real Dr. House," *Discover*, July 19, 2007, https://www.discovermagazine.com/environ ment/the-real-dr-house. On simplicity and learning how to think, see A. L. Alter, "Popular Science," Point, June 12, 2014, https://thepointmag.com/criticism/pop ular-science/; D. Ponka and M. Kirlew, "Top 10 Differential Diagnoses in Family Medicine: Cough," *Canadian Family Physician* 53 (2007): 690–91.

126 *Emma Coats published twenty-two tweets summarizing*: C. Lamar, "The 22 Rules of Storytelling, According to Pixar," Gizmodo, June 8, 2012, https://gizmodo .com/the-22-rules-of-storytelling-according-to-pixar-5916970; K. Miyamoto, "10 Screenplay Structures That Screenwriters Can Use," Screencraft, January

16, 2018, https://screencraft.org/2018/01/16/10-screenplay-structures-that-screen writers-can-use/.

127 *Parker and Matt Stone, the creators of* South Park: H. Hale, "But . . . Therefore . . . ," YouTube, March 2, 2018, https://www.youtube.com/watch?v=j9jEg9uiLOU.

128 *A couple of years ago, Leidy Klotz, an engineer*: L. Klotz, *Subtract: The Untapped Science of Less* (New York: Flatiron Books, 2021). See also L. Klotz, "Subtract: Why Getting to Less Can Mean Thinking More," *Behavioral Scientist*, April 12, 2021, https://behavioralscientist.org/subtract-why-getting-to-less-can-mean -thinking-more/; G. S. Adams et al., "People Systematically Overlook Subtractive Changes," *Nature* 592 (2021): 258–61.

129 *On her Twitter bio, she writes*: https://twitter.com/lawnrocket.

130 *"This was the destruction of my dream of becoming an artist"*: P. Hansen, "Embrace the Shake," TED, n.d., https://www.ted.com/talks/phil_hansen_embrace_the _shake. Also see Hansen's website: https://www.philinthecircle.com/.

133 *a group of researchers examined twenty-eight thousand basketball games*: J. S. Chen and P. Garg, "Dancing with the Stars: Benefits of a Star Employee's Temporary Absence for Organizational Performance," *Strategic Management Journal* 39 (2018): 1239–67.

134 *A team of economists wondered whether the strike*: T. Vanderbilt, "The Pandemic Gives Us a Chance to Change How We Get Around," *Wired*, December 2, 2020, https://www.wired.com/story/cities-micro-mobility/; S. Larcom, F. Rauch, and T. Willems, "The Benefits of Forced Experimentation: Striking Evidence from the London Underground Network," *Quarterly Journal of Economics* 132 (2017): 1969–2018.

135 *One well-known example is business titan Warren Buffett's*: See, for example, T. Po-pomaronis, "Warren Buffett Loves Teaching This '20-Slot' Rule at Business Schools—and It's Not Just about Getting Rich," CNBC, May 28, 2020, https:// www.cnbc.com/2020/05/28/billionaire-warren-buffett-teaches-this-20-slot-rule -to-getting-rich-at-business-schools.html; E. Kaplan, "Why Warren Buffett's '20-Slot Rule' Will Make You Insanely Successful and Wealthy," *Inc.*, July 22, 2016, https://www.inc.com/elle-kaplan/why-warren-buffett-s-20-slot-rule-will-make-you-insanely-wealthy-and-successful.html; P. W. Kunhardt, director, *Becoming Warren Buffett* (online video), HBO, 2017; M. Housel, *The Psychology of Money* (London: Harriman House, 2021).

135 *Since 1979, French artist Pierre Soulages has painted exclusively*: N. Siegal, "Black Is Still the Only Color for Pierre Soulages," *New York Times*, November 29, 2019, https://www.nytimes.com/2019/11/29/arts/design/pierre-soulages-louvre.html. More broadly on why constraints inspire innovation, see O. A. Acar, M. Tarakci, and D. van Knippenberg, "Why Constraints Are Good for Innovation," *Harvard Business Review*, November 22, 2019, https://hbr.org/2019/11/why-constraints -are-good-for-innovation.

Chapter 8: Recombination and Pivoting

137 *Browsing a local record store, Zimmerman bought a copy*: This section on Bob Dylan owes much to D. Garner, "Remember Odetta, Whose Powerful Voice Met a Powerful Moment," *New York Times*, August 24, 2020, https://www.nytimes.com/2020 /08/24/books/review-odetta-biography-ian-zack-one-grain-of-sand-matthew-frye -jacobson.html; and K. Ferguson, "Everything Is a Remix, Part 1 (2021)," YouTube, September 7, 2021, https://www.youtube.com/watch?v=MZ2GuvUWaP8. Ferguson's YouTube videos, beginning in 2010, cataloged the extent to which modern culture, particularly music, borrows from the past. C. Heylin, *Bob Dylan: Behind the Shades, the Biography—Take Two* (London: Penguin, 2001); S. P. Farrell, "Last Word: Odetta," *New York Times*, December 2, 2008, https://www.nytimes.com /video/arts/music/1194832844841/last-word-odetta.html; A. Billet, "Charleston, Juneteenth and 'No More Auction Block for Me,'" *Red Wedge*, June 19, 2015, http:// www.redwedgemagazine.com/atonal-notes/charleston-juneteenth-and-no-more -auction-block-for-me; M. Haddon, "Matrices of 'Love and Theft': Joan Baez Imitates Bob Dylan," *Twentieth Century Music* 18 (2021): 249–79.

139 *The second explanation is that people are naturally cryptomnesic*: A. S. Brown and D. R. Murphy, "Cryptomnesia: Delineating Inadvertent Plagiarism," *Journal of Experimental Psychology: Learning, Memory, and Cognition* 15 (1989): 432–42; J. Preston and D. M. Wegner, "The Eureka Error: Inadvertent Plagiarism by Misattributions of Effort," *Journal of Personality and Social Psychology* 92 (2007): 575–84.

140 *Grohl was disarmingly open about borrowing ideas*: D. Grohl, director, *From Cradle to Stage* (documentary), Live Nation Productions, 2021.

142 *One of my favorite examples of recombination was the brainchild of Arlene Harris*: See, for example, D. Pogue, "Brilliant Ideas That Found a Welcome," *New York Times*, December 28, 2006, https://www.nytimes.com/2006/12/28/technology/28pogue .html; K. Terrell, "AARP Study: Americans 50 and Older Would Be World's Third-Largest Economy," AARP, December 19, 2019, http://aarp.org/politics -society/advocacy/info-2019/older-americans-economic-impact-growth.html; R. Booth, "Young Adults Have Less to Spend on Non-essentials, Study Says," *Guardian*, June 19, 2019, https://www.theguardian.com/inequality/2019/jun/20 /young-adults-have-less-to-spend-on-non-essentials-study-says; L. Gardiner, "Life as a Millennial Is Far Less Extravagant Than You Might Think," Resolution Foundation, June 20, 2019, https://www.resolutionfoundation.org/comment/life -as-a-millennial-is-far-less-extravagant-than-you-might-think/; L. Judge, "Young People Are No Longer Footloose and Fancy Free—and Rent Rises Are to Blame," Resolution Foundation, June 6, 2019, https://www.resolutionfoundation.org /comment/young-people-are-no-longer-footloose-and-fancy-free-and-rent-rises -are-to-blame/; C. Ford, "Arlene Harris," YouTube, October 10, 2011, https:// www.youtube.com/watch?v=tKyYLfKGxI4.

144 *Idea #487: An alarm clock mat that you have*: Ruggie, https://ruggie.co/.

144 *Idea #522: Netflix's "postplay" feature, which changed the default setting*: Tech-Crunch's description of postplay: R. Lawler, "Netflix Launches Post-Play, So You Never Have to Interrupt TV or Movie Marathons," TechCrunch, August 15, 2012, https://techcrunch.com/2012/08/15/netflix-post-play/.

144 *In the book I wrote before this one,* Irresistible: A. L. Alter, *Irresistible: The Rise of Addictive Technology and the Business of Keeping Us Hooked* (New York: Penguin, 2017).

145 *a not-truly-original-but-effective innovation*: On pivoting in this way in business, see P. K. Chintagunta, "Let Your Customers Tell You When to Pivot," *Chicago Booth Review*, January 20, 2020, https://www.chicagobooth.edu/review/let-your-customers-tell-you-when-pivot; S. J. Anderson, P. K. Chintagunta, and N. Vilcassim, "Connections across Markets: Stimulating Business Model Innovation and Examining the Impact on Firm Sales in Uganda," working paper, 2021.

145 *"You should be holding the golf club with the same pressure"*: See, for example, Golf.com staff, "How to Hold a Golf Club: The Proper Grip," Golf, April 25, 2019, https://golf.com/instruction/how-to-hold-a-golf-club-the-proper-golf-grip/.

146 *One of the most striking examples of pivoting*: See, for example, M. Reynolds, "Viagra Can Teach Us a Lot about Treating Rare Diseases," *Wired UK*, October 7, 2021, https://www.wired.co.uk/article/healx-rare-diseases. The Viagra origin story isn't unusual in the world of pharmaceuticals. Among other examples, a recent clinical trial found that an arthritis drug called Ilaris was an effective heart disease drug. In 2008, researchers discovered that a glaucoma medication to treat high pressure in the eye also thickened the eyelashes of users. It went on to sell as Latisse, with the same basic compound approved for two very different uses. The baldness treatment Propecia had a similar origin story: the drug was once used to treat prostate abnormalities, and patients noticed their hair grew in thicker and stronger after using it. In each case, someone like Brown needed to recognize and run with the idea that a drug might have a superior use. See K. E. Foley, "Viagra's Famously Surprising Origin Story Is Actually a Pretty Common Way to Find New Drugs," Quartz, September 10, 2017, https://qz.com/1070732/viagras-famously-surprising-origin-story-is-actually-a-pretty-common-way-to-find-new-drugs/.

148 *"He began with nothing," a* New York Times *obituary*: "William Wrigley Dies at 70," *New York Times*, January 27, 1932, https://www.nytimes.com/1932/01/27/archives/william-wrigley-dies-at-age-of-70-chicagoan-who-made-millions-from.html.

150 *This is the approach that Ties Carlier, the cofounder*: B. Bracken, "TV, or Not TV: The Story of Our Bike Box," *Inside VanMoof* (blog), August 5, 2019, https://www.vanmoof.com/blog/en/tv-bike-box; J. Prisco, "This Box Protects Your $3,000 Bike during Shipping," CNN Business, October 3, 2017, https://money.cnn.com/2017/10/03/smallbusiness/vanmoof-bike-box-tv/index.html.

152 *they aren't bound by the shackles of knowledge*: For more on this idea, see Adam Grant's excellent *Think Again* (New York: Viking, 2021).

153 *in one study in which researchers asked two groups of students*: Y. J. Kim and C.-B Zhong, "Ideas Rise from Chaos: Information Structure and Creativity," *Organizational Behavior and Human Decision Processes* 138 (2017): 15–27. See also H. A. Simon, *The Architecture of Complexity* (Cambridge, MA: MIT Press, 1962).

154 *In 2021, Rick Beato, a music producer and YouTube personality*: R. Beato, "What Makes This Song Great?, Ep. 105 SEAL," YouTube, June 8, 2021, https://www.youtube.com/watch?v=Hhgoli8klLA.

155 *A couple of months after interviewing Seal, Beato interviewed Sting*: R. Beato, "The Sting Interview," YouTube, November 18, 2021, https://www.youtube.com/watch?v=efRQh2vspVc.

Chapter 9: Diversity and Crowdsourcing

157 *That's exactly what has happened over the past sixty years*: See G. Soda, P. V. Mannucci, and R. S. Burt, "Networks, Creativity, and Time: Staying Creative through Brokerage and Network Rejuvenation," *Academy of Management Journal* 64 (2021): 1164–90; J. Surowiecki, *Wisdom of Crowds* (New York: Anchor Books, 2004); R. S. Burt, "Structural Holes and Good Ideas," *American Journal of Sociology* 110 (2004): 349–99.

161 *Instead, Pixar's founders sought nonredundancy*: H. Rao, R. Sutton, and A. Webb, "Innovation Lessons from Pixar: An Interview with Oscar-Winning Director Brad Bird," *McKinsey Quarterly*, April 1, 2008, https://www.mckinsey.com/business-functions/strategy-and-corporate-finance/our-insights/innovation-lessons-from-pixar-an-interview-with-oscar-winning-director-brad-bird. For a case study focusing on a group of musicians, see M. Hill, B. Hill, and R. Walsh, "Conflict in Collaborative Musical Composition: A Case Study," *Psychology of Music* 46 (2018): 192–207.

163 *According to one study, for example, we believe top performers*: D. E. Levari, D. T. Gilbert, and T. D. Wilson, "Tips from the Top: Do the Best Performers Really Give the Best Advice?," *Psychological Science* 29 (2022): 504–20.

164 *The bots may have been "noisy," but they also helped*: H. Shirado and N. A. Christakis, "Locally Noisy Autonomous Agents Improve Global Human Coordination in Network Experiments," *Nature* 545 (2017): 370–74.

164 *As more women entered the medical profession*: See, for example, G. Jackson, "The Female Problem: How Male Bias in Medical Trials Ruined Women's Health," *Guardian*, November 13, 2019, https://www.theguardian.com/lifeandstyle/2019/nov/13/the-female-problem-male-bias-in-medical-trials; N. Dusenbery, *Doing Harm* (New York: HarperOne, 2017); H. Etzkowitz, C. Kemelgor, and B. Uzzi, *Athena Unbound: The Advancement of Women in Science and Technology* (Cambridge, UK: Cambridge University Press, 2000); Y. Ma et al., "Women Who Win Prizes Get Less Money and Prestige," *Nature* 565 (2019): 287–88; A. W. Woolley et al., "Evidence for a Collective Intelligence Factor in the Performance of Groups," *Science* 330 (2010): 686–88; A. W. Woolley et al., "The Effects of Team

Strategic Orientation on Team Process and Information Search," *Organizational Behavior and Human Decision Processes* 122 (2013): 114–26; L. M. Ataman et al., "Quantifying the Growth of Oncofertility," *Biology of Reproduction* 99 (2018): 263–65; Y. Yang et al., "Gender Diverse Teams Produce More Innovative and Influential Ideas in Medical Research," working paper, 2022.

165 *The same is true of the business world*: S. Turban, D. Wu, and L. Zhang, "Research: When Gender Diversity Makes Firms More Productive," *Harvard Business Review*, February 11, 2019, https://hbr.org/2019/02/research-when-gender-diversity-makes-firms-more-productive; L. Zhang, "An Institutional Approach to Gender Diversity and Firm Performance," *Organization Science* 31 (2020): 439–57; S. Hoogendoorn, H. Oosterbeek, and M. van Praag, "The Impact of Gender Diversity on the Performance of Business Teams: Evidence from a Field Experiment," *Management Science* 59 (2013): 1514–28.

166 *One of the great case studies in diversity as an unsticking agent*: J. Flack and C. Massey, "All Stars: Is a Great Team More Than the Sum of Its Players?," Aeon, November 27, 2020, https://aeon.co/essays/what-complexity-science-says-about-what-makes-a-winning-team; M. Lewis, "The No-Stats All-Star," *New York Times Magazine*, February 13, 2009, https://www.nytimes.com/2009/02/15/magazine/15Battier-t.html; D. Myers, "About Box Plus/Minus," Basketball Reference, February 2020, https://www.basketball-reference.com/about/bpm2.html.

168 *There's a mountain of research about exactly when diverse ideas*: See, for example, J. Sulik, B. Bahrami, and O. Deroy, "The Diversity Gap: When Diversity Matters for Knowledge," *Perspectives on Psychological Science* 17 (2022): 752–67; M. Basadur and M. Head, "Team Performance and Satisfaction: A Link to Cognitive Style within a Process Framework," *Journal of Creative Behavior* 35 (2001): 227–48; S. T. Bell et al., "Getting Specific about Demographic Diversity Variable and Team Performance Relationships: A Meta-Analysis," *Journal of Management* 37 (2011): 709–43; C. A. Bowers, J. A. Pharmer, and E. Salas, "When Member Homogeneity Is Needed in Work Teams: A Meta-Analysis," *Small Group Research* 31 (2000): 305–27; A. Cooke and T. Kemeny, "Cities, Immigrant Diversity, and Complex Problem Solving," *Research Policy* 46 (2017): 1175–85; A. D. Galinsky et al., "Maximizing the Gains and Minimizing the Pains of Diversity: A Policy Perspective," *Perspectives on Psychological Science* 10 (2015): 742–48; I. J. Hoever et al., "Fostering Team Creativity: Perspective Taking as Key to Unlocking Diversity's Potential," *Journal of Applied Psychology* 97 (2012): 982–96; A. K.-Y. Leung and C. Chiu, "Multicultural Experience, Idea Receptiveness, and Creativity," *Journal of Cross-Cultural Psychology* 41 (2010): 723–41; E. Mannix and M. A. Neale, "What Differences Make a Difference? The Promise and Reality of Diverse Teams in Organizations," *Psychological Science in the Public Interest* 6 (2005): 31–55; A. L. Mello and J. R. Rentsch, "Cognitive Diversity in Teams: A Multidisciplinary Review," *Small Group Research* 46 (2015): 623–58; S. E. Page, "Where Diversity Comes From and Why It Matters?," *European Journal of Social Psychology* 44 (2014):

267–79; P. Parrotta, D. Pozzoli, and M. Pytlikova, "The Nexus between Labor Diversity and Firm's Innovation," *Journal of Population Economics* 27 (2014): 303–64; P. B. Paulus, K. I. van der Zee, and J. Kenworthy, "Cultural Diversity and Team Creativity," in *The Palgrave Handbook of Creativity and Culture Research*, ed. V. P. Glaveanu (London: Springer, 2016), 57–76; J. T. Polzer, L. P. Milton, and W. B. Swarm, "Capitalizing on Diversity: Interpersonal Congruence in Small Work Groups," *Administrative Science Quarterly* 47 (2002): 296–324; G. K. Stahl et al., "Unraveling the Effects of Cultural Diversity in Teams: A Meta-Analysis of Research on Multicultural Work Groups," *Journal of International Business Studies* 41 (2010): 690–709; H. Van Dijk, M. L. Van Engen, and D. Van Knippenberg, "Defying Conventional Wisdom: A Meta-Analytical Examination of the Differences between Demographic and Job-Related Diversity Relationships with Performance," *Organizational Behavior and Human Decision Processes* 119 (2012): 38–53; J. Wang et al., "Team Creativity/Innovation in Culturally Diverse Teams: A Meta-Analysis," *Journal of Organizational Behavior* 40 (2019): 693–708; K. Y. Williams and C. A. O'Reilly, "Demography and Diversity in Organizations: A Review of 40 Years of Research," *Research in Organizational Behavior* 20 (1998): 77–140. Also note, immigrants are overrepresented as entrepreneurs in the United States. Immigrants make up 25 percent of all founders in the United States, despite constituting just 15 percent of the population. There are, in other words, 66 percent more immigrant founders than you might expect based on the immigrant population of the United States. (Almost 40 percent of founding teams include one immigrant.) From S. P. Kerr and W. R. Kerr, "Immigrant Entrepreneurship," Harvard Business School Working Paper 17-011, June 2016, https://www.hbs.edu/ris/Publication%20Files/17-011_da2c1cf4-a999-4159 -ab95-457c783e3fff.pdf. A second paper suggests that a minimum of 30 percent of all US innovation since 1974 has come from immigrants (twice their share of the population). If you replaced every immigrant to the United States with a native-born person, the United States would have 13 percent less innovative output: S. Bernstein et al., "The Contribution of High-Skilled Immigrants to Innovation in the United States," Stanford Graduate School of Business Working Paper, July 11, 2019, https://web.stanford.edu/~diamondr/BDMP_2019_0709.pdf.

169 *which inspired Heyman to found CrowdMed in 2012*: J. Kerber, "In the Wild West of Online Medicine, Crowd Sourcing Is the Next Frontier," *Peninsula Press*, January 6, 2020, https://peninsulapress.com/2020/01/06/in-the-wild-west-of -online-medicine-crowdsourcing-is-the-next-frontier/; A. N. Meyer, C. A. Longhurst, and H. Singh, "Crowdsourcing Diagnosis for Patients with Undiagnosed Illnesses: An Evaluation of CrowdMed," *Journal of Medical Internet Research* 18 (2016): e12. In general, this section was inspired by Lisa Sanders' Diagnosis column in the *New York Times*, and her *Diagnosis* show on Netflix.

170 *On December 27, 2020, Choi posted a brief video*: K. Sanchez, "Parkinson's Meds Are Hard to Grab, So TikTok Users Crowdsource a Solution," Verge, January 23, 2021, https://

www.theverge.com/2021/1/23/22244673/parkinsons-tiktok-crowdsourced-pill-bottle. See the original video at J. Choi, @jcfoxninja, "Hey Pharma Companies," TikTok, December 27, 2020, https://www.tiktok.com/@jcfoxninja/video/6911148251982925061?is _from_webapp=1&sender_device=pc&web_id7051421448719713798.

172   *In 2019, a team of psychologists created a virtual reality environment*: M. Slater et al., "An Experimental Study of a Virtual Reality Counselling Paradigm Using Embodied Self-Dialogue," *Scientific Reports* 9 (2019): 10903; M. Slater, "An Experimental Study of a Virtual Reality Counselling Paradigm Using Embodied Self-Dialogue," YouTube, August 9, 2021, https://www.youtube.com/watch?v=G J6cAVxQOwo.

173   *In 2008, two cognitive psychologists proposed the "wisdom of inner crowds"*: E. Vul and H. Pashler, "Measuring the Crowd Within: Probabilistic Representations within Individuals," *Psychological Science* 19 (2008): 645–47. See also S. M. Herzog and R. Hertwig, "The Wisdom of Many in One Mind: Improving Individual Judgments with Dialectical Bootstrapping," *Psychological Science* 20 (2009): 231–37; S. M. Herzog and R. Hertwig, "Think Twice and Then: Combining or Choosing in Dialectical Bootstrapping?," *Journal of Experimental Psychology: Learning, Memory, and Cognition* 40 (2014): 218–32; S. M. Herzog and R. Hertwig, "Harnessing the Wisdom of the Inner Crowd," *Trends in Cognitive Sciences* 18 (2014): 504–6; P. Van de Calseyde and E. Efendić, "Taking a Disagreeing Perspective Improves the Accuracy of People's Quantitative Estimates," *Psychological Science* 33 (2022): 971–83; R. P. Larrick and J. B. Soll, "Intuitions about Combining Opinions: Misappreciation of the Averaging Principle," *Management Science* 52 (2006): 111–27; J. M. Berg, "When Silver Is Gold: Forecasting the Potential Creativity of Initial Ideas," *Organizational Behavior and Human Decision Processes* 154 (2019): 96–117.

Chapter 10: Experimentation

179   *Elite male swimmers are generally tall, broad shouldered, and dedicated*: For a fascinating book on natural gifts in sport, see D. Epstein, *The Sports Gene: Inside the Science of Extraordinary Athletic Talent* (New York: Portfolio, 2013). See also C. Bellefonds, "Why Michael Phelps Has the Perfect Body for Swimming," Biography.com, May 14, 2020, https://www.biography.com/news/michael-phelp-per fect-body-swimming.

179   *Dave Berkoff, an ambitious collegiate backstroke swimmer in the mid-1980s*: Much of the information on Dave Berkoff comes from a discussion we had in early 2021. See also S. Eschenbach, "David Berkoff," A for Athlete, undated, https://aforath lete.fandom.com/wiki/David_Berkoff; "FINA Swimming Rules," FINA, September 21, 2017, https://www.fina.org/swimming/rules; R. Hughes, "1987 NCAA Swimming Championships, 100 Yard Backstroke (Austin, TX), Berkoff Blastoff," YouTube, November 9, 2015, https://www.youtube.com/watch?v=F-OPR_yoOEM; F. Litsky, "Swimming; Fastest Backstroker Loses a Revolution," *New York Times*, March 31,

1989, https://www.nytimes.com/1989/03/31/sports/swimming-fastest-backstroker-loses-a-revolution.html; WestNyackTwins, "1988 Olympic Games—Swimming—Men's 100 Meter Backstroke—Daichi Suzuki JPN," YouTube, July 8, 2016, https://www.youtube.com/watch?v=R-DSrQQaggQ.

179 *Australian swimming coach Laurie Lawrence met Berkoff in 1988*: L. Lawrence, "Champions Come in All Shapes and Sizes—David Berkoff," Laurie Lawrence, *Stuff the Silver, We Are Going for Gold*, February 11, 2020, https://laurielawrence.com.au/podcasts/champions-come-in-all-shapes-and-sizes-david-berkoff/.

183 *Colonel John Boyd was a fighter pilot who, like Berkoff*: C. Coram, *Boyd: The Fighter Pilot Who Changed the Art of War* (New York: Little, Brown, 2003).

186 *This philosophy drove an English wine merchant*: E. Asimov, "Steven Spurrier, Who Upended Wine World with a Tasting, Dies at 79," *New York Times*, March 31, 2021, https://www.nytimes.com/2021/03/16/dining/steven-spurrier-dead.html; M. Godoy, "The Judgment of Paris: The Blind Taste Test That Decanted the Wine World," *All Things Considered*, NPR, May 24, 2016, https://www.npr.org/sections/thesalt/2016/05/24/479163882/the-judgment-of-paris-the-blind-taste-test-that-decanted-the-wine-world.

187 *much of the developed world is stuck on the idea that the full-time workweek*: See, for example, K. Sawyer, "200 Years Ago—the 12-Hour Day, the 6-Day Week," *Washington Post*, December 25, 1977, https://www.washingtonpost.com/archive/politics/1977/12/25/200-years-ago-the-12-hour-day-the-6-day-week/8a0f3c78-b7a0-4db4-ac33-00649519d1eb/; E. A. Roy, "Work Four Days, Get Paid for Five: New Zealand Company's New Shorter Week," *Guardian*, February 8, 2018, https://www.theguardian.com/world/2018/feb/09/work-four-days-get-paid-for-five-new-zealand-companys-new-shorter-week; R. Stock, "Perpetual Guardian's Four-Day Work Week Trail Going Well," Stuff, March 31, 2018, https://www.stuff.co.nz/business/102741507/perpetual-guardians-fourday-working-week-trial-going-well; J. Yeung, "A New Zealand Company Tried a Four-Day Work Week. It Was a 'Resounding Success,'" CNN Money, July 19, 2018, https://money.cnn.com/2018/07/19/news/economy/new-zealand-four-day-work-week-perpetual-guardian/index.html; E. A. Roy, "Work Less, Get More: New Zealand Firm's Four-Day Week an 'Unmitigated Success,'" *Guardian*, July 18, 2018, https://www.theguardian.com/world/2018/jul/19/work-less-get-more-new-zealand-firms-four-day-week-an-unmitigated-success; C. Graham-McLay, "A Four-Day Workweek? A Test Run Shows a Surprising Result," *New York Times*, July 19, 2018, https://www.nytimes.com/2018/07/19/world/asia/four-day-workweek-new-zealand.html; 4 Day Week Global, https://www.4dayweek.com/; N. Kobie, "What Really Happened in Iceland's Four-Day Week Trial?," *Wired UK*, December 7, 2021, https://www.wired.co.uk/article/iceland-four-day-work-week.

189 *Globally curious adults are rare, but children are almost universally*: On curiosity, see L. P. Hagtvedt et al., "Curiosity Made the Cat More Creative: Specific Curiosity as a Driver of Creativity," *Organizational Behavior and Human Decision Processes*

150 (2019): 1–13; G. Loewenstein, "The Psychology of Curiosity: A Review and Reinterpretation," *Psychological Bulletin* 116 (1994): 75–98; C. D. Speilberger and L. M. Starr, "Curiosity and Exploratory Behavior," in *Motivation: Theory and Research*, ed. H. F. O. Neil Jr. and M. Drillings (Hillsdale, NJ: Lawrence Erlbaum, 1994), 221–43. I also discuss the human instinct to be curious in my book *Irresistible* (New York: Penguin, 2017), in chapter 9, on cliff-hangers and the curiosity gap.

190 *That was the case when I spoke to Max Deutsch*: Most of the information in this section comes from my interview with Deutsch. See also his *Medium* blog, https://medium.com/@maxdeutsch, and his posts on mastering new skills: https://medium.com/@maxdeutsch/m2m-day-1-completing-12-ridiculously-hard-challenges-in-12-months-9843700c741f.

195 *Until several years ago, few teams showed much interest*: NBA scoring-data visualization: API via data.world @sportsvizsunday, design by Ryan Soares; K. Goldsberry, "How Mapping Shots in the NBA Changed It Forever," FiveThirtyEight, May 2, 2019, https://fivethirtyeight.com/features/how-mapping-shots-in-the-nba-changed-it-forever/.

Chapter 11: Exploring and Exploiting

199 *In 2018, a team of researchers examined the career paths*: L. Liu et al., "Hot Streaks in Artistic, Cultural, and Scientific Careers," *Nature* 559 (2018): 396–99.

199 *A new team including many of the original researchers*: Y. Yin et al., "Quantifying the Dynamics of Failure across Science, Startups, and Security," *Nature* 575 (2019): 190–97. For related work, see R. Sinatra et al., "Quantifying the Evolution of Individual Scientific Impact," *Science* 354 (2016): 596–604.

199 *The answer came three years later, in a second piece*: L. Liu et al., "Understanding the Onset of Hot Streaks across Artistic, Cultural, and Scientific Careers," *Nature Communications* 12 (2021): 1–10. See also Z.-L. He and P.-K. Wong, "Exploration vs. Exploitation: An Empirical Test of the Ambidexterity Hypothesis," *Organization Science* 15 (2004): 481–94; C. Bidmon, S. Boe-Lillegraven, and R. Koch, "Now, Switch! Individuals' Responses to Imposed Switches between Exploration and Exploitation," *Long Range Planning* 53 (2001): 1019–28.

205 *White truffles are absurdly expensive*: See, for example, D. Farley, "The Truth about Italy's White Truffles," BBC, January 9, 2018, https://www.bbc.com/travel/article/20180108-the-truth-about-italys-white-truffles; B. Wilson, "The Best Truffle Hunters in Italy," *Forbes*, January 9, 2017, https://www.forbes.com/sites/breannawilson/2017/01/19/the-best-truffle-hunters-in-italy-a-morning-hunt-with-the-family-who-found-a-330000-white-truffle/.

206 *This bull's-eye analogy is a specific case of the eighty-twenty rule*: R. Koch, *The 80/20 Principle: The Secret to Achieving More with Less* (Sydney, Australia: Currency, 1999).

207 *This "just keep going" mentality was central to the insights of Robert Merton*: L. Crampton, "Serendipity: The Role of Chance in Scientific Discoveries," Owlcation, April 23, 2021, https://owlcation.com/stem/Serendipity-The-Role -of-Chance-in-Making-Scientific-Discoveries; L. McKay-Peet and E. G. Toms, "Investigating Serendipity: How It Unfolds and What May Influence It," *Journal of the Association of Information Science and Technology* 66 (2015): 1463–76; W. B. Cannon, "The Role of Chance in Discovery," *Scientific Monthly* 50 (1940): 304–9.

209 *Walter Gratzer published a book cataloging the role of serendipity*: W. Gratzer, *Eurekas and Euphorias: The Oxford Book of Scientific Anecdotes* (Oxford, UK: Oxford University Press, 2004).

211 *In 2019, three psychologists asked hundreds of physicists*: S. L. Gable, E. A. Hopper, and J. W. Schooler, "When the Muses Strike: Creative Ideas of Physicists and Writers Routinely Occur during Mind Wandering," *Psychological Science* 30 (2019): 396–404. See also K. Christoff et al., "Mind-Wandering as Spontaneous Thought: A Dynamic Framework," *Nature Reviews Neuroscience* 17 (2016): 718–31; J. E. Davidson, "The Suddenness of Insight," in *The Nature of Insight*, ed. R. J. Sternberg and J. E. Davidson (Cambridge, MA: MIT Press, 1995), 125–55. On mind wandering's benefits and costs, see also M. A. Killingsworth and D. T. Gilbert, "A Wandering Mind Is an Unhappy Mind," *Science* 330 (2010): 932; E. J. Masicampo and R. F. Baumeister, "Consider It Done! Plan Making Can Eliminate the Cognitive Effects of Unfulfilled Goals," *Journal of Personality and Social Psychology* 101 (2011): 667–83; J. Smallwood and J. W. Schooler, "The Science of Mind Wandering: Empirically Navigating the Stream of Consciousness," *Annual Review of Psychology* 66 (2015): 487–518; B. Baird et al., "Inspired by Distraction: Mind Wandering Facilitates Creative Incubation," *Psychological Science* 23 (2012): 1117–22; C. M. Zedelius and J. W. Schooler, "Mind Wandering 'Ahas' versus Mindful Reasoning: Alternative Routes to Creative Solutions," *Frontiers in Psychology* 6 (2015): 834; C. M. Zedelius and J. W. Schooler, "The Richness of Inner Experience: Relating Styles of Daydreaming to Creative Processes," *Frontiers in Psychology* 6 (2016): 2063; P. T. Palhares, D. Branco, and O. F. Goncalves, "Mind Wandering and Musical Creativity in Jazz Improvisation," *Psychology of Music* 50 (2022): 1212–24; D. Breslin, "Off-Task Social Breaks and Group Creativity," *Journal of Creative Behavior* 53 (2019): 496–507; M. S. Franklin et al., "The Silver Lining of a Mind in the Clouds: Interesting Musings Are Associated with Positive Mood While Mind-Wandering," *Frontiers in Psychology* 4 (2013): 583; J. Rummel et al., "The Role of Attention for Insight Problem Solving: Effects of Mindless and Mindful Incubation Periods," *Journal of Cognitive Psychology* 33 (2021): 757–69.

214 *in the 1930s it drove a Russian physicist named Lev Landau*: See, for example, A. Livanova, *Landau: A Great Physicist and Teacher* (New York: Pergamon Press, 1980); P. Ratner, "Landau Genius Scale Ranking of the Smartest Physicists Ever," Big

Think, September 28, 2020, https://bigthink.com/hard-science/landau-genius-scale-ranking-of-the-smartest-physicists-ever/.

215 *This insight—that striking gold and continuing to fail*: Y. Wang, B. F. Jones, and D. Wang, "Early-Career Setbacks and Future Career Impact," *Nature Communications* 10 (2019): 1–10; J. Li et al., "Nobel Laureates Are Almost the Same as Us," *Nature Reviews: Physics* 1 (2019): 301–3. On asking the right kinds of questions when assessing your understanding, see A. L. Alter, D. M. Oppenheimer, and J. C. Zemla, "Missing the Trees for the Forest: A Construal Level Account of the Illusion of Explanatory Depth," *Journal of Personality and Social Psychology* 99 (2010): 436–51; W. J. McGuire, "Inducing Resistance to Persuasion: Some Contemporary Approaches," in *Advances in Experimental Social Psychology*, vol. 1, ed. L. Berkowitz (New York: Academic Press, 1964), 191–229; G. Bush, P. Luu, and M. I. Posner, "Cognitive and Emotional Influences in Anterior Cingulate Cortex," *Trends in Cognitive Sciences* 4 (2000): 215–22.

Chapter 12: Action above All

219 *You can find those interviews online*: "Paul Simon on His Writing Process for 'Bridge over Troubled Water,'" *The Dick Cavett Show*, YouTube, January 27, 2020, https://www.youtube.com/watch?v=qFtocP-klQI; "Paul Simon Deconstructs 'Mrs. Robinson,'" *The Dick Cavett Show*, YouTube, February 3, 2020, https://www.youtube.com/watch?v=sDqIsuIpVy4.

221 *You may have heard the idea, for example, that smiling*: Embodied cognition, as the phenomenon is known, is controversial in scientific circles. Some of the effects demonstrated in embodied-cognition papers have been difficult to replicate, and some seem to be outright fabrications. Still, there's plenty of evidence for the general idea that our actions and body positions have the power to shape how we think and feel. See, for example, P. M. Niedenthal, "Embodying Emotion," *Science* 316 (2007): 1002–5; N. A. Coles et al., "Fact or Artifact? Demand Characteristics and Participants' Beliefs Can Moderate, but Do Not Fully Account for, the Effects of Facial Feedback on Emotional Experience," *Journal of Personality and Social Psychology*, 2022, forthcoming; E. W. Carr, A. Kever, and P. Winkielman, "Embodiment of Emotion and Its Situated Nature," in *The Oxford Handbook of 4E Cognition*, 4th ed., ed. A. Newen, L. De Bruin, and S. Gallagher (Oxford, UK: Oxford University Press, 2018), 528–52; P. Winkielman, P. M. Niedenthal, and L. Oberman, "The Embodied Emotional Mind," in *Embodied Grounding*, ed. G. R. Semin and E. R. Smith (Cambridge, UK: Cambridge University Press, 2008), 263–88; G. K. Wells and R. E. Petty, "The Effects of Head Movements on Persuasion: Compatibility and Incompatibility of Responses," *Basic and Applied Social Psychology* 1 (1980): 219–30; S. E. Duclos et al., "Emotion-Specific Effects of Facial Expressions and Postures on Emotional Experience," *Journal of Personality and Social Psychology* 57 (1989): 100–108.

222 *The best way to predict whether health-care workers will wash*: A. S. Wellsjo, "Simple Actions, Complex Habits: Lessons from Hospital Hand Hygiene," working paper (Berkeley: University of California, 2022), https://www.alexwellsjo.com/.

222 *Action also matters because it changes how we see ourselves*: C. J. Bryan et al., "Motivating Voter Turnout by Invoking the Self," *Proceedings of the National Academy of Sciences* 108 (2011): 12653–56; C. J. Bryan, A. Master, and G. M. Walton, "'Helping' versus 'Being a Helper': Invoking the Self to Increase Helping in Young Children," *Child Development* 85 (2014): 1836–42; R. K. Mallett and K. J. Melchiori, "Creating a Water-Saver Self-Identity Reduces Water Use in Residence Halls," *Journal of Environmental Psychology* 47 (2016): 223–29; S. Franssens et al., "Nudging Commuters to Increase Public Transport Use: A Field Experiment in Rotterdam," *Frontiers in Psychology* 12 (2021): 633865, https://doi.org/10.3389/fpsyg.2021.633865.

223 *The value of action doesn't speak against taking one of Tara Brach's*: See, for example, T. Brach, "The Sacred Pause," *Psychology Today*, December 4, 2014, https://www.psychologytoday.com/us/blog/finding-true-refuge/201412/the-sacred-pause; T. Brach, *Radical Acceptance: Embracing Your Life with the Heart of a Buddha* (New York: Random House, 2004). I discussed this topic in depth in chapter 5.

224 *But structure turns out to be freeing when you're stuck*: On the benefits and drawbacks of scheduling, and of measuring how we live our lives more generally, see G. N. Tonietto and S. A. Malkoc, "The Calendar Mindset: Scheduling Takes the Fun Out and Puts the Work In," *Journal of Marketing Research* 53 (2016): 922–36; S. Devoe and J. Pfeffer, "Time Is Tight: How Higher Economic Value of Time Increases Feelings of Time Pressure," *Journal of Applied Psychology* 96 (2011): 665–76; S. Bellezza, N. Paharia, and A. Keinan, "Conspicuous Consumption of Time: When Busyness and Lack of Leisure Time Become a Status Symbol," *Journal of Consumer Research* 44 (2016): 118–38; J. Etkin, "The Hidden Cost of Personal Quantification," *Journal of Consumer Research* 42 (2016): 967–84.

225 *Several years ago two architects were poring over a data set*: On the benefits of movement for fluid and creative thinking, and for studies describing the relationship between walkability and entrepreneurship, see L. Zimmerman and A. Chakravarti, "Not Just for Your Health Alone: Regular Exercisers' Decision-Making in Unrelated Domains," *Journal of Experimental Psychology: Applied*, 2022, forthcoming; C. Chen et al., "Regular Vigorous-Intensity Physical Activity and Walking Are Associated with Divergent but Not Convergent Thinking in Japanese Young Adults," *Brain Sciences* 11 (2021): 1046; K. Aga et al., "The Effect of Acute Aerobic Exercise on Divergent and Convergent Thinking and Its Influence by Mood," *Brain Sciences* 11 (2021): 546; A. Bollimbala, P. S. James, and S. Ganguli, "Impact of Physical Activity on an Individual's Creativity: A Day-Level Analysis," *American Journal of Psychology* 134 (2021): 93–105; S. Imaizumi, U. Tagami, and Y. Yang, "Fluid Movements Enhance Creative Fluency: A Replication of Slepian and Ambady (2012)," *PLOS One* 15 (2020): e0236825; M. L. Slepian and N. Am-

bady, "Fluid Movement and Creativity," *Journal of Experimental Psychology: General* 141 (2012): 625–29; K. J. Main et al., "Change It Up: Inactivity and Repetitive Activity Reduce Creative Thinking," *Journal of Creative Behavior* 54 (2020): 395–406; B. Bereitschaft, "Are Walkable Places Tech Incubators? Evidence from Nebraska's 'Silicon Prairie,'" *Regional Studies, Regional Science* 6 (2019): 339–56; E. Labonte-LeMoyne et al., "The Delayed Effect of Treadmill Desk Usage on Recall and Attention," *Computers in Human Behavior* 46 (2015): 1–5; A. P. Knight and M. Baer, "Get Up, Stand Up: The Effects of a Non-sedentary Workspace on Information Elaboration and Group Performance," *Social Psychological and Personality Science* 5 (2014): 910–17; S. Hamidi and A. Zandiatashbar, "Does Urban Form Matter for Innovation Productivity? A National Multi-level Study of the Association between Neighborhood Innovation Capacity and Urban Sprawl," *Urban Studies* 56 (2018): 1–19.

227 *Strategically lowering your standards is another excellent way*: J.-C. Goulet-Pelletier, P. Gaudreau, and D. Cousineau, "Is Perfectionism a Killer of Creative Thinking? A Test of the Model of Excellencism and Perfectionism," *British Journal of Psychology* 113 (2022): 176–207.

227 *That's the position of Jeff Tweedy*: E. Klein, "Wilco's Jeff Tweedy Wants You to Be Bad at Something. For Your Own Good," *New York Times*, July 2, 2021, https://www.nytimes.com/2021/07/02/opinion/ezra-klein-podcast-jeff-tweedy.html; J. Tweedy, *How to Write One Song* (New York: Dutton, 2020).

230 *quality follows from quantity*: R. E. Jung et al., "Quantity Yields Quality When It Comes to Creativity: A Brain and Behavioral Test of the Equal-Odds Rule," *Frontiers in Psychology* 6 (2015): 864.

230 *or you can learn by doing*: On the benefits of learning by doing, and Hamilton Naki's experience, see J. Clark and G. White, "Experiential Learning: A Definitive Edge in the Job Market," *American Journal of Business Education* 3 (2010): 115–18; R. Loo, "A Meta-Analytic Examination of Kolb's Learning Style Preferences among Business Majors," *Journal of Education for Business* 77 (2002): 252–56; R. DuFour et al., *Learning by Doing: A Handbook for Professional Learning Communities at Work*, 3rd ed. (Bloomington, IN: Solution Tree, 2016); M. Wines, "Accounts of South African's Career Now Seen as Overstated," *New York Times*, August 27, 2005, https://www.nytimes.com/2005/08/27/world/africa/accounts-of-south-africans-career-now-seen-as-overstated.html; J. Abrahams, "Special Assignment: The Hamilton Naki Story," SABC News, June 2, 2009, https://web.archive.org/web/20110723010408/http://www.sabcnews.co.za/SABCnews.com/Documents/SpecialAssignment/HEART-SCRIPT.pdf; C. Logan, *Celebrity Surgeon: Christiaan Barnard, a Life* (Johannesburg, South Africa: Jonathan Ball, 2003).

INDEX